MW01443184

Undaunted Gladiator

Colonel Dan Wilson

Copyright © 2024 Daniel Hunter Wilson

All rights reserved. Cover Graphic designed by Shane Violette of Loud House Audio Studio, Myrtle Beach, SC.

ISBN: 979-8-8836-8850-7

DEDICATION

I dedicate this book to my Higher Power whom I know as GOD…a God of my understanding…loving, compassionate, and merciful, who wants what is best for me. I believe that my life has played out exactly the way that God intended for it to. I'm convinced that God's plan for my life is vastly better than anything I could ever have imagined.

My goal, every day now, is to seek greater conscious contact with the God of my understanding through prayer and meditation. He guides and directs my daily actions, and my prayer each morning is that Thy will be done on earth, as it is in heaven. I derive my spiritual strength from my daily connection with God. God sustained me through many trying experiences, because I always kept my faith in His power, and knew that He was always with me. I firmly hold on to the verse in the Bible which asserts that I can do all things through Him who strengthens me. Another meaningful verse from the Bible, for me, is that He will never leave me nor forsake me. I am forever grateful to God for the life that He has blessed me with, and therefore would be remiss if I did not dedicate this book, and the rest of my life, to God.

DISCLAIMER

I am in a retired status from the United States Marine Corps. Therefore, any ideas or opinions I express in this book are my very own, and in no way represent an official position by the United States Marine Corps, the United States Armed Forces, or any government agency. No classified information is contained in this book.

Throughout this book, I have inserted from my official record of trial those remarks and testimony which I deemed significant in describing my case. The record of trial occupies the equivalent of nineteen 300-page books. I made an author's cut where necessary, to avoid producing an interminable tome. I have removed all personal names, or name references in testimony except for my own, and only in those instances where my wife is specifically referred to as Mrs. Wilson.

The transcript sections were taken from the record of trial; any grammatical inconsistencies represent my desire to remain true to the trial documentation. My goal is to put you as close to the facts of the trial as possible.

ACKNOWLEDGMENTS

Exodus 20_22: And the Lord said…you have seen for yourselves that I have talked with you from heaven.

Exodus 23_20: Behold, I send an angel before you to guard you on the way.

[The Bible – DRV]

First and foremost, I give all credit and thanks to my Higher Power for giving me strength to do all things, including finishing, this, my very first book. "Let the words of my mouth and the meditation of my heart, be acceptable in your sight, O Lord, my rock and my redeemer."

My wife and daughters deserve honorable mention for their loyalty and devotion throughout. I forever owe you gals a huge debt of gratitude for the suffering you endured. Each of you rate a Medal of Honor, our nation's highest award for valor, for your demonstrated gallantry and intrepidity in the face of unimaginable adversity. You ladies are my heavenly angels. Thank you for everything from the bottom of my heart. I love you guys forever!

My dad was the greatest man, and most charismatic preacher, I have known in life. He taught me all about leadership by the way he led his "flock." The night prior to his passing, my sister called me from his bedside and said that my dad's final request was for me to sing him Marine Corps cadences. She put the phone to his ear, and I could hear his labored breathing as I sang cadences that we refer to as "ditties" in the Marines. I went on and on for about fifteen minutes, because I remembered all of them from when I was a Sergeant of Marines. A few ones like these:

> Running through the jungle with my M-Sixteen…
>
> I'm a mean motor-scooter, I'm a U.S. Marine.
>
> C-130 rolling down the strip,
>
> Dad and I gonna take a little trip.
>
> Stand up, buckle up, and shuffle to the door,
>
> Jump right out and shout, "Marine Corps!"
>
> If Dad's chute don't open wide,
>
> Dad's got another one by his side.
>
> And, if that chute don't blossom round,
>
> Dad'll be the first one on the ground!

My sister got back on the phone and said that dad had a huge smile on his face and mouthed "ooohraaah," which is a Marine exclamation of unbridled enthusiasm. God took dad home a few hours later, but I was blessed to have had the opportunity to bolster his spirits before he departed. Talmage certainly was a difference maker in my life, as well as in the lives of tens of thousands of other human beings. May you rest in eternal peace, dad, and thank you for being the most amazing father ever.

Thank you to my eldest sister and two brothers for supporting your brother and his wife with love and material support. And to my beloved mother…thanks, Mom – I love you! My father and uncle were my two role models in life and taught me all about leadership before I ever came in the Marines. What you two greats of the greatest generation did in life will continue to echo through eternity. May you both rest in eternal peace.

Daisy was our beloved dog who visited me at Camp Pendleton's Brig, after my wife got her certified as her "emotional support" pet. It meant the world to me when my wife would come to visit me with Daisy in tow. I was always on an emotional high for the rest of the week until her next visit. Daisy showered sixteen years of love on our family. May you rest in peace, Daisy. Daddy loves you!

I must acknowledge my 100-year-old friend, Bob – a World War II veteran of the Army Air Corps. He helped put a stop to World War II. I'm privileged to spend precious time visiting Bob every week and he has become a dear friend and mentor to me, making a huge difference in my life with his sage advice. Bob told me recently that "father time is undefeated," which is ironic coming from a Centurion who has stared "father time" in the face for over one hundred years. Thank you, Bob, for all the wisdom you continue to share with me, and for our "band of brothers" friendship. I salute you, sir…Semper Fi, soldier!

Thank you, Katie and Andy Cherkasky, both esteemed Esquires, for treating me special – as if I was your only client. Katie, your Appellant's Brief on my behalf was brilliant legal work. I'm thinking that your 82-page brief to the NMCCA will be studied by future students of military law for generations to come. I was fortunate to be able to study it every day for nine months and six days, after you filed it with the Appellate Court. Every time I reread it, I was 100 percent sure that I was going to be exonerated based on your first assignment of error – factual and legal insufficiency. You are an amazing person and my Angel for life!

I had a superb defense team, backing me up at my court martial. Especially, Mark, Phil, and Ben. You guys put forth a tremendous effort on my behalf. Thank you, Gentlemen, for giving your utmost in defending me. I am very grateful to you all.

BOOK UNDAUNTED GLADIATOR

I would like to give a special "shout out" to all the prisoners, detainees, guards, and prison staff whom I spent thirty-three months of my life getting to know intimately. I like to tell people since my release that "some of the finest Marines I served with; I met in prison." A legendary Marine general – Lieutenant General Chesty Puller – once remarked to his driver, "take me to the Brig, I want to meet some real Marines." So very true, Chesty, wherever you are. I remain friends with many of them today. Special thanks to Mark (aka: the Professor), Brandon (aka: the Viking), Matt (aka: The Chief), Clarence (aka: The Champ), Army, Carlos (aka: The Jackal), Preston (aka: Patient Zero), Charlie, the Gunny, Dakoda (aka: Hootie), Kevin, Nate (aka: Nasty), the Senator, William (aka: Top Gun), Yobany (aka: Mexican Mafia), John (aka: Mr. Mossad), Booth (aka: the Assassin), Anthony (aka: the King), Eddie (aka: Agua), Carlton (aka: Wild Man), Austin (aka: Hamburger, or Big Mac Hanny), Will (aka: Monster Asian Man), Peter (aka: the Dog Whisperer), Woodrow (aka: Blade), Josh (aka: Surfer), Esteban (aka: Autobaan), Walter, Patrick (aka: Nascar Racer), Timothy (aka: Steve Irvin's Brother), Tristan (aka: Sparky), A.J., Kevin (aka: Maxwell Smart), Arriaga (aka: Caesar), Chris (aka: Slick Willy), Tristan (aka: Parks & Recreation), Tomas (aka: Cockroach), Trey (aka: Tatoo Man, or Arteestay), Ben (aka: Checkmate), Brian (aka: Barker), Miguel (aka: Tixi), Joe, the Kenyan kid (aka: Bwana, or Jomo Kenyatta), Jose, Andras (aka: Chappy), Omar (aka: Hern-dog), Stilleto (aka: Pistol Pete), Caleb, Daniel (aka: Budda), Darrius (aka: Upstager), Chris (aka: Penya), Eddie, Neeke (aka: the Artist), Jon (aka: Meet Joe Black), Twerk, Darren (aka: Dimmer), Kylan (aka: Sully), Mike (aka: Pew Pew), J_Marcus (aka: Franky goes to Hollywood – also the youngest Marine detainee at 17, and the funniest!), Joey, Oscar (aka: CPIPS_Estrada), Paul (aka: Voor the Dutchman), Eugene (aka: SVU), Barraza (aka: Smiley), Steve (aka: Poorman), Izrafil (aka: the King Maker), Cody (aka: 007-James Bond), George (aka: Lullaby), Luke (aka: Cool Hand), Justin, Anthony (aka: MJ), Jay, Jake (aka: the Snake), Oscar (aka: De la Renta), SteveO (aka: the Grand Master), "Woody", Staff Sergeant (aka: the Recruiter), Tyler (aka: Bart), and of course, Lance Corporal Benatz (aka: Rifleman Ramos), my favorite guard. I thoroughly enjoyed meeting and interacting with all the prisoners and detainees, so thanks to you all for the unforgettable memories.

I must acknowledge and thank Mr. Sloan and the staff at MILITARYCORRUPTION.COM for believing in me from the very start and frequently spotlighting my case to their audience. He does "Yeoman's work" in alerting citizens to corruption in the military. Mr. Sloan fights for truth, justice and the American way, by exposing the corrupt, and trying to fix what is broken. He is also committed to helping me fix the military "justice" system. Subsequent to my retirement, he has helped me out personally in many ways, including sharing his wisdom and advice on numerous topics. Thank you, Shipmate, from the bottom of my heart.

Earl *"The Pearl"* is an Army Veteran, having served as an infantry officer. Earl now spends the majority of his time giving back to fellow veterans. He established and runs a non-profit organization whose sole purpose is to help veterans in need, called VETERANS AMERICA. Earl serves as an advocate for veterans with the Veterans Administration, which can be a daunting task for most veterans. However, Earl has been highly successful in helping veterans get the benefits they deserve from the Veterans Administration. I am fortunate to count Earl as a dear friend, and I deeply appreciate all that he has done for me. I salute you, Earl, and "Semper Fi" Soldier!

Thank you to my spiritual advisor, Mary, also known as "Thunder Sky." She has given me priceless advice since my release and has continually inspired me to share my story.

Huge gratitude to the multitude of friends who supported me with letters, books, cards, and even by sharing your diary entries (Susie) with me in prison. They are priceless mementoes to me, and I have kept every single one of them. You know who you are – thank you from the bottom of my heart!

I would like to thank my Grand Uncle, Bill Wilson, who founded a spiritual program to help sufferers of the disease of alcoholism. His divinely inspired program has help millions of alcoholics around the world break the bonds of alcoholism and become rocketed into a fourth dimension of existence – I am one of them. For this alcoholic, the key to staying sober every day is through maintaining a connection with my Higher Power and working on my spiritual growth. Maintaining a fit spiritual condition is what keeps me away from the booze. I have always considered the Marines the finest organization in the world, but I now have to admit that my Uncle Bill's program, and fellowship, is truly the greatest show on earth. I have so many new family members, thanks to recovery, that it's difficult to keep track of them all: Joe, Mike, DanO, Bill, Mister Ed, Ru, Bob, Jake, Bo, Brenda, Bret, Carson, Reed, Veda, Dale, Darrin, Eric, Jane, Phil, Signe, Wally, Lowman, Randy, Miller, Lee, Larry, Dennis, Danny, Otis, Steve, Floyd, Nancy, Aimee,

BOOK UNDAUNTED GLADIATOR

Lacey, Kelly, Deana, Andy, Brian, Diane, Dianna, Beth, Billy, Liana, Jenny, Susan, Billy, Karl, Godzilla, Gary, Leon, Leo, Eva, Brett, Rob, Tim, Brad, Phil, Amanda, Larry, Lou, Alex, Harry, Donna, Cherry, Winifred, Savannah, Sylvia, Katie, Big John, Jack, Jim, Bill, Paul, Bruce, Mary Ann, Caroline, Linda, Kerry, Martha, Jennifer, Nimit, Kristen, Emerson, Page, David, Ted, Coop, Tom, Lori, Bobbie, Dennis, Keshava, Joel, Terry, Derek, Joe, Haley, Brittany, Frank, Rachel, Nancy, Karon, Joshua, Natalie, Nancy, John, Catherine, Fernanda, Jeannie, Joyce, Skip, Sully, Erik, Don, Cody, Dan, Roger, Jim, Mark, Leon, Chris, Matt, Pat, Alex, Charles, Shipmate Joe, Happy Dave, Toad, Nicky, Butch, Matea, Tim, Jack's Back, Bernie, Jean, Preston, Fran, Whit, Gordon, Clive, Walter, John, SteveO, Bob, Phil, Erica, Daniel, Anthony, Ryan, Rich, Milt, Tracy, Jo Anna, Kristie, James, Jimmy, Jac, Candace, Drew, Joshua, Matthew, Skeeter, Marsha, Tyson, Paul, Charlie, Don, Patrick, Scott, Tony, Brian, Dale, Josh, Edwin, Kevin, Dean, Eric, Gil, Jean, Tabitha, Jenn, Jenni, Tyler, Joseph, Katy, Mick, Norm, Pat, Pete, Russ, Blake, Terry, Sam, Scott, Stacy, Wes, and Rhett.

Every day, I play Pickleball in Myrtle Beach with the likes of John & Scotty, Larry (who originally taught me to the basics) and Bonnie, Jenn, Jasa, Angelina, Ernst, Al, Jeff, Mark, Eric, Frank, Mike, Sally, Big Mike, Bobby, Stokes, Dave, Chuck, Al, Andy, Angie, Barry, Elizabeth, Stan, Vicky, Tran, Allan, Mike, JR, Laura, Jim, Rick, Lee, Dennis, Mary, Lou, Leon, Phil, Chris, Gary, Jerry, Jim, John, Bill (world champ for the 88 year old age group), Ricky, Carson, and Brian.

A special thanks to the many fellow warrior friends who visited me in prison, like Jerry, the coolest sergeant ever and who is like my "brother from another mother." Greg & Tod, legendary machine gunners who served side-by-side with me in Desert Storm and were awarded for their heroism in combat. Jimbo from the Magnificent Bastard's Battalion and currently the most successful realtor in Southern California. Sergeant Major "Rock," a legendary Marine I served with on recruiting duty. Eric from Parris Island who went on to work for Elon at SpaceX. Craig whom I was honored to retire at 8th & I. A.J. "Jut Jut," a fellow Colonel I served with as a Lieutenant. My adopted son Ryan (aka: The Beast). Drew, who is now a general. "Crazy Horse" Rick, another fellow Mustang & Colonel. Adria, who was like a daughter to my wife and I and now serves proudly in the Air Force. Dennis and Kathy whom I served with at my first duty station. Tony, another PI Marine friend. Chris whom I promoted to captain and made one of my company commanders and who is now himself a lawyer at the esteemed rank of Lieutenant Colonel. Marty, whom I met on Okinawa. Drew (aka: Nurse Ratchet), Brian (aka: The Great Cornholio). Then the unforgettable Drill Instructor I served with on Parris Island who "bamboozled" his way into the Brig to visit me on the declaration of being my "command representative," and was recently serving at Notre Dame.

Thank you to the Headquarters Battalion Legal Advisor and his support crew for helping me with out-processing from the Marines to the best of their ability upon my release from Camp Pendleton's Brig. Especially to Sandy, the Marine Chief Warrant Officer Five in charge of IPAC who did her level best to restore me to a "full up round."

My final salute is to all the Marines, military service members, and civilian employees whom I was honored and privileged to have served with on active duty. I served shoulder-to-shoulder with legions of heroic Marine Warriors and service members. I'm always reminded of the Shakespearean quote from the Henry the Fifth Play when I talk about warriors and our camaraderie that is forged in the crucible of combat. "For he today, that sheds his blood with me, shall forever be my brother." In retirement, I'm blessed to still be in contact with many warriors whom I was fortunate to have served with. In regard to your service, my friends, I like to harken back to my first Commander-In-Chief, Ronald Wilson Reagan who wrote to a Marine Lance Corporal, "some people go their entire lives wondering if they've made a difference; Marines don't have that problem." Each of you made a difference in my life, and I'm a better man for having served with you. Thank you for your service and friendship. May God bless you all for your honorable and patriotic service to our great nation – thank you!

MILITARY TERMS & ACRONYMS

ASAP: As soon as possible!
AWOL: Absence without leave. Also known in the military as unauthorized absence (UA).
Boot: Newbie. "Nick, the new guy." Anyone in the Marine Corps with one day less in service than yourself.
Bravo Zulu: Good job, way to go, or great effort…congrats.
Brig: Prison, or military confinement facility.
BOHICA: Bend over, here it comes again!
Bulkhead: Wall.
CA: Convening Authority. The officer imbued with the authority, by virtue of their rank and billet, to convene legal proceedings against a military member of their unit (i.e. a court martial). Typically, the Commanding Officer of a unit with the rank of Lieutenant Colonel (O-5) or higher.
CAAF: The United States Court of Appeals for the Armed Forces. This is the second tier of appeals for a military member. First is their service appellate court, next is CAAF. CAAF's mission is to ensure that the various military departments are implementing the UCMJ and Manual for Courts Martial equally and similarly. CAAF Judges are tasked with leveling the legal playing field.
CAC: Child Advocacy Center.
CG: Commanding General. A general officer with specific command authority over a subordinate unit within a military service. A Commanding General is also a Convening Authority, authorized to convene the highest level of courts martial, a General Court Martial.
Chit: An official form in military prisons, used to initiate all interactions with, or requests to the staff. For example, if you want to speak with your lawyer, it first requires you to drop a chit in a box to your counselor. Your staff counselor then has 5 business days to process your request. Chits are collected from the box every weekday morning, except holidays, and routed to the appropriate staff members.
CO: Commanding Officer. The top officer in a unit with specified command and legal authorities.
COS: Chief-of-Staff.
Deck: Floor.

Detainee: A military member in a status, awaiting a court martial, or other legal action (SILT, or dismissal of charges), wearing blue.
Devil Dog: A term used by Marines to refer to each other, particularly senior Marines when addressing junior Marines. As in, "put a cover (hat) on your grape (head), Devil Dog!" Can be used in an endearing manner like, "you're my favorite Devil Dog." Recently, considered by many younger Marines as a term of derision, and some are offended by it. Devil Dog is the literal translation from the German, Teufil Hunden. German soldiers in World War I bestowed the term on Marines out of respect, when describing the ferocious fighting spirit of Marines in battle.
DV: Distinguished Visitor.
EOTG: Expeditionary Operations & Training Group. Formerly SOTG.
FO: Flag officer. Officers in the Navy, equivalent in rank to general officers in the other military services. Officers in the grades of O-7 through O-10 (1 star through 4 stars).
FOB: Forward Operating Base.
FUBAR: F'd up beyond all recognition.
GO: General Officer. Officers in every service, except the Navy, in the grades of O-7 through O-10 (1 star through 4 stars).
GP: General population. The area of the Brig, housing detainees and prisoners who are not specifically confined to Special Quarters (SQ) – solitary confinement cells.
Grunt: Generic term of affection for infantrymen. The infantryman on the ground, engaging the enemy directly, enduring all the hardships of combat, and living in an austere environment. Revered by his countrymen for taking the fight to our nation's foes. Feared by our enemies who know the grunts' ferocious, tenacious, and courageous fighting spirit.
Hatch: Door, or entryway.
IOC: Infantry Officers Course. All students selected for the 0302 MOS, must attend, complete, and graduate from IOC. It is about a 10-week course with heavy emphasis on infantry tactics, and leadership.
IRO: Initial Review Officer. After a military member is placed in confinement by direction of their Convening Authority, a member has a legal right to a hearing within 5 days, in order to determine if the confinement, prior to legal proceedings is appropriate and warranted. The IRO is typically a Major (O-4) who regularly comes to the confinement facility to hold hearings.
Judge Advocate: A lawyer in the Marine Corps.

KISS: Keep It Simple, Stupid! Typically, relates to planning. Keep things simple, so they are easy to comprehend, and perform during execution; especially in combat with bullets flying amidst the "fog of war."
MAGTF: Marine Air Ground Task Force. A Marine Corps unit, specifically organized to be self-contained and self-sustaining, able to project combat power anywhere in the world on short notice for a specified time frame.
MarForPac: Marine Forces Pacific.
MARSOC: Marine Special Operations Command.
MCCS: Marine Corps Community Services.
MCI: Marine Corps Installations.
MCM: Manual for Courts Martial.
MCMAP: Marine Corps Martial Arts Program. When you find yourself on the battlefield, and your bullets have run out with the enemy in your face, you must be trained to kill with your hands and feet, or with anything that can be used as a weapon (i.e. rock, stick, belt, etc.) – "one mind, any weapon."
MCRD: Marine Corps Recruit Depot. Boot Camp. Two in the Marine Corps. One is on Parris Island for all recruits from East of the Mississippi River, and in San Diego for all recruits from West of the Mississippi River.
MECEP: Marine Corps Enlisted Commissioning and Education Program. A special enlisted-to-officer (aka Green to Gold) program wherein board-selected enlisted members are sent to a preparatory school for 3 months, then on to the university of their choice.
MEF: Marine Expeditionary Force. The highest-level of MAGTF in the Marine Corps. There are three MEFs in the Marine Corps. I MEF is headquartered at Camp Pendleton, California, II MEF is headquartered at Camp Lejeune, North Carolina, and III MEF is headquartered on Okinawa, Japan.
MOS: Military Occupational Specialty – a four-digit, numeric code, that spells out your basic duties; what you do in the military…your job description. For example, an 0311 in the Marine Corps is an infantryman. The infantryman is considered the heart & soul of the Marine Corps, and his mission is to "locate, close with, and destroy the enemy by fire and maneuver, or by fire and close combat." Everyone else in the Marine Corps exists to support the infantryman. The 0302 Infantry Officer (my officer MOS) leads the enlisted infantrymen of the 03XX MOS's.
MPO: Military Protective Order. Similar in nature to a restraining order. Issued by a Convening Authority to one of his military members, spelling out what they can, or can't, do. If the MPO is violated in any way, the member

risks additional charges for failure to obey orders from a senior commissioned officer.
M.R.E.: Military Rules of Evidence. Court room guidance for military lawyers.
Mustang: An officer who served first as an enlisted Marine for a minimum of one four-year enlistment, before being commissioned as an officer.
NCIS: Naval Criminal Investigative Service. NCIS investigates all cases involving allegations of sexual misconduct in the Department of the Navy, which includes the Navy, and the United States Marine Corps.
NCO: Non-commissioned Officer. An enlisted Marine in the rank of Corporal, or Sergeant (E-4 & E-5).
NMCCA: The Navy-Marine Corps Court of Criminal Appeals. The first level of appellate review for the Department of the Navy, which includes both the U.S. Navy and U.S. Marine Corps.
OCS: Officer Candidate School. The Marine Corps' officer screening program in Quantico, Virginia. OCS is designed to answer the question, does a candidate have what it takes to be an officer in the United States Marine Corps?
Officer Panel: The senior military members, comprising what is essentially the jury. Unlike in the civilian judicial system, the jury is not comprised of your peers. All members of the officer panel in a court martial are senior to the defendant, and the jury-pool is hand-picked by the same individual directing your prosecution – your Boss or Convening Authority (through his lawyers). Twelve jurors are not required in military courts. Five is the minimum requirement.
OIC: Officer-in-Charge. The person in charge of a specialized military unit. Sort of like a Commanding Officer, but not imbued with the same legal and command authorities. Like wardens of Marine Corps Brigs, typically a Chief Warrant Officer.
POG: Person other than a GRUNT. Pronounced "pogue.".
POS: Position. What is your current POS? – pronounced pause – (i.e. where are you located right now?).
POS: Piece of Shit.
Prisoner: Confined in a post-Trial status, serving time for convictions, wearing an orange suit.
Proper Prior Planning, Prevents Piss-Poor Performance: A military concept, and mindset, for making sure that the mission is executed with precision.

PTA: Pretrial agreement. An agreement, wherein the accused agrees to plead guilty to specific charges in order to get a guaranteed sentence, worked out between the prosecution and defense lawyers, prior to legal proceedings. The vast majority of military members facing a Special or General courts martial sign a pretrial agreement before stepping into the courtroom, because our defense attorneys scare them into it. Less work for the lawyer. Military lawyers get the same paycheck whether or not they win or lose a case. Most just want a hasty agreement so they can move on to the next case.
Rack: Bed.
SILT: Separation in lieu of a trial. An agreement worked out by a detainee's defense attorney, wherein he accepts administrative separation from the Marine Corps instead of going to a court martial.
SJA: Staff Judge Advocate. A Marine Corps lawyer on a staff who provides legal advice to the commander.
SNCO: Staff Non-commissioned Officer. Enlisted Marines in the ranks of Staff Sergeant through Sergeant Major, or Master Gunnery Sergeant (E-6 – E-9).
SOTG: Special Operations & Training Group. Now EOTG.
SQ: Special Quarters. The section of Marine Corps confinement facilities considered solitary confinement in regular prisons. Individual cells isolated from the general population.
TBS: The Basic School. All newly commissioned Marine officers attend TBS in Quantico, Virginia for about four months prior to attending their MOS specialty school. The officer instructors at TBS teach the students all about the Marine Corps, and the different occupational specialties.
The 5 Ws: The details of a planned event: Who, What, Where, When, and Why.
UA: Unauthorized absence. Also known in the military as absence without leave (AWOL).
UCMJ: The Uniform Code of Military Justice.
VLC: Victim's Legal Counsel. Every "victim" is assigned their very own lawyer now in addition to all other lawyers on the prosecution's team.
WILCO: Will comply…roger that…good to go.
XO: Executive Officer. The number two person in a unit large enough to have a Commanding Officer.

INTRODUCTION

This is my story of surviving a vicious attack on my character. I was accused of a heinous crime out of left field, after 35 years of service. I had been a Colonel for five years in July of 2016 and had been just notified by higher headquarters that I was being considered for selection to general when a woman claimed that I had sexually assaulted her daughter. I was immediately treated by investigating agents and military prosecution lawyers as guilty, and they set about to collect as much dirt as they possibly could, putting my entire career under the microscope. Three separate investigations ensued prior to my court martial. Six months into the investigations, a second woman went to NCIS, accusing me of sexual assault. My boss immediately ordered that I be placed in pretrial confinement, where I languished for seven months awaiting my day in court.

My new mission in life is to put justice back into the military justice system. My prosecution was a direct result of bad policies forced on the military. What happened to me, happens routinely to junior service members in the military. I can assure you that the military's justice system is exponentially worse than the civilian judiciary. It doesn't seem right that the people willing to die to protect your rights should have less rights. I need your help in fixing the military justice system. Please elect national leaders who will return the sole concern of our Armed Forces to fighting and winning wars – our national security. We need leaders who will not allow for social experimentation in the military and who will prevent further destructive policies from tearing at the fabric of our military's mission. Those same leaders will also be required to reform our military justice system that is rotten to the core.

TABLE OF CONTENTS

DEDICATION		iii
DISCLAIMER		iv
ACKNOWLEDGMENTS		v
MILITARY TERMS & ACRONYMS		xii
INTRODUCTION		xvii
CHAPTER 1	CAN'T HANDLE THE TRUTH!	1
CHAPTER 2	OUT OF AFRICA, AND INTO THE CORPS	5
CHAPTER 3	DINNER PARTY IMPLOSION	11
CHAPTER 4	WITCH HUNT	18
CHAPTER 5	ME TWO!	33
CHAPTER 6	FRIDAY, THE 13TH	37
CHAPTER 7	THE WAITING GAME	44
CHAPTER 8	INTO THE ARENA	69
CHAPTER 9	HELL HATH NO FURY	135
CHAPTER 10	LAND DOWN UNDER	157
CHAPTER 11	CLOSING ACT	176
CHAPTER 12	A JURY OF COWARDS	185
CHAPTER 13	CASE #22	203
CHAPTER 14	DOUBLE RAINBOW	218
CHAPTER 15	THE DIRTY DEAL	228
CHAPTER 16	BREAKING BAD	236
CHAPTER 17	THE LIFE OF RILEY	250
CHAPTER 18	POSTSCRIPT	255

CHAPTER 1
CAN'T HANDLE THE TRUTH

Like McCarthyism in the Red Scare, the #MeToo Movement weaponized finger-pointing as proof-positive of guilt, wrongfully destroying countless innocent lives with false allegations.

"**You are being charged with the rape of a child**," the NCIS agent informed me, to my utter astonishment. He pointed to the charge sheet on his table and told me that he was going to read me my rights. I don't remember him reading me my rights. I was too stunned, and shocked to my core with emotions of dismay, anger, and disbelief, all intermingling explosively – I thought my head was going to burst! Deep down inside, however, I wasn't overly concerned about the charge, because I had done no such thing. I believed that I would be quickly cleared when the investigative team started looking into this charge. How could anyone in their right mind believe that I had raped, or molested, a six-year-old child, while sitting in my living room and having a professional conversation with her father and a visiting academic? I sat next to the girl's father on my couch the entire evening talking shop and swapping war stories with their father and a guest. All the while that we were conversing, the girl, her twin sister, and nine-year-old sister were scampering about the house like hell on wheels, reminding me of angry little bees buzzing around us all evening long. I remember remarking to my wife at some point during the evening that "I can't wait till these hellions go home!"

Instead of recognizing that the charge was absolutely unbelievable, NCIS launched a fourteen-month investigation with all the resources of the United States government at their disposal. NCIS weaponized the investigative process with the sole aim of digging up any dirt they could uncover from my entire career in the Marine Corps. At one point, prior to my court martial, there were twenty-seven charges, twenty-six of which had been stacked onto the original charge of raping a child in my living room in front of her father with the other two sisters and a visitor present. Many of the additional charges were so frivolous as to beg incredulity that they were actually to be taken into a court room.

At the very moment NCIS agents were talking to me at their headquarters building at Camp Lejeune, North Carolina, six other NCIS agents had stormed our home on base, flashing their badges menacingly at my wife, and demanding that she immediately open up our front door. Not fully understanding her own legal rights, they coerced my wife into speaking with two agents, while the other agents ripped through our home, snapping pictures, collecting DNA samples, and helping themselves to whatever they wanted to take. The mess they left in our home looked like the aftermath of a hurricane.

NCIS agents interrogated my wife, as you might imagine they would a terrorism suspect, telling her upfront that they already knew so much more than she did. They insisted that she tell them everything she knew; come clean with them, so to speak. *Are you aware of your husband's infidelities? Does he pay you to be married to him? How many women do think he's slept with? We heard that he fraternized with Marines in the past. Tell us what you know about his fraternization. Did he ever molest your daughter? Did he ever molest your son? Do you know if he ever molested his own daughter? Tell us about your husband's sexual proclivities? Have you ever suspected that he has a sexual interest in children? Are you aware of him viewing or downloading any child pornography? Does he have a porn stash that you can show us? Does he watch a lot of porn?*

On and on, the agents interrogated my terrified wife with salacious, probing, questions, representing the true character of their entire fourteen-month investigation against me. They were on a fishing expedition, not at all concerned about conducting a fair investigation. In the end, dozens of NCIS agents around the globe, employed similar under-handed techniques in their quest to dig up as much dirt as they could for the prosecution at my court martial. They ignored the basic truth in my case - my innocence, because they couldn't handle the truth! NCIS agents even trumped up the mother's initial charge of "inappropriately touching" her daughter into "rape of a child under twelve." They desperately wanted everything to line up with their incomprehensible narrative.

Meanwhile, back at the NCIS office on Camp Lejeune, NCIS agents wanted to talk to me. By the very nature of the charge, I knew that no questions for which I provided answers would cause them to dismiss the charge and close out the investigation. I knew intuitively that there would be a lengthy investigation, and that the heinous charge would only be resolved in a legal venue, like a court martial. Therefore, anything I said to investigators would only be used against me in a court of law, and never to exculpate me. I therefore informed the agents that I had nothing to say to them, but that I would fully cooperate in providing whatever else they needed from me. They appeared very disappointed and pressed me several times, before it sunk in that I wasn't going to consent to an interview. They took pictures of me, finger-printed me, and collected samples of my DNA. When they were done a senior NCIS agent came into their office and said that he was required to escort me back to my headquarters building. He explained that it was a new NCIS policy for suicide prevention. Pretty crazy, I thought, realizing it was to cover their own asses. He followed me to the parking lot, and we both got in separate vehicles. Had he been serious about suicide prevention, he should have had me ride with him. Instead, he tailed me to my headquarters building, and we walked up to the office of the Chief-of-Staff for II Marine Expeditionary Force (II MEF), where he handed me off to a fellow Colonel. I sarcastically asked the NCIS agent to make sure he annotated in his report that I had displayed no suicidal ideations!

There were three of us in the Chief's office. The II MEF Chief-of-Staff, myself, and another Colonel from my office. I had just taken over as the G-3 Operations Officer for II MEF, and didn't know either of them that well, having never previously served with them.

The Chief announced that I was being relieved of my duties, and that I would be given a new office. He asked for my government-issued mobile phone (Blackberry), which I gave him. He asked that I not return for any reason to my G-3 office. He stated that through the course of the investigation, I could come and go as I pleased. That I had no reporting instructions, but he asked that I maintain phone contact with the Colonel from my office. I was also to make myself available, if he needed to meet with me for any reason. He finally asked me not to return home until he called me to let me know that NCIS was done, and out of my neighborhood.

NCIS agents took possession less than an hour later of my government computer, government laptop, the Blackberry, and numerous external hard drives, both government and personal that contained everything I had stored up for the previous two decades. Literally thousands of documents, pictures, and email files, fitness reports, and power point presentations. I had no private laptop or personal computer, but NCIS had a treasure trove of my electronic history.

I returned to the parking lot with the Colonel from my office, and we sat in my Ford Expedition, while I waited for the all clear signal. I was angry and vented to the junior Colonel. He was a decent fellow, and we had become friends in the relatively short time that he had worked for me. I pointed out that this was a unique opportunity for him to take charge as the Operations Officer. It would be a huge feather in his cap, leading the 75-person G-3 Operations Directorate of II MEF, and might lead to his being selected for command. Turns out that I was right – he was awarded a plum command assignment about a year later in the summer of 2017, just prior to the start of my court martial.

Finally, getting the all clear signal, the junior Colonel exited my vehicle, and I returned home. My wife was a nervous wreck, after the intense interrogation she had endured from NCIS. I tried my best to calm her down and reassure her that everything was going to be okay. I told her it was going to be a long road ahead, but that it would all work out in the end. I just didn't realize that Friday evening, 15 July of 2016, how long that road was going to actually be.

CHAPTER 2
OUT OF AFRICA, AND INTO THE CORPS

*I got MERCENARY and MISSIONARY
mixed up, landing me in a Marine Corps
recruiting office.*

Who is Dan Wilson? Shortly after I was born, my parents flew out to Africa with me and my three elder siblings. I spent the majority of my childhood, growing up in various African countries where they were

**The Bamboo Enclosure into the Nile River, Sudan
Dad holding me in his left arm (Circa 1962)**

missionaries. My mom, a medical doctor, provided free health care to locals in desperate need of her services. My dad was a schoolteacher and pastor.

Both were devoted Christians, spreading the word of God to anyone willing to listen. It was their life's work. I lived at various times in the Sudan, South Africa, Namibia, and Kenya. I learned to swim in the Nile River when I was three years old. I grew up playing soccer and rugby, but I also learned to play basketball at a missionary boarding school in Kenya. I got to climb Mt. Kilimanjaro when I was fourteen and travel the length of Africa from Cape Town to Cairo, which is more than five thousand miles on rough roads. We had no TV, and I stayed entertained by playing with local kids my age and reading books. I also loved riding my bike around and became a proficient bike mechanic.

Fixing Bikes in Rumbek, Sudan (Circa 1975)

In Namibia, I had a bushman friend who taught me how to track and stalk game along with other survival techniques. I was fluent in the local languages wherever we lived, being proficient in seven during my childhood: Dinka, Nuer, Shilluk, Arabic, Zulu, Afrikaans, and Swahili. I took French in high school, but the only French I remember now is from a song, *Voule Vous*.

I was bred to be a United States Marine, and obviously destined to be one. God chose me to be one of the few, one of the proud, and my upbringing in Africa helped prepare me for being a Marine. Prior to joining the Marines as a twenty-year-old, I had traveled to forty countries, had interacted with several other cultures, had learned to speak a few languages, and had demonstrated an ability to get along with people who couldn't have been more different.

I felt like I belonged in the Marines when I first stepped onto the Yellow Footprints in Boot Camp. I excelled in Boot Camp, graduating as the Platoon and Series Honor Man, as well as earning the distinction as the fittest recruit in our Series of 300-plus men. I was also the only recruit in the company to survive the highest qualification in the swimming pool, a day long series of swimming tests, which concluded with one having to tread water in cammies and boots for an hour, while two drill instructors tried to drown you. I was bursting with pride on graduation day in my full Dress Blue uniform with my dad seated in the stands.

My enlisted job, or military occupational specialty was 2631, which is an Electronic Intelligence (ELINT) Operator. It became 2632 when I was assigned to VMAQ-2 Squadron at Cherry Point, North Carolina, after additional training in California. It involved working with top secret stuff all day and was fascinating. It was important work pertaining directly to our national security, and I felt like I was making a difference. My superiors felt my performance was outstanding as well. Shortly after graduating at the top of my class from NCO School, I was promoted meritoriously to Sergeant on 2 February 1983, a mere sixteen months after graduating from Boot Camp. Prior to that, I had been promoted meritoriously to Private First Class, Lance Corporal, and Corporal. I had maintained proficiency & conduct markings throughout of 5.0/4.9. Following my first tour at Cherry Point, I was selected to be an instructor in our trade craft and sent to Point Mugu, California to teach the newcomers to our MOS of 2632. While there, I was selected for Staff Sergeant, and I submitted my application for the Marine Corps Enlisted Commissioning and Educational Program (MECEP). I was shortly thereafter selected for the academic year of 1986, and attended the University of Arizona in Tucson, Arizona.

I graduated from the University of Arizona magna cum laude…a 3.45 GPA…with a Bachelor of Science degree in Business Administration on 22 December 1988. In the MECEP program, you are not commissioned after completing Officer Candidates School (OCS), but must first graduate from the university you're attending, and have your bachelor's degree in hand. I had previously attended OCS as a Staff Sergeant during the summer of 1987.

I then attended The Basic School (TBS) in 1989, which is a required six-month school that all newly commissioned Lieutenants must attend, prior to going to their MOS school. I was the top-scoring pistol shooter of our company and graduated third in my TBS company of 222 men. I wanted to be an infantry officer, and based on my TBS class standing, I was able the get the exact MOS that I desired. I graduated from the Infantry Office Course with The Wheeler Award for infantry excellence and a new MOS of 0302.

I commanded four different platoons, three separate companies, and four battalions as an officer. I was the security detachment commander on the USS Kitty Hawk for three years. I served a two-year stint at Marine Corps Recruit Depot, San Diego, as the Executive Officer and Commanding Officer of Third Recruit Training Battalion, and was the Commanding Officer of Recruiting Station, San Diego for three years. I attended the Marine Corps Command and Staff College, graduating with distinction and with a master's degree. I attended the National War College at Fort McNair, graduating as the top student in four of the nine courses I completed, and with a second master's degree. I served in the Pentagon on the Joint Staff for two years, as the Colonel in charge of a division that was dedicated to supporting our forces in Afghanistan. I was selected for O-6 command while at the Pentagon, and subsequently served a two-year stint as the Commanding Officer of Weapons and Field Training Battalion, Parris Island, South Carolina. I served for two years as the Chief-of-Staff for Third Marine Division on Okinawa, followed by a short stint as the Officer-in-Charge (OIC) of III MEF's Special Operations and Training Group.

I deployed eleven times for a total of five and a half years in support of our national security objectives, and many times into harm's way. I participated in combat operations in Kuwait, and Iraq, and I made three trips to Afghanistan. I was shot at repeatedly and withstood numerous indirect fire attacks on our bases. I was blown up during the Second Battle of Fallujah when the vehicle I was riding in hit an improvised explosive device (IED). By my count of my official records, I was awarded fifty-two ribbons and medals during my career with my final medal, a Legion of Merit, being awarded in 2013. Further awards that were in the system in 2016 were erased on account of my pending litigation. I was awarded a Bronze Star and Navy-Marine Corps Achievement Medal for my performance during combat operations, and the V for valor on my Navy-Marine Corps Achievement Medal denotes heroism during Operation Desert Storm. I was also awarded a Navy-Marine Corps

Commendation Medal for saving a civilian man's life.

I absolutely loved serving on active duty in the Marines, and my only regret in life is that I have but one life to give to my Corps and Country. Semper Fi!

Pics from my childhood

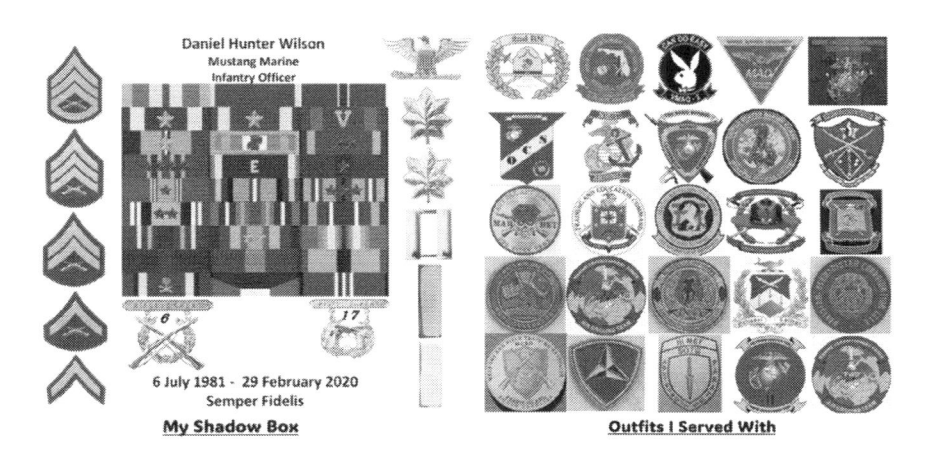

6 July 1981 - 29 February 2020
Semper Fidelis
My Shadow Box

Outfits I Served With

Career Pics

CHAPTER 3
DINNER PARTY IMPLOSION

I first met the junior officer in January 2008 when he was a Captain, and on temporary orders to Camp Pendleton, California, where I was stationed. Seven years later he was working for me, after I took over as the Officer-In-Charge of III MEF's Special Operations and Training Group on Okinawa, Japan. Before I returned to the States from my thirty-three-month stint on Okinawa, he asked me to help him get orders to an infantry battalion at Camp Pendleton. I linked him up that same day, via email, with an old friend of mine, who was the Commanding Officer of 1st Marine Regiment at Camp Pendleton.

Four months later in June of 2016, shortly after I had assumed my duties as the Operations Officer for II MEF at Camp Lejeune, North Carolina, I was surprised to hear that they were moving to Camp Lejeune, because I had thought he was hell-bent on going to Camp Pendleton. He told me later that he had heard a mentor of his was taking command of an infantry battalion at Camp Lejeune and he had successfully lobbied to get the position as his Executive Officer.

A few weeks later, I was sitting in the front yard on base when he pulled into my driveway with his family. They were temporarily staying out in Jacksonville in an extended stay motel, while they awaited a home on base to open up. They had wanted to check in with me, so they had driven all around the neighborhood until they found our home. As we were catching up, my wife drove up into the driveway, returning from buying groceries at the commissary. I introduced them to my wife, who was meeting them for the first time. After hearing his wife mention that she was doing the family's laundry at a decrepit laundromat in Jacksonville, my wife told her that she was welcome to come over to our house any time to use our washer, dryer, or to just hang out. My wife is a very nurturing person and was always volunteering to help out any of my Marines, or their family members. She was a morale multiplier for me, always doing meaningful things for my Marines' spouses and families that I would never have thought of. My wife exchanged phone numbers with his wife, and during the next few weeks, they got together several times, while he and I were on duty. My wife took them to Walmart and bought the girls toys. She paid for all of them to have manicures and pedicures. My wife quickly assumed the role of a beloved Aunt to their three daughters and that of a best friend to his wife.

Our Home and View of the New River at Camp Lejeune

He and I decided to start working out together at the functional fitness (CrossFit) facility on Camp Lejeune. We met at 0515 weekday mornings to perform the workout of the day (WOD). In early July 2016, he asked for my help in getting a guest speaker to speak to his battalion. His battalion did not have the funds to pay for the guest speaker, so he was asking that I arrange for the funding through the operations division of II MEF. He was proposing that the professional military education (PME) opportunity be opened up for any officer in II MEF to attend, and that my office would be the sponsor. I agreed, and had my administrative folk make the arrangements for a gentleman to come educate us on U.S.A.I.D. and what they do around the globe for the U.S. government. The guest flew into Jacksonville airport, the afternoon of 13 July 2016. Following our CrossFit workout that morning, the junior officer had surprised me by asking that I pick up the guest from the airport that afternoon. He claimed that he couldn't pull away from pressing duties at his battalion. I agreed, as I had a few days prior, when he had asked that we host the dinner party for the guest at my home instead of his. His reason being that they had just moved in there two weeks prior, and it wasn't ready yet to host guests at a dinner party. My wife and his wife worked out who was going to be responsible for what at the dinner party.

I left my office around 1400 on the afternoon of 13 July 2016 to go pick up the guest from Jacksonville's airport. The first stop was to check him in at the All Points Inn, which is about a half mile from where my home was. My administrative clerk had not only arranged for the guest's plane tickets but had also secured one of the VIP suites for him. We tossed his bags in the room and drove over to my home, arriving about 1600. My wife opened a bottle of wine, and we sat down in our living room to chat, before the junior officer's family arrived. I poured myself some whiskey, which had become my beverage of choice in the recent five years. On a previous evening when they had been at our house, one of the twins had asked me what I was drinking. "Apple juice," I replied, "do you want some?" Her parents laughed, and it was clear to everyone in the living room that I was joking. I would have never allowed her to even have touched my glass.

The dinner guest had served with USAID for decades, including several years of service in the Sudan. He and I had plenty to talk about that evening, given that I had spent my childhood growing up in Africa with seven years living in the Southern Sudan. We were bonding and dropping names about people we both knew in the military and government, once again validating my postulate that there is less than one degree of separation in the Marine Corps. Lost in our conversation, and content to keep chatting the rest of the evening, the junior officer's family arrived at our doorstep. It was like a whirlwind of locusts descending on our home. The girls demanded to be the center of attention in the living room, and I became their primary target. They were like a swarm of angry bees around me. I was trying to converse with the guest and their father, when out of nowhere, one of them would kick me in the shin, or slug me in the shoulder. At one point, and in a moment that would later become consequential in the trial, they interrupted what I was saying to their dad and the guest and demanded that I judge which of them had the cutest belly button. I looked over at their dad for guidance, and he just smiled and gave me a whatever shrug with his shoulders. The twins saw his look and pulled up their shirts, baring their belly buttons, and demanded that I render my judgement. I did a quick eeny, meeny, miny, moe, and pointed at one of the twins. She immediately wanted to know what her prize was for winning. Just to get rid of her, I shot back that she could go upstairs and grab my wallet from my bed-stand, and have whatever bill was left in my wallet. I was pretty sure that there was only one bill, which was either a one-dollar, five-dollar, or ten-dollar bill. She quickly returned, holding up a ten-dollar bill in victory.

Later on that evening, one of the twins was sitting on my knee in the living room and interrupted our conversation to suggest that her mother come sit on my lap. "Come sit on Colonel Dan's lap, mom. You should try it. Please?" All of us adults merely grinned at her comment, knowing that kids say crazy things. Well, her mom, actually got up from her seat, walked over, and sat down, right next to me on the couch, saying, "I'm not going to sit on his lap, but I'll sit next to him." I put my arm around her in a family kind of way, and she smiled. She got back up, soon thereafter, and went back to gossiping, and drinking cocktails with my wife in our kitchen.

There came a time in the evening when I just had to take a time-out and get some fresh air. This was the only time in the evening that I was ever by myself. At least, I thought I was by myself. I stepped out the front door and took a seat in my front lawn on a swaying bench. It was relaxing to look out at the New River in all her glory with the summer sun starting to set, while rocking slowly, back and forth on the bench. I sat there for about five minutes, when I felt a hard blow to the back of my head. I heard it too. Crack! It was loud and it hurt. My neighbor, a Lieutenant Colonel who worked for me at II MEF, heard and watched it from his driveway as well, and started to walk over in my direction, asking if I was going to be okay. Never wanting to ruin my image as a hardcore Marine infantry officer, I told him that it was no big deal, and that I was good-to-go. I couldn't admit to an artillery officer, one of my subordinates in the Operations section, that I was a weak sister. One of the twins, must have been the evil twin, snuck out the back door, after I had gone out the front, found a dead tree-limb, crept up on me like a ninja, then had used the tree-limb like a baseball bat to whack the back of my head. I returned immediately to the living room and the conversation with her father, and the dinner guest. No, I did not throw her under the bus by snitching on her.

The evening continued with drinking and conversation, mainly between the junior officer, our dinner guest, and I. My wife and the junior officer's wife went back and forth between the living room and the kitchen, which was adjacent to, and connected to the living room by a short foyer. Walk out of the living room, turn right, and you are out the front door in six feet. Walk out of the living room, and turn left, you are in the kitchen in about ten feet. You can be in the kitchen and clearly hear people talking in the living room. My wife and the junior officer's wife were having their own conversation, which was mainly gossip, while they enjoyed cocktails. They would wander into the living room from time to time, and inject themselves into our conversation, or interact with the three girls. The twins had not tired of harassing and rough-housing with Colonel Dan – me. Kids that age typically have a mandatory bedtime in the middle of the week. I continued hoping it was sooner, rather than later.

The dinner party came to an abrupt end around 2100. Ten minutes before the end, one twin was chasing the other out of the dining room into the living room. Their father was standing by the fireplace to the left side of our wall-mounted, big-screen, TV. The twin in the front, rounded the corner from the dining room into the living room at a full sprint, and smacked right into her dad's right thigh. She immediately fell; her head banging off the hard wood floor with a loud thud. Her contact with the floor was significant enough, that I volunteered to call for emergency medical personnel to come evaluate the blow to her head. Their father didn't think that was necessary, picked his daughter up in his arms, and carried her into the kitchen to get her mother's attention and sympathy. My wife, also in the kitchen, decided to give them a moment alone, and encouraged the other two girls to go upstairs with her to look at jewelry. She had them each pick out a piece of fake jewelry for themselves, and something to give to the injured twin.

The dinner guest, the girls' father, and I, continued our conversation in the living room, as if nothing serious had happened. The kid was having a good cry with her mom, but we all thought she would be okay. My wife and the girls came back downstairs, and they seemed happy about the new jewelry from their auntie. My wife came over and sat down next to me in the living room.

A few minutes later our conversation was rudely interrupted by the junior officer's wife. Her demeanor was completely opposite of what it had been up till that point in the evening. She was standing in the foyer with the girls flanking her and screaming at the top of her lungs. It soon became apparent that she was screaming at me. "What did you do to my daughter?," she demanded to know of me. "I didn't do anything to your daughter," I shot back. "You know what you did to my daughter," she yelled back at me. At this point, I'm thinking she is trying to pin the blame for her daughter's accident on me. Maybe she thought that her daughter had run into my leg, then hit her head on the floor on my account. I was confused and said, "I don't know what you're talking about." She immediately replied with, "you know exactly what I'm talking about." Before I could answer her, she loudly blurted out, "you might be a Colonel, but I'm going to take you the 'f' down!" I had stood up when she first started her tirade, and I now looked over at the junior officer, and asked him "what the hell is going on, Brother?" He shrugged his shoulders, and said "I have no idea, sir." She then walked over to her husband and insisted that they leave my house immediately, that it was for his safety. Our dinner guest was standing at this point, also looking confused, while the family was exiting our home, heading out to load up their van. He went outside to talk to them, and returned shortly to tell my wife and I that he would be leaving with them, and this was a situation that would need to be discussed with the junior officer in the morning. He then left our house and rode in their van back to their home. My wife and I stood in our living room for a while, asking ourselves what had just happened.

  The next morning when I fired up my work computer, I had an email from the dinner guest, suggesting that I needed to talk to the junior officer as soon as possible to work things out, and that he, the guest, was bailing on his presentation, and returning to DC immediately. Would I be so kind as to have my clerk get his tickets changed to the first flight out of Jacksonville? I immediately forwarded his email to my clerk, and the guest had his tickets changed, flying out a few hours later. I then sent an email to the junior officer, asking what was up with his wife, and suggesting that we get together for lunch to have a face-to-face chat. Crickets! Silence on the net. I didn't hear back from him the entire day. When I returned home after work, my wife and I continued to speculate as to what had set off the junior officer's wife. We were dumbfounded. My wife told me that she had tried to text her several times during the day, but with no success. I was tired and went upstairs around 2000 to relax in our bedroom and watch TV. My wife got a phone call, right as I was lying down. It was the junior officer, and he wanted to talk to me. It didn't register as odd at the time that he was calling my wife's phone to speak with me, even though he had my phone number on speed dial. He began our conversation by informing me that his wife believed that I had inappropriately touched one of their twin daughters. I told him that "no" I had never inappropriately touched any of his daughters. I assured him that his daughters were like my own granddaughters, and that if I ever suspected that anyone had inappropriately touched either of his daughters, or my daughters, I would have pulled a *Dexter* on them by taking justice into my own hands. When I mentioned that we had all been together in the living room, and that I had never been alone with any of the girls, he said that his wife thought that it may have occurred on a previous visit to our home. I reiterated that I had never been alone with any of his daughters at any time. We went back and forth, until he finally asked me what would I do, if I were him. "What would you do, sir?" I told him that I would recommend that he do what I would advise any Marine to do: to go with his gut, and to do what he feels is the right thing. Thus ended our phone call.

    The following morning, Friday 15 July 2016, I had finished a meeting with my staff, and was back in my office at II MEF. Earlier in the morning at 0700, I had provided an operational briefing to the Deputy Commanding General, as our Commanding General was out of town. I typically provided the Boss an around-the-world operational brief, first thing every Monday, Wednesday, and Friday morning. The Commanding General was in Quantico, Virginia, attending to Marine Corps matters, which is Marine-speak for sitting on a selection board. Now, back in my office, the phone rang, and I looked at my digital clock. It read 1044. I answered, and an NCIS agent asked me to kindly come over to their headquarters building and ask to speak to agent so and so. I then knew for sure that the junior officer and his wife had gone to NCIS. I got a sick feeling in my stomach, anticipating the worst of all possible scenarios.

CHAPTER 4
WITCH HUNT

"Show me the man and I'll show you the crime." Lavrentiy Beria

Stalin's most ruthless and longest-serving Secret Police Chief, Lavrentiy Beria, bragged that he could prove misconduct on anyone, even the innocent. "Show me the man and I'll show you the crime" was Beria's legendary boast. Beria would be delighted to know that NCIS adheres to his same investigative strategy. In fact, in my experience, it's a strategy employed by the majority of military investigating officers. They treat service members under investigation as "guilty," then the investigating officer "finds" the evidence they need to prove "guilt" in a court of law. If they are unable to come up with any evidence for the crime accused of, they will continue to investigate the "target" in order to find evidence of other "crimes." They will always find something to hand over to the prosecution, regardless of whom is being investigated. No person out there is squeaky clean. This "no hold's barred" strategy has been bolstered by the MeToo movement, because investigators never put any credence in what an accused might say. They always believe the "victim" first.

From 15 July 2016 onward, I was under investigation by NCIS, and then a separate Command Investigation, conducted by a Marine lawyer. His sole mission in life was to assassinate the character of a fellow Colonel whom he had never met and have his investigation compliment NCIS's investigation. He did a tremendous job of dredging up private remarks I had made to a few individuals in my past in order to conclude in his investigation that indeed I was a sexual predator. He based his conclusion on "guy talk" from private conversations between myself and friends, which to be clear, although inappropriate, never involved any discussions about children. His hit piece was so impressive that he was subsequently promoted to be the senior Staff Judge Advocate (SJA) to my boss, the Commanding General of II MEF. In that new role, the very individual who had conducted an investigation of me was now the man advising my boss on what to do, before, during, and after my court martial. At a motion hearing prior to the court martial, it was revealed that he was best friends with the presiding Judge in my case.

    Early on, I couldn't even talk to military defense lawyers. The senior defense counsel at Camp Lejeune told me that I would have to wait until charges were proffered by my boss, the convening authority (CA). Charges weren't proffered until four long months later. The first four days after being informed of the original charge by NCIS, I was convinced that I would represent myself at a court martial, and I was certain that it was going to a court martial. I thought I would have plenty of time to study up, prepare, and give it my best shot as my own layman lawyer. We had a term for that when I was an enlisted Marine, a sea lawyer. I believed that if I could look my jury in the eyes, they would see my honesty and sincerity, and sense that I was innocent of the despicable charge. The following week, I decided to seek advice from a friend, who is himself a Marine lawyer. The old phone-a-friend lifeline. I had known him for nearly two decades and trusted his advice. He advised me to not represent myself, explaining several reasons why it was not a good idea. I will never forget a phrase he used in our conversation. He said, "sir, a man who represents himself, has a fool for a client." I may never be the smartest man in any room, but I am smart enough to know when to take sound advice. He quickly stifled my desire to represent myself. He then recommended the name of an officer to be my senior military defense lawyer, if the allegation went to a court martial.

    I was initially given an office at the headquarters of the unit that was in charge of base operations. Ironically, my office was adjacent to the offices of their staff lawyers. I quickly discovered that they were not on my side, and even hostile toward me. The female lawyer in the office next to mine was the only friendly face. We had been stationed together, four years prior at Parris Island. The young Captain had then briefed me several times on cases involving my Marines. I had given her some marksmanship tips when she was doing her annual qualification on our pistol range. We had a good, friendly, professional relationship, and I could tell that she sympathized with my situation. One day I walked into her office and asked for her legal advice. She proceeded to give me several good tips and said that I needed a female lawyer on my team. A female lawyer, she explained, would be able to ask the difficult questions of females in the court room without coming across like a bully to the jury, as a male lawyer might. I immediately asked her, if she would consider being on my defense team. She said she would love to, but had just left the defense section, and was certain that her current bosses wouldn't allow it. Her intuition was confirmed the next day, when her direct superior asked if he could chat with me. He was obviously very nervous and uncomfortable. I think he was intimidated by both my rank and physical stature. He said that he knew I had spoken with the female captain and was respectfully asking me not to discuss my case anymore with anyone on his staff. I felt like standing up and bitch-slapping the little pogue, but I took the high road, and agreed that I wouldn't discuss my situation with her, or any of the other lawyers.

I did come and go from my office, exactly how I pleased, which was the only guidance I had received from the Chief-of-Staff when I was relieved of my duties at II MEF. On days that I did come in, I would check my military email account, and answer the mail. Nearly every week, I had requests from former Marines of mine to write them a letter of recommendation (LOR), for a special program in the Marine Corps, or a civilian job. Rarely did I ever get any feedback regarding how things went for them, which made this feedback from a former Marine of mine all the more significant. "I am fortunate to have belonged to the Corps and to have had leaders like you. There were 500 applicants for the job, and they picked one…me. They said they picked me based on your recommendation in the letter you wrote on my behalf. Thank you, sir."

I was also asked to perform ceremonies for Marines, while I was under investigation, which kept me busy in a meaningful way. The first request was from a Staff Sergeant, stationed at King's Bay, Georgia, who wanted me to promote him to Gunnery Sergeant. I immediately agreed, recognizing the side benefit of a road trip on my 2012 Harley-Davidson Ultra-Classic Electra-glide. I enjoyed a 500-mile ride on my Harley to King's Bay, Georgia, and was honored to promote a deserving Marine to the rank of Gunnery Sergeant.

A female Corporal insisted that I also re-enlist her. I had first met her at a Marine Corps Ball on Okinawa, when she was dating one of my Navy Corpsman from SOTG. She had since moved to Camp Lejeune and was feeling depressed about being separated from her beau. The Corpsman had contacted me a few months earlier, asking that I stop by where she worked to boost her spirits. I did as he had asked, and she had wanted a few pics on my Harley. I had accomplished the mission of improving her morale. I was honored to re-enlist her on the banks of the beautiful New River for four more years.

I was privileged to promote two Marines on 1 October 2016. We had all served together on Parris Island, and they were then on recruiting duty in central North Carolina. About a week prior, I had received a note in Facebook Messenger from one of the Sergeants: "Good morning sir, I just received confirmation that I will be promoted October first, and I would be honored if you can come out here to promote me." I was there and promoted the both of them at their recruiting office.

The ceremony of all ceremonies was as the retiring officer for a Master Sergeant serving at the Mecca of the Marine Corps in DC. It is the oldest Marine Corps post, constructed in 1801, and it is where our Commandant resides. It was the only set of buildings not burned by the British in Washington D.C., during the War of 1812. They refused to burn the Marine Barracks out of respect for the Marines' fighting spirit. He was set to retire in early December 2016 and asked me to come up to DC to serve as his retiring officer. Right before I was to drive up, the story about the charges against me became public. I called him up, and we discussed the recent press reports about me. I said, "I will completely understand, if you are now uncomfortable with me being your retiring officer. I don't want to be the elephant in the room that distracts from the ceremony, which is a celebration of your Marine Corps career." He immediately shot back at me, "sir, I would rather no one else retire me than you. Now, get your ass up here and retire me!" I left for DC the next morning and spent the next two nights at their home. The morning of 2 December 2016, I retired the Master Sergeant on what all Marines consider the hallowed grounds of 8th & I. While I was making my remarks, trying to give him a memorable send-off, I could see various Marines in the audience looking at me, and the lightbulb flashing on in their eyes, thinking, that's the Colonel I just read about. Hmmm. It was a magnificent ceremony, and a fitting tribute to his amazing career in the Marine Corps. He remains a loyal friend.

Many days, I just wouldn't go into the office at all, staying at home, and binge-watching different TV series. To prepare for the upcoming legal proceedings, I watched the entire series of Suits, which is about lawyers and legal stuff. I fell into a funk and fell even deeper into the whiskey bottle. I was feeling sorry for myself, and having pity parties, which typically involved hard drinking to dull the reality of what was to come. Several days, I would start drinking before breakfast. There were times when I would inspire myself to stop drinking for a few days and try to get back on track with sobriety. One such day, I got up early, went for a 3-mile run, and was relaxing afterward in the sway-bench on our front lawn. I soaked up the bright morning sunlight, and suddenly noticed a large evergreen tree on the other side of the street. It had a huge dark gash from about its chest-level, running down below its midsection. I instantly realized that it must have been struck by lightning, years earlier. I had never noticed it before, but here it was, demanding my attention. It was like it had a message for me, I took a huge, unexpected blow, and have continued to grow and thrive. "What is your problem?" Then, I heard a voice in the back of my head. It felt like the voice of God. The voice was exhorting me to "be like that tree!" Kind of like the old TV commercial, "be like Mike." I took it as a divine admonishment to stop feeling sorry for myself, and to have faith that the good Lord above has a plan for my life; all of our lives. I needed to step back and take my own advice. I had preached for decades to my Marines who were going through difficult times that everything happens for a reason. We don't always understand what that reason is at the time, but down the road at some point, you will look back and understand the reason why.

I took a concealed carry class one weekend, while under investigation. I was being accused of a despicable crime and I needed to protect myself and my family. I spent eight hours at a fire station near Richlands, North Carolina, receiving instruction on all the applicable laws and regulations for carrying a concealed pistol. This was one of the few times in my life that the thought of suicide entered my mind. In class that day, I had an internal debate with myself about suicide. I was extremely depressed to be falsely accused of an awful crime, being relieved of duties, and not knowing how long the investigation was going to take. Essentially, I was making a case for feeling sorry for myself, and just making all the pain go away by committing suicide.

The angel in my debate pointed out the immense pain my suicide would cause my family and friends and had me remember the helpless angst that I had experienced in the past when a Marine or friend I knew had committed suicide. I would ask myself if there had maybe been something that I could have done, or said, to have prevented the person from taking their own life. I imagined my daughters feeling the same angst and how it would likely scar them psychologically for life, if their dad committed suicide. The other thought was that if I did commit suicide, it would be tantamount to admitting that I was guilty as charged. This would be wholly unacceptable, given I was innocent. In the end, after many hours of back and forth between the angel and the devil in me, I concluded that, for me, suicide would be taking the easy way out, and that it would have unknowable, but adverse, second and third order effects on my family and friends. By the end of the day, the thought of suicide had vanished from my mind, and I was still able to pass the written test in spite of being distracted from the instruction by my internal debate. However, when we went out to a local farmer's field to complete the mandatory qualification, my hands were shaking like a leaf. Coincidentally, we were firing adjacent to a small cemetery, which briefly brought back the thought of suicide. Initially, I had a misfire, because I loaded the wrong ammunition into my pistol. I wasn't paying attention. After an embarrassing moment, when the instructor corrected me, I fired the rounds into the target. In spite of my shakiness, I was able to meet the qualification standard. I rode my Harley home that evening, giving thanks to God for giving me a new lease on life and ever more determined to keep the faith through whatever travails lay ahead.

    I decided to set up my own gym in our garage to avoid any of the base gyms, where I might risk violating my military protective order (MPO). The Chief-of-Staff had come over to my new office to hand-deliver the MPOs which stated that I wasn't allowed anywhere near my accuser or her family members. I ordered a barbell, bumper plates, kettlebells, and a wall ball. I installed a pull-up bar in the garage and constructed my own box jump. I put down special green rubber matting. I christened it the Big Foot gym and tried to do some kind of workout every day. I spent many hours in my garage gym, reducing my stress through sheer physical exertion. I'm not a physiologist, but I am convinced that there is a definite connection between the physical and the mental. Endorphins are generated during physical exertion, and they produce a soothing and satisfying effect in my brain. This was critical therapy for me to work out when I was put on ice, during the investigation.

The only thing I was asked to do by my command in the first six months under investigation was to get evaluated by the substance abuse counseling office (SACO). I dutifully reported for my evaluation the following day and blew a 0.0 on their breathalyzer. I was pleasantly surprised since I had consumed some whiskey the night prior, but was pleased, nonetheless. I knew that my command was hoping to label me as an "alcoholic," and I did not want to give them that additional weapon to use against me. Clearly, I'm not an alcoholic, I reassured myself. After-all, I can go for six months on a deployment without a drop to drink, and I can stop drinking on any given day. I left their office many hours later with a clean bill of health…no addictions whatsoever…and felt like that was my first victory in the legal battle that was looming on the horizon.

I started to get numerous phone calls, text messages and emails from family members, and Marines I had served with. I was very careful about what I said, because I suspected immediately that my phone had been tapped by NCIS, and that everything I was saying or writing was being silently recorded by their agents. Five months later in December 2016, I was finally assigned government counsel, and they confirmed my suspicions, as did the civilian lawyer I hired in December 2016.

The conversations I had with everyone gave me insight into the nature of all three of the investigations. I began to get a growing list of Marines contacting me, just to let me know that they had been interviewed by NCIS, and they had nothing but good things to say about me, my leadership, honor, and integrity. A Marine Major stationed on Okinawa, messaged me that NCIS had interviewed him and his wife. I had been his commanding officer at two different commands, where we had served together. The interview was short, because the couple only had good things to say about me, and NCIS was fishing for "dirt" on Colonel Dan Wilson. His wife messaged me separately about the interview, and to say how much her husband and her respected me, and always had.

My first wife contacted me. We were divorced in 1986, and I hadn't heard from her in the intervening thirty years. She told me that two NCIS agents had visited her at her home in Louisiana. They first verified that she had been married to me, then informed her of the nature of the charges against me. Their plea to her was, "do you have any dirt from your marriage that we can use against Colonel Wilson?" She fired right back at them, "I have nothing but good things to say about Dan Wilson...now, get the 'f' outta my house!" I smiled remembering what a firecracker that red-headed lady could be when fired up.

A female Major called me from Okinawa, where I had been stationed from August 2013 through March 2016. NCIS agents interviewed her and her husband, also a Major. "We heard that in September of 2013, Colonel Wilson may have touched your thigh in an inappropriate manner at the officers' club. Can you substantiate that, and would you be willing to testify against him?" She told the NCIS agents, "No. Colonel Wilson never at any time touched my thigh in an inappropriate manner, and my husband was sitting right next to me the entire time we were at the officers' club. Besides, Colonel Wilson is a good man and a dear friend of our family."

NCIS agents tracked down a Marine I had served with at Parris Island, where civilians east of the Mississippi River are transformed into United States Marines...one of our two Boot Camps. He emailed me their interaction the same day it occurred. NCIS agent: "We understand that you served with Colonel Wilson on Parris Island, and that he had you court martialed. You must be resentful of the asshole. Now's your chance to get back at him by sharing any dirt you might have had on him while you served together." The Marine I had sent to a Summary Court Martial four years earlier told NCIS, "Colonel Wilson is the best commanding officer I had in the Marines, and I want to testify on his behalf." Suddenly, the NCIS agents didn't want to talk to him anymore.

My own children let me know that NCIS agents were snooping around their places of residence and reaching out to each of them for interviews. What were they to do? I told them that I couldn't give them any advice, because then I would likely be charged with obstruction of justice, or intimidating witnesses. That they would have to seek legal advice from their friends who were lawyers. Whatever advice they did get was spot on, because neither of the three sat down with any investigating agent. They understood that all the good things they had to say about me would be for naught...that the investigating agents were only looking for dirt on their dad.

I got a phone call from a Sergeant Major, stationed in Hawaii, that shed light on the investigative processes used by the Colonel lawyer who was tasked with taking me down, and also collecting additional dirt for my prosecution. The Sergeant Major and I had served for two years on Okinawa from the summer of 2013 to the summer of 2015. "Sir, I just had to let you know that I had a conversation with Colonel Pogue lawyer who is conducting an investigation on you. He sent me a summary of our conversation, asking that I sign off on it. It was at least seventy-five percent inaccurate, sir. He had me saying negative stuff about you that I had never said. Everything I told him about you was glowing. I literally had to rewrite the transcript with the help of my lawyers before I signed it and returned it to the Colonel investigating you. Just wanted to give you a head's up about the dude investigating you. He's doing you no favors, sir. He is out to take you down. Watch your six, sir!" I later learned that the Colonel used his strong-arm tactic to manipulate one of my friends into testifying against me by threatening to prosecute him for a different crime, if he refused to cooperate.

It wasn't until 21 November 2016 that I was finally informed of the first tranche of charges by the II MEF Chief-of-Staff. He also had present in his office, the Sergeant Major, the Staff Judge Advocate, and a handful of other Colonels to be witness to the event. He issued me new military protective orders from the general, banning me from the main roads on base that might pass near to the home of my accuser, and the local elementary school. He also asked that I allow a fellow Colonel to escort me to my home, collect all my weapons, and accompany him to the armory to turn them in. I did, and later that same evening, agents from the Criminal Investigative Division (CID) showed up at my doorstep, demanding to come in and search my home for weapons. The base general had directed CID to search and seize my weapons, after learning that I had only turned in two pistols instead of the four I had registered. I explained to the CID agents, as I had to my escort earlier in the day, that I had given away one of my pistols to a Marine for winning a competition, and the other pistol was in the possession of a retired Marine who was going to fix it for me. CID wasn't buying my explanations and ripped apart our home. Hours later they concluded their search, coming up empty-handed. Just as had previously happened after NCIS agents had torn through our home, my wife and I labored for hours to pick up the pieces and restore our home to normalcy.

When my case was turned over to government lawyers for prosecution, they conducted their own investigation, trying to gin up even more charges to stack onto my case. I got a phone call from a captain who had worked for me years prior, talking about how a lawyer from the prosecution team had reached out to him, asking if he had any dirt on me, and would he be willing to testify against me in court. My former subordinate said that he told the prosecution lawyer, "I don't have any dirt on Colonel Wilson, and good luck finding anyone who has anything bad to say about him. He was a great officer to work for."

The prosecution lawyers certainly tried to find someone with dirt on me. They heard about a beautiful female Marine who was out of the Corps but had served four years earlier with me on Parris Island. They called her, "we heard that you used to work for Colonel Wilson, and he is now being charged with heinous crimes. Did he ever come on to you in an inappropriate manner that you can testify to in court against him?" God bless her for telling them, "Colonel Wilson was the best commanding officer I worked for, and I want to come testify on his behalf!" All of a sudden, her phone went dead...click, dial-tone, and she never heard back from them.

Five months into the three investigations on me, I decided to write an email to "Uncle Bob," the Commandant of the Marine Corps. I had served twice with General Bob Neller; once at Camp Fallujah, Iraq, and a second time in the Pentagon. I had taught him a few words of Swahili, while we were at Camp Fallujah, because he wanted to chat with the soldiers from Uganda serving with us and he found out that I knew how to speak Swahili, from attending high school in Kenya. In fact, he overheard me speaking Swahili with the Ugandan soldiers one day, and wanted to know what we were saying that was so hilarious. In December of 2016, I just knew he was being hounded by the press about the notorious Colonel Dan Wilson. I also knew that all of the information about me and the investigations was being fed to him by military lawyers. I wanted "Uncle Bob" to know the real story, directly from me, since we had had a great professional and personal relationship for over a decade:

      From: **Colonel Daniel H. Wilson**
      To: **General Robert B. Neller**
      Subj: **Clearing the Air with my Commandant**
      Date: 22 December 2016 at 2:02 p.m.

Uncle Bob (most affectionately and respectfully),

I apologize in advance that this will be lengthy, but this has been welling up inside me for the past 5 months! I'm only sharing this with you, because I've known you for 11 years and we have served together twice in combat zones...Iraq and The Pentagon! We inhaled the same noxious fumes from Camp Fallujah's trash pits, I taught you bits and pieces of Swahili, we anguished together during the recovery effort of our Marines who were tragically swept away in the 7 ton, trying to cross the flooded river bed, and I'll never forget how you tried to get me command of 3/1 when the Bn Cmdr was fired, or when you emailed me 29 points for improving my presentations to VIPs/visitors, or when you extended me that last month in Iraq by calling Col Padilla to shift my change-of-command for ITB, or when we high-five'd each other going into the Pentagon, the morning after Osama was killed. Just a few of our many great memories together. Up to this point, you've only heard one side of my case. Since this is a PR black eye for the Marine Corps, particularly after one-sided and sensational articles have been published about me, and since we have a long history together, you need to know my side, so you have a balanced picture as our Commandant and on an officer you know so well.

On July 15th, 2016, I was summoned to NCIS where two agents informed me that I was being accused by a fellow Marine's wife of raping one of her three daughters at a dinner party, hosted at my quarters on July 13th. Days later, I found out that she had also accused me of adultery and fraternization, while I was "unaccompanied" on Okinawa, prior to executing orders to Lejeune in April. Her sources for the other allegations were rumors, gossip, and "third shitter from the left!" The agents assured me that their investigation would be "fair and balanced"... yeah, right! It so happens that I served with this Marine on Okinawa, and he was like a son to me. When they arrived on Lejeune the third week of June, my wife and I welcomed them like family. Needless to say, the allegations crushed our souls!

My command had absolutely no probable cause to strip me of my second amendment rights on 21 November when they "served" me with charges, as I had demonstrated no suicidal or homicidal tendencies in the intervening 5 months...it was purely a CYA move, where I was escorted to my quarters by a junior colonel to retrieve my pistols and turn them into the armory. I additionally accounted for my other two pistols, which were with friends. Later that evening, four CID agents were dispatched to my home and searched our quarters from top to bottom, because a senior Colonel is not to be trusted.

Getting back to day one...while I was at NCIS HQ, five NCIS agents descended on my wife like Gestapo, waving their badges in her face and demanding to talk to her. Not knowing what her rights were, she talked to them freely for two hours. When I returned home, she was absolutely distraught from the ordeal. They asked her demeaning questions, like "does he pay you to be married to him?" Implying a sham marriage! "Did he ever inappropriately touch your daughter or his daughter, or your son?" On and on, they grilled her for two hours!
Dozens of agents around the world, interviewed hundreds of people who knew me, or who had only briefly met me. All three of our children contacted me and said, NCIS wants to talk to us, what should we do, and I had many other Marines contact me and ask what they should do...in every case I

told them that I couldn't tell them what to do, or I would be slapped with obstruction of justice charges...that if they needed advice to consult with the legal experts...lawyers. NCIS agents tracked down my first wife in Louisiana...we got divorced in November of 1986 when I was a Sergeant...30 years ago! They questioned her on whether or not she had any "dirt" on me! She told them, "I only have good things to say about Dan Wilson!" I know, because she immediately contacted me after their visit. In the end, none of the three investigations have found anything to substantiate my accuser's original allegations.

My wife and I have stoically borne the burden of those who feel that one is "guilty" until proven innocent, but when it comes from your own command, it really feels like you've been hit below the belt. Particularly, when you couple it with their obvious strategy of "take him down, no matter what!"

In the end, I will be acquitted and exonerated, because the original charges are lies. However, my good name and reputation, built on leading Marines and treating them right for 35 1/2 years is forever tarnished, thanks to the articles that only sensationalized the charges and failed to mention the lack of substantiation, after thousands of man-hours wasted examining my entire career in three separate investigations. It will be a long slog till I get my day in court, where I will be acquitted and exonerated, but no one will write an article to highlight that! It will be costly and, on my dime...my civilian lawyer alone will cost me in excess of 100 grand, but I can't take any chances with all the multiple unrelated charges they've added to the mix. Like you say, I have to protect what I've earned for my family and I!

On the positive side, it has brought our family closer together than ever before. I have been overwhelmed by their support and from my Marine tribe. Since the first article on 30 November...my 56th birthday, literally hundreds of Marines and folk I've served with through the years have contacted me with encouraging email, texts, and phone calls...absolutely overwhelming, because I never expected it! I had a Corporal I served with years ago on Parris Island call me up at 0222 the other night...I took his call and we spoke for an hour. He told me that I was like a father to him and he insisted on paying for my defense.

I wake up each day and write down the things I'm thankful for, and ask myself how I can leverage what I'm going through to help other Marines or friends in need of good advice. They picked a fight with the wrong Marine. Getting shot at and blown up by an enemy who wants to kill you in several combat zones, has imbued in me an unbroken resiliency, Sir!

I went for a run Saturday morning, 16 July...the day after NCIS informed me of the charge. Afterward, I was sitting on a bench in my front lawn, looking at the New River...beautiful view! I noticed a tree directly across the street that has a gash from about two thirds up and down below its mid-section...an obvious lightning strike! Yet, the tree continues to grow and get stronger! To me it was a divinely inspired metaphor for what hit me, and I could almost hear God screaming at me to, "be like that tree!"

If you've read this far, I apologize for my ramblings, but I have to say it has been cathartic for me...thank you for listening, Sir! I will probably be counseled for contacting you directly, and if the prosecution finds out, it will likely end up as an additional charge for my court martial, but I could care less! You needed to hear this directly from me, Boss...no filter...just the irreverent me. "Irreverent," as you said "Dan Wilson" is to my new general when you were down here in May, after our field exercises.

All my very best to you, sir, and Merry Christmas!
Semper Fi until I die!
Respectfully,
Col Dan Wilson

I never did hear anything back from "Uncle Bob," but I didn't expect to. I knew from inside sources within his office that he did get my email. My lawyers were apoplectic, thinking that the prosecution might get ahold of my email and somehow use it to manufacture additional charges. My attitude was, "go ahead, make my day – charge me for breaking the chain-of-command...sue me, while you're at it!"

CHAPTER 5
ME TWO!

A few months into the investigation, a woman married to a sailor on base befriended my wife. She had fallen on the outs with the officer wives club on account of her unacceptable behavior. To exact revenge on one neighbor who had aggrieved her, she had spray-painted a penis on the neighbor's car, and on the American flag that was displayed by their front door. My wife felt sorry for the lady and took her under her wing. Towards Christmastime, she let it be known that she planned to divorce her fourth husband. She told my wife and I one day that she had trained to be a dominatrix in New York City and was planning to start up her own business to make a boatload of money on men who had such predilections.

One day she begged me to take her seven-year-old daughter out for a ride on my Harley motorcycle. I told her the optics would not be good given the current charge against me, but she persisted. I relented, but only after getting assurances from her that she and my wife would travel right behind us for the entire ride. I rode the kid out to Camp Lejeune's beach about ten miles from our home on base, where we all walked on the sand for a bit. We then returned home with my wife and the kid's mother in tow.

She spent Thanksgiving Day 2016 with us, because she didn't want to be near her husband. Around that time, she started giving me advice about my case. She had the perfect civilian lawyer in town whom she wanted me to hire, and she seemed to know who the real culprit was, but knew it wasn't me. Again, on Christmas she came over to celebrate with my wife and I. Her husband and his two kids came over, but they quickly bailed to go see a movie. It was my first time meeting him, and we did not make any kind of connection. I got the feeling that he was intimidated by my rank and physicality. Ironic, as he was a big sailor, a good two inches taller than I. I also found out that their marriage was ending in large part on account of her going to NCIS a year prior and accusing him of raping her. NCIS investigated and he was set to face a Board of Inquiry to boot him out of the Navy when she refused to testify. She had realized that if he was booted out and paid at a lesser rank in retirement then she would get less alimony should they divorce. She immediately changed her tune, and he was retained in the Navy, escaping a certain drop kick by the board.

Following his departure, she started insisting that I go with her and my wife to Beaufort, South Carolina to go house hunting. She wanted to find a place to escape to, after leaving her husband. My wife had mentioned to her what a beautiful area that Beaufort is, and they had been planning a trip there for weeks. I did not want to go, but they both persisted until I was finally persuaded before the end of the night to drive them down there. We left mid-morning, Monday, the day after Christmas, and checked into the officer's temporary lodging facility on base that evening aboard Marine Corps Air Station, Beaufort. I was given the luxury suite normally reserved for generals. We had a large bedroom, a living room, and a kitchen. The ladies elected to sleep in the bedroom, leaving me the pullout couch in the living room. Shortly after arriving, I passed out watching TV in the living room, only to be startled awake by the both of them standing over me and laughing. The lady had a bottle of eyeliner in her hand and was sticking the brush back into the bottle when I came to. I suspected foul play immediately and went to a mirror to check it out. She had drawn a penis on my cheek, and they had taken pictures of it. Her MO seemed to be drawing penises on people, places, and things. I didn't think it was as funny as she did.

The ladies went house-hunting for the next few days, and my wife's friend asked me if we could stay until Friday instead of leaving Wednesday, as previously planned. I had nothing going on at Camp Lejeune and everyone up there was on basket leave anyway in the short period between Christmas and New Year's Day. Besides, I was my own boss and had no reporting instructions. Before we left on Friday, she wanted to show me the condo she'd picked out in Beaufort to buy. All she needed was a $10,000.00 loan to make a down payment…hint, hint. I certainly didn't have that kind of money, having just contracted with my civilian lawyer to retain his services for a cool $125,000.00. She probably thought that all Colonels are rich, and of course I'm going to give her the money she needed to buy the place. Her attitude toward me soured on the trip home, as it sunk in that I was not going to be her white knight in shining armor, financially speaking. I had my own two daughters to think about, before sinking a ton of money into some lady who had just come into our lives.

She texted me, after we returned from Beaufort to thank me, and emphasize how much she loved my wife and I. Ten days after our return, her and my wife were drinking and texting each other one evening when they went sideways of each other. My wife broke up their friendship, which enraged her friend who had been spurned by other officers' wives. She felt like a woman scorned. And, like that old saying, "hell hath no fury, like a woman scorned!" A few days later, she sauntered into NCIS headquarters, where she had recently been putting her own husband on report and told two agents that I had raped her repeatedly one night in front of my wife, while we were in Beaufort. She didn't have any article of clothing with my DNA on it, but they just needed to take her word for it. She also did not mention that she was so angry at my wife for having ended their friendship that she was only making her report to get back at my wife. She knew that it would hurt my wife deeply, if I was remanded to pretrial confinement, and that her allegation was certain to send me there. NCIS did believe her, because they had all received the same sexual assault prevention training that all of us Marine Corps officers had been indoctrinated with for the previous four years. "You must always believe the 'victim,' over the accused, especially if the 'victim' is a female, and the accused is a male." That mantra was contained in the mandatory training forced on the military by the Obama administration. Along with, "you must prosecute all claims of sexual assault, no matter how baseless the claim." NCIS agents glommed on to her story during their sit-down, and even offered her suggestions to strengthen her story. She sat on a couch, relaxed, and sipping her favorite blend of coffee from Starbucks, while spinning her tale of woe, and how the monster, Colonel Wilson, had even leaped on her repeatedly to rape her, all the while she was lying next to my wife in their queen-sized bed.

Following her interview with NCIS agents, the agents literally sprinted over to my boss to inform him of this new development and ask him that I be remanded to custody. They quickly convinced him, and he issued verbal orders that I be remanded into custody immediately, while I awaited my trial date.

CHAPTER 6
FRIDAY, THE 13TH

I started off the year of 2017 with a deep-seated desire to stop drinking. It was my only New Year's resolution. During the course of the investigations, I had sunk deeper and deeper into the whiskey bottle. I was starting to feel pangs of pain in my liver in the mornings, that didn't go away, until I'd had a few drinks of whiskey. I realized that I was poisoning myself, and that it would lead to my untimely death if I didn't do something. I also appreciated that my body was the Temple of God, and was this any proper way to treat God's Temple? I have rarely asked for help as a Marine. I have always been the leader of Marines, and the guy they looked to fix their problems. In my own case, I never really had any problems that I couldn't fix myself. I knew this was the time to ask for help. I called the II MEF Chief-of-Staff on Tuesday, 10 January 2017. I needed to get my command's permission, before I committed to a treatment program that would sequester me for thirty days. He was immediately agreeable to the idea and gave me two thumbs up. I then called the substance abuse control office on base and set up an appointment for the following morning. I was required to be screened, before they could determine a plan of action.

I showed up on time for my second appointment at the SACO office on 11 January 2017. This one was a self-referral. I was asking for help for myself, and I was there freely of my own volition. After hours of poking and prodding, and answering hundreds of questions, the Director of the Clinic personally talked to me, confirmed that I indeed help, and laid out the plan. The way ahead was five days in detoxification, followed by thirty days at the farm in Virginia. I was surprised, and disappointed, that the good doctor wanted me admitted to the detox facility that same evening. Truth be known, my demons wanted a few days of final binging on whiskey, before giving it up for good. That same day at 1800 (6 p.m. for civilians), I was to be escorted to the detox facility in Jacksonville, North Carolina, by a Lieutenant Colonel from my command (II Marine Expeditionary Force) with a non-commissioned officer driving. Everyone at the SACO office treated me with utmost respect, as if I was some kind of VIP patient. They collectively set everything up for me, without my having to lift a finger. I hope that I adequately conveyed my appreciation to them, before I returned home to get ready. I remember driving home, feeling relieved in having taken such a monumental step, and thinking, this is truly the first day of the rest of my life – rejoice and be glad in it.

I spent all afternoon – you guessed it – drinking whiskey and watching The Revenant. Ironically, the name of the movie, The Revenant, is from the French word, revenir, which is one who has returned, as if from the dead. I had seen some low points in my Marine Corps career, but by seizing the initiative in my own life, I felt like I was returning from somewhere.

I was picked up like clockwork that evening. Part of the check-in process at the rehab facility was a breathalyzer test. I tested at 1.6 BAC; more than double the amount to be considered legally intoxicated. I was a functional drunk, though, and processed seamlessly into a wing of the facility, reserved for military members. My valuables were collected and placed in a mini-safe, to include my iPhone. I was assigned a two-person room, but I didn't have a roommate. It was a nice room and included a bathroom with a shower. Doors were to be kept open for roving nurses to observe patients at all times, and there were cameras everywhere. It had the feel of a detention facility, but the staff were as nice as could be.

I felt pretty good, waking up Friday morning, the 13th of January 2017. I had spent two restful nights in detoxification and had started to develop friendships with several of the other military guys in the program. In three more days, I was scheduled to be transferred to a 30-day, in-house, alcohol rehabilitation program in Virginia. I was finally taking a bended knee and seeking help for my addiction to whiskey. Yes, whiskey, straight up with no ice. I might as well have been pouring bleach into my body. However, I was now committed and excited at the prospect of transitioning to a sober lifestyle. Camp Lejeune was my twilight tour, as they say in the military, and I wanted to retire being remembered as a warrior, and not as a drunk. I had been a hard-drinking, tobacco-dipping, infantry Marine for decades, but I was now determined to rid myself of those destructive, and expensive, addictions. No excuses, or apologies; it was just the way I was at the time, but things were beginning to change for the better. I was feeling good about taking the first steps in what I knew was the right direction. I had spent two hours, the previous day, pouring out my heart to the chief psychologist. We had developed an instant bond. I could tell he respected me when he had mentioned that I reminded him of a modern-day John Wayne.

Shortly after breakfast, I got on my iPhone, and made my final payment on my 2012 Harley motorcycle loan. It felt good to fully own my beast, and I day-dreamed about riding her again when I completed the rehab program. I was housed in a wing of the facility, devoted solely to military members. Everyone was in their own stage of recovery, and for different reasons. However, we did have a schedule of activities, which included everyone. Our first activity that fateful Friday was a group discussion about superstition. Various guys spoke up about being superstitious, while others scoffed at the concept. I was in the latter group – I had never been superstitious about the number 13, or Friday, the 13th in particular. In fact, one of my most memorable events was on Friday, the 13th of April 2007. I was the Commanding Officer of Infantry Training Battalion on Camp Pendleton, and we held a Warriors' Night.

I hadn't developed any bad associations with the number 13, and emphasized that to the group, when I had an opportunity to speak my mind. In fact, a few hours previously, I had made another positive association with 13, having paid off my Harley loan in full. Everyone knows the fantastic feeling of making a final payment on any loan. I was stoked to have zero debts for the first time in my adult life. Every group has its dissenters, as did the one I participated in that morning. Several of the guys related stories to support their superstitions about Friday, the 13th. I remember thinking that there may be something to it, but I had yet to experience it in my five and a half decades of life.

Shortly after lunch, I returned to my room for a nap. Residents were encouraged to take naps during their detox period of five days. I've never needed any encouragement to take a nap. I've always thought that even a quick, five to ten-minute nap, is an excellent way of recharging my internal batteries. The Chief Psychiatrist interrupted my nap at about 1400 by entering my room with a nurse. They had somber looks on their faces, and I wondered why the long faces? I soon found out, when he informed me that he had received a call from my command, and that NCIS agents were inbound to take me into custody. It was his belief that my boss had directed that I be placed in pretrial confinement immediately for reasons unknown. My heart sank. The doctor had called his supervisor, demanding to speak directly with my boss, but had been denied. He was hoping to convince my general to at least keep me in the rehab program through its duration, before sending me into pretrial confinement. It was not to be. My boss had made his mind up, and my health was not a consideration. The fact that a second woman had pointed an accusing finger at me was the deciding factor. No one at NCIS informed my boss of the second woman's history of making false allegations. NCIS should have shown due diligence in providing him with a complete picture of her lack of credibility, which would have cast her allegations against me in a different light. Bad call, general.

The doctor, himself, escorted me out to the lobby, when he received word that NCIS agents had arrived to arrest me. I walked into the lobby to a spectacle. There were eight NCIS agents surrounding the interior of the lobby with only about six feet between them. All agents had holsters with pistols showing. They looked at me, as if I was America's Most Wanted, and they had somehow managed to trap a very dangerous man. I just could not believe in the excessive show of force for a 56-year-old Colonel who had never been sideways with the law. Also present was the II MEF Chief-of-Staff who just days prior had okayed my desire to enter the rehab program. Several other Marines were in the lobby, and outside in the parking lot. An NCIS agent stepped toward me, identified himself, and asked that I place my hands behind my back so he could handcuff me; the first time that I had ever been handcuffed in my life. I immediately asked him why I was being handcuffed with my hands behind me. The agent didn't expect my question, and stammered something along the lines of, it's for your safety. I told him that was ridiculous, and that they were just trying to humiliate me in public for no good reason. It was uncomfortable, after I was loaded into the front seat of a van, sitting there with my hands behind my back.

In the van ride to NCIS headquarters, the agents accompanying me tried to act like they were on my side, and sympathetic toward me. I ignored them, consumed in my own thoughts about what lay ahead. Two new agents at their headquarters, informed me of the new charges against me. My wife's friend had told NCIS agents that I had raped her repeatedly, the first night of our trip to Beaufort, South Carolina. Again, no agent asked her any hard questions to undermine her insane allegation. For example, why didn't you call 911 in between the rapes? Colonel Wilson raped you repeatedly the first night, yet you were the one who asked him to extend the trip until Friday? If he had raped you Monday night, why would you want him to see the place you had selected to live, before going back to Camp Lejeune on Friday? You say you were wearing pajamas; why would you knowingly launder what you had to know would be critical DNA evidence? Is it true that you were right here in our headquarters, a year and a half ago, making allegations of rape against your own husband, which later turned out to be false?

The NCIS agent told me that he would get my side of the story, after he had collected my DNA, taken my fingerprints, and snapped pictures of me. I told him straight up, "listen young man, I have absolutely nothing to say to you, so be prepared to skip that part. I'll save what I have to say for where it actually counts for something." He seemed disappointed, and tried classic bonding techniques, in the hopes of changing my mind. You are probably familiar with one of the techniques; get the target to answer yes to as many questions as you can, because then when you ask for his cooperation, it is much more difficult for the target to say no. Another one is to try and identify in a positive way with the target, like you're from Washington State? I've visited my grandparents up there several times. It is beautiful up there, but it sure rains a lot. Or you must be a Seattle Seahawk's fan then. Russel Wilson and the Seahawks really crushed Peyton Manning and the Bronco's in Super Bowl 48. I'm betting you were pretty happy to be a Wilson on Ground Hog's Day in 2014.

I didn't respond the way the young agents were hoping I would, but I wasn't your typical Marine either. I had no fear of what lay ahead, because I was innocent, and I knew that at some point the system would work as intended, and that I would be exonerated. Thirty minutes later, we were back in the van, and heading to the MEF headquarters building for a medical exam. Their staff weren't present that late in the evening on a Friday night, so we had to go to the hospital for my blood pressure, blood draw, and other medical checks required, prior to placing a Marine in confinement. NCIS had taken all of my belongings including my iPhone upon leaving the rehab facility but failed to fill out an inventory and have me sign it, along with a chain-of-custody sheet.

During the ride to the hospital, one of the NCIS agents had the bright idea that he was going to solve my case, by getting me to talk. He started with the bonding routine, and when I responded to one of his questions about football, I noticed him not-so-casually reach down to his iPhone and start the voice recorder. I confronted him with, "are you really trying to record me right now? Well, you aren't too slick about it, are you? We are done talking, young man." At the hospital, a female Navy nurse approached me to draw blood for the mandatory HIV test. I've always held Navy Corpsmen and Navy medical personnel in the highest regard. They are good Patriots, and Corpsmen are especially revered by the infantrymen, whom they accompany into battle.

The hospital was the final stop, before Camp Lejeune's Brig. I had only been by the Brig one time. Ironically, it had been when I was giving my wife's friend's grade-school-aged daughter a ride to Onslow Beach, the previous month on my Harley. A portion of the main road to the beach had been closed for repairs, and the detour took us right by the Brig. I thought about that on the way to the Brig that night and wondered if a) it had been a premonition, or b) if the ride had taken place on 13 December, potentially confirming the superstitious nature of the number thirteen.

The Brig's Reception and Release Room was a gaggle of who's who in the zoo, when I was escorted in by NCIS agents about 1800. They immediately turned me over to the duty Marine guards. Several more Colonels were present, including the warden's Battalion Commander. The warden was there, and as I look back at that night, I realize that it was likely the latest she had ever stayed at the Brig on a Friday night. She was there to demonstrate to me, and her superiors that she was in charge, and that even though I was a senior ranking officer, she was not about to be pushed around. The first thing I was required to do was change into my new prison garb; light blue pajamas with a top and bottom. I was then asked to place my back against a wall with measuring markers behind me. The standard arrest photo, but this one was for my prison badge. After the picture, the warden stepped in front of me and read me the riot act. She emphasized several times that she was in charge, and that I was to obey all her orders and the orders of her staff. That my rank didn't matter in the Brig, even though I hadn't had my day in court. She seemed to take glee in informing me that I would be appropriately punished, if I violated any of the prison's rules and regulations.

It took about three hours to process me. The duty staff went through their checklist, to make sure they didn't screw up my in-take. I was the highest-ranking Marine officer to ever be placed in pretrial custody at Camp Lejeune's Brig. They did not want to be the ones to get my in-processing wrong. I filled out as many different forms as I did when I enlisted in the Marine Corps. I was required to pee in a little bottle to make sure I wasn't on any illicit drugs. I wasn't, but I was on a ton of other medications, prescribed for the detoxification process. Tough shit, now I would be detoxifying the old-fashioned way; cold turkey with no medications at all. I was finally escorted down to Special Quarters, where I would be spending the next five days in solitary confinement, before being allowed into General Quarters. I started to make order out of my cell, by making my rack and putting all of my stuff in the one drawer under my rack. It was an unreal feeling to be on the inside of the caged door, looking out. I thought to myself, there's a first time for everything in life.

CHAPTER 7
THE WAITING GAME

For the first time in my career, I issued Commander's Guidance to myself…
"**YOU** will not just **SURVIVE** in here; you will **THRIVE** in here!"

I was initially placed in the special section of the Brig with individual cells – solitary confinement. It was referred to as Special Quarters (SQ). All incoming detainees and prisoners are required to spend a cooling down period in SQ, before being allowed into general population (GP). All newbies are provided with a copy of the Brig rules and are required to pass a written test on the rules in order to earn your way into GP. Additionally, SQ housed anyone who was in a disciplinary status, or was considered a danger to himself and other prisoners. There was a former guard in SQ, when I arrived, who was placed in protective custody, pending his court martial. He had supposedly been an asshole guard – plenty of those around – and the prison staff feared for his safety. Snitches who might get stitches were also placed in protective custody.

I had a tiny cell, painted white, with a drab cement floor. There was a steel platform, built into the back wall where I slept. The cell had a co-joined toilet and sink. A tiny steel desk with steel stool, bolted securely into the deck and bulkhead, was where you were required to sit, when not on your rack. A guard immediately handed me an inspection sheet, and I was directed to annotate any and all discrepancies in the cell. Detainees are required to reimburse the government, should you cause any damage to the cell during your stay. Quite frankly, the cells were filthy shitholes.

You were forbidden from sleeping during the day, and a roving guard passed by your grated, steel bar, entryway, every five minutes to ensure compliance. Mid-morning of my first day, I committed an unpardonable sin by stretching out on my rack and shutting my eyes. A guard rudely interrupted my reverie, Detainee Wilson, wake up, or I'll write you up for a rule's violation. You are not allowed to sleep. I'm not sleeping, Devil Dog, I'm meditating, I answered him. Well, I say you were sleeping, so wake up, he replied. I was angry and cranky, and shot back with shut the f up, you pogue, bitch-ass boot. I thought he was about to cry as he timidly replied, you don't have to be disrespectful to me. I told him that if he showed me some respect, he would get my respect in return. He sulked off, and I didn't see him for another five minutes. He couldn't meet my gaze for the remainder of his watch, and there remained animosity between us for my entire stay at Camp Lejeune's Brig.

I was placed in solitary confinement, the Friday night of a long, four-day, weekend - a 96, as we refer to it in the Marine Corps. The Brig Staff always get the full measure of a 72 (three-day weekend), or 96. The guard force is broken into watches, and they have their own schedule, which does not include the normal time off that the Brig Staff enjoys. Let me assure you that they get plenty of time off too. Members of the Marine Corps in other job specialties are green with envy when they find out how skate the guards' schedule is. The Brig Staff have an even lighter schedule. If a 96 begins on a Thursday, you can be sure that the Brig parking lot is empty around noon on Wednesday, and the first car won't be parking on the back end, until noon on Monday. You can tell a lot about the morale of a unit by observing their parking lot. A unit with high levels of morale has a full parking lot from early in the morning till late in the evening. They enjoy what they do, and they want to be there. A unit with its morale in the dumps, has a parking lot that is relatively empty till mid-morning, and empties out again in the mid-afternoon. I knew from the get-go that the morale at Camp Lejeune's Brig was very low.

I was issued two sets of blue prison-garb, indicating that I was in a pretrial status. I had nothing else. I didn't even have a pair of glasses to read the tiny font in the Rules & Regulations handbook. I was authorized to read a Bible, or my religious book of choice, but I didn't have one. For hours, during that long weekend, I just sat and stared at the white walls. I felt like a psychiatric patient in a rubber room and thought that maybe I was going insane. The medications I was taking to help ease me through detoxification at the Rehab Center were quickly wearing off. I began craving alcohol and nicotine and started to feel serious withdrawal symptoms. There were splotches of darker color in the concrete floor of my cell, in different shades of grey. I stared at them for hours, until various shapes took form. I saw a lion's head, but if I adjusted my position slightly, it appeared to be something altogether different, like the profile of a Silver Back Gorilla. It reminded me of riding my Harley motorcycle on the I-395 southbound in Arlington, Virginia. If you quickly glance up at the Air Force Memorial, just after you cross the bridge from DC and pass by the Pentagon on the right, it appears that there are only two stainless steel spires – the spires that soar 270 feet high and represent contrails of the Air Force Thunderbirds as they disperse in a bomb-burst maneuver. Ride along further, and glance up again at the Air Force Memorial, and you will see all three spires in their full glory. It is a life-lesson on perspective. Depending on which position you are observing something, anything, you will have a unique perspective, and swear by it. I could of sworn at one point on the 395 that the Air Force Memorial had two spires without knowing that the third was perfectly tucked in behind one of the other two spires. It also led me to understand that given two or more perspectives in life, one will actually reflect reality, or the truth. Or, maybe your reality changes in life, as your perspective changes. I'm sure many philosophers have grappled with these concepts, since the beginning of mankind. Somehow, as I kept staring at my cell floor from different angles, I wondered what really was the truth, was it a Lion's head, or a Silver Back Gorilla. I just confused myself by overthinking it and couldn't seem to make sense of my perspective's theory. I did know for sure that I was in confinement, and it seemed so very wrong. A righteous rage burned deep within my soul, throughout my time in confinement.

Shortly after my blow-out with the guard on day one, I caught myself feeling sorry for myself. How could this happen to me at the twilight of my decades-long career? Why would God allow this to happen to his son? This led me to think about Job in the Bible, and how he kept his faith in God, no matter what the Devil tormented him with. Job's attitude was "God giveth, and God taketh away, blessed be the name of God." I wondered to myself if I could be as loyal and faithful as Job and keep the faith in the depths of my despair. I'm a Marine, I've been shot at repeatedly, mortared, rocketed, and have survived an IED attack on my vehicle, during the Second Battle of Fallujah, I thought, of course you're going to survive this experience, and on the far side of this experience, you will be that much stronger. In the back of my head, I could hear a voice encouraging me to be like that tree! Or, I thought, like the old commercial for Timex watches, it takes a licking, and keeps on ticking. And then there is the verse in the Bible that I had memorized as a child along with the entire book of James. "Count it all joy my brethren when you meet various trials, for you know that the testing of your faith produces steadfastness. And let steadfastness have its full effect that you may be perfect and complete, lacking in nothing."

I spent hours having back and forth conversations with myself, without speaking a word. There was nothing else to do in my cell. At some point, I had a burst of inspiration, and decided to issue myself, my very own Commander's Guidance. Marines will immediately understand what I'm talking about. Whenever I took command of a new unit, I used to draft up a one-page sheet of my Commander's Guidance. Within my first week as their new leader, I would sit down with my Marines and explain it to them, Barney-style. It would have such pearls of wisdom as; I trust each and every one of you implicitly. It is up to you to prove me wrong. Training for combat is our most important mission but taking care of each other as a family is equally important. I will treat each of you, as I would want you to treat me. I expect you to do the same with each other. Treat the little guy like a King! You get the drift. I liked to keep my published guidance to a page or less. In my experience, Marines don't like to read much, and particularly not, if it is longer than one page. Infantry Marines prefer coloring books and crayons!

My own guidance to myself just came to me. A thought that God conveniently placed in my head. Timing is everything and God's timing is impeccable. Instead of a full page, my guiding thought for whatever amount of time I was to be confined would be, you will not just SURVIVE in here, you will THRIVE in here. I can still hear myself saying, aye, aye, Colonel Wilson – WILCO (will comply). The THRIVE statement is in my first diary entry, exactly a week later on January 20th 2017, after I was released from solitary confinement and was able to purchase a composition notebook to use as a diary. That thought set the tone and gave me a guiding compass heading for the remainder of my time behind bars. No more wasted time, wallowing in self-pity. I was going to learn everything I could about the military legal system; the good, the bad, and the ugly. I was going to keep a diary and make entries as often as possible. I was going to read as many books as I could to gain knowledge. I was going to start a daily push-up routine in my cell, along with other calisthenics, to keep my body strong and healthy. During recreation call, I was going to lead high intensity, CrossFit style, workouts and welcome any others who wanted to join me. I was going to listen to other prisoners' problems and give them my fatherly advice. I was going to get good at playing chess and any of the other games we were allowed to play, like Scrabble, Risk, and Monopoly. I was going to be a dignified role model for other detainees to emulate. I also wanted to be undaunted like Job, no matter what came my way. My commander's guidance thought had literally launched a thousand other positive ideas that would shape my experiences and allow me to grow in so many different areas of my life.

My wife was able to get permission to visit me that first weekend, but not without the personal intervention of the commander of the battalion the Brig Company was assigned to. Every detainee is required to prepare and maintain a Mail and Visitation Roster. To take receipt of a letter from someone, or for a visitor to visit you, their name must be on your authorized roster. For example, I would get a letter at least once a week from someone I didn't expect to. You have to have ESP in order to know that someone is going to write you a letter, before they actually do. The mail clerk, normally a guard taking a six-month break from their normal duties, would come around once a day, if we were lucky. If you had a letter from a person, not on your authorized list, the mail clerk would hold your letter hostage, until you received official approval for their address to be added to your Mail and Visitation Roster. Every request to do anything at all in a military prison is written out on a chit, explaining what your request is, and which staff section it needs to go to. Lord help you, if you send it to the wrong section! When the staff member receives your request to add an address, they make sure the address is valid, and not on your prohibited persons contact list. This address approval process can take up ten days. Throw in long weekends, or federal holidays, and it might take longer. I can't explain how frustrating it is to know you have a letter from someone, and you have to wait ten more days to actually read it. Furthermore, you are required to update your Mail and Visitation Roster, every three months, and if you transfer to a new facility, you start from scratch, all over again. Inside of a few months, I had over 80 names on my Mail and Visitation Roster. It would take me four hours to neatly pen in all the addresses of people who were writing me or visiting me on the weekends. During those hand-cramping four hours, I would remind myself of all the inspiration I would benefit from, through their visits and future mail. I would also repeatedly thank God that he had blessed me with so many friends in life. My daughter's letters were pure inspiration, and she wrote me at least three times a week. I would repeatedly reread her letters, and my spirits would be instantly boosted.

My wife showed up that first Sunday. I asked her to bring a pair of my civilian glasses with her the following day to visitation. I was going to try and get a permission slip from the prison's duty Corpsman, authorizing me to receive the glasses from my wife. Usually, a military member is only allowed to wear military-issued glasses in military prisons, but I didn't have any at that time. It would take me four months to get a pair through the military; another slow process when you are in the Brig. Detainees and prisoners are the lowest priority for medical and dental services. My wife and I discussed how quickly I had been thrown into confinement and how my boss should have looked into the accuser's credibility before his knee-jerk reaction. I told my wife that I would have an Initial Reviewing Officer (IRO) hearing by Thursday of the next week to determine whether I would be released or continue in confinement. I made it clear to her that I believed there to be less than a ten percent chance that the IRO would release me. After all, he was a Lieutenant Colonel. If he released me, he would in essence be metaphorically slapping my boss in the face. Releasing me would be sending a message to my boss from the IRO that you got this one so very wrong, general, and I'm going to fix your mistake by releasing Colonel Wilson until the court martial. Bad career move. I knew the IRO was unlikely to possess the requisite moral courage to make that call; he simply didn't have the balls to do it, and I knew it before I ever even met him. Additionally, the particular IRO assigned to review my case had been the same officer who had prepared the paperwork to have me banned from base. His decision would likely be biased against me. My wife didn't like hearing that, but I never wanted to give her false hope. I estimated that my court martial wouldn't commence for at least another four months, but likely longer. Per the Manual for Courts Martial, the prosecution has 120 days from the day that charges are proffered until the beginning of a court martial, to ensure speedy justice. In reality, this is rarely the case, like it was in mine. For one reason or another, court martials always seem to be delayed. I tried to encourage my wife as much as I could to stay strong, and to take good care of our four-legged babies. My wife was upset, because she had been served with a restraining order against her former friend. The woman claimed to local authorities that she was terrified that after I was placed in confinement on account of her false allegations, my wife was going to find her, and murder her. The two hours of visitation goes by in what seems like five minutes, especially when the guards have taken their sweet-ass time in clearing visitors, which cuts into your time with them by as much as twenty minutes on some days.

Following the departure of visitors, I had my first experience with the ugly side of visitation, the strip search. We were marched up to the Reception & Release (R & R) room and ordered to stand in line at the position of modified parade rest, outside the hatch. Three at a time were brought into the room with two guards observing the procedure. It was done by the numbers, while standing and facing the guards:

> "Remove your boot bands and place them on the bench behind you. Remove your boots, turn them upside-down, and bang them together three times. Place them on the floor behind you. Take off your socks, turn them inside-out, and shake them three times. Put your socks on the bench behind you. Now, take off your blouse. Grab your blouse by the bottom and shake it hard three times. Okay, lay your blouse on the bench behind you. Take off your trousers, shake them three times, and lay them on the bench behind you. Pull your skivvies down to your ankles. With your right hand, grab your privates. Move them up, move them down, move them to the left, move them to the right. Now, turn around, bend over, and cough three times. Now hurry up and get dressed!"

Not until everyone was dressed, were we directed to form a new line outside R&R, and wait, until an available guard escorted us back down to SQ or GP. I returned to my cell with my morale boosted by my wife's visit. During the strip-search, I caught myself paying close attention to the process and procedures, and thinking about how I could beat the system, if I really wanted to smuggle something into the Brig. My propensity to always be evaluating people and systems is a product of my infantry training to always be on the lookout to exploit my enemy's weakness.

I got a second visit from my wife the next day, and she brought me a new pair of glasses. Suddenly, I was able to start reading, at least the Bible and the Brig Rules & Regulations. The II MEF Chaplain had visited me on Saturday, and I now had a Gideon Bible to read. I wanted to spend as little time as possible in SQ, so I went through the regulations several times to make sure I passed the entrance exam to GP. I'm a social guy, and at least in GP I would be interacting with other Marines.

    True to form, the Brig Staff didn't return until mid-day on the Tuesday, following the MLK-Day weekend. Nothing got accomplished that day, because they were operating at ten percent capacity, fighting their hangovers from over-consumption of booze. The next day, I was administered the Rules & Regulations test by a staff member and passed with flying colors. Prior to my transfer into GP, the Brig Psychiatrist wanted to have a chat with me. He was very concerned about my safety, given the nature of the charges against me. I assured him that I was innocent, and that I could handle myself. He was also concerned for my safety, given that I represented the Man to the prisoners. I was an officer, a Colonel, and most of the kids associated me with the guy who punishes them when they get in trouble. Many of the kids in the Brig were put in there by a guy who looked a lot like me. I had been a convening authority myself for seven years in three different billets. However, I told the good Doctor that I had two combat action awards, was a Black Belt in MCMAP, and very confident that I could handle myself in any situation. Later that evening, I was escorted into GP, and assigned a cell, right next to the duty guards' enclosure. The positioning of my cell came to have its ups and downs, but generally I liked being Malcolm in the middle. The greatest advantage to being in the middle is that you are literally hidden within plain sight, and the guards generally direct their attention to the periphery.

    I became an instant curiosity to the other detainees and prisoners in GP. Never in their wildest imaginations did they ever expect to encounter a Colonel in the Brig. I fascinated the millennials, including the guards. Only, the guards did their level best not to show it. The majority were recent graduates of boot camp, and the school in Texas that teaches them their MOS of being a Marine Corrections Specialist (MOS 5831). Their schoolhouse teaches them from the start that they are first and foremost a Corrections Specialist, then a Marine. The exact opposite of what every other Marine is taught, you are a Marine first. The schoolhouse warns the future guards not to give out any personal information, or to develop any personal relationships with detainees or prisoners. The new guards are constantly reminded that they will be taken advantage of in every situation, should a relationship develop.

The first Brig Staff member I met was a Gunnery Sergeant. He was going to be my Staff Counselor. I was escorted to his office, thinking to myself, I recognize that name. Indeed, fifteen years earlier, he had been a Sergeant, and one of my recruiters at Recruiting Station San Diego. He had two framed pictures in his office of me presenting him awards for his recruiting prowess. Instead of a counseling session it was more like a reunion. Every time I went to his office, during the next few months, we would chat about old times together. He was preparing for retirement, and had definitely dropped his pack, as we Marines say about those who don't carry their weight anymore. The Gunny had spent his entire career in the Corrections' MOS and had been on exactly one deployment oversees. He had been picked to train guards in Iraq at the infamous Abu Ghraib prison. Corrections Marines never deploy like nearly every other Marine. I had eleven six-month deployments, as I sat there listing to my counselor bragging about his one deployment. We didn't meet much after that first session. He was too busy, preparing for retirement. Counselors are required to meet with their assigned detainees or prisoners at least once a week, but there is no oversight, and reports can be easily fudged. With anyone of the counselors assigned to me, it was catch, as catch can. If you needed to see your counselor for any reason, you were required to drop a chit, and wait till they were ready to see you. The old, don't call us, we'll call you, except that it was a paper request. The chit (form) had to be filled out properly and placed in a box. The box was emptied by a staff member on weekdays they were present for duty, and all chits were routed to the appropriate staff member. Per their internal regulations, the staff member had five business days to respond to your chit. I had a counselor remind me of that, after I complained that I needed to make an important legal call to my lawyer, you know, Prisoner Wilson, I'm doing you a huge favor. I technically have five days to get back to you.

A day or two after I was transferred into general population, I had my hearing with the IRO to determine whether or not he was going to release me from pretrial confinement, pending my court martial. Unsurprisingly, he did not release me. It wasn't a huge letdown for me, because I had anticipated his decision. My family was very disappointed to hear the news, as they were not allowed to attend the IRO hearing.

I began to look forward to anything that got me out of the Brig for a few hours, or more. It was a logistical nightmare for II MEF, whenever I left the Brig. A Colonel, accompanied by a Staff non-commissioned officer (SNCO), was required to escort me, anywhere I had to go. An NCO served as our driver. I was required to be hand-cuffed, but in uniform for any legal meetings on base, or anytime I was escorted off base. Twice, I was taken to New Bern for blue light treatments on the back of my hands to destroy pre-cancer spots, called squamous cell carcinoma. I got some strange looks, while handcuffed and waiting in the lobby for treatment. I spent hours both times waiting for treatment, and the escorts refused my request for a simple cup of coffee. I remarked to one, well, if I can't even get a cup of coffee, then I guess a dip is out of the question. I thought I was being humorous, but the next morning the warden confronted me about my remark, I could charge you for trying to bribe your escorts for a dip of tobacco. She didn't like it too much when I explained the concept of bribery to her. You actually have to have something to offer, in order to be in a position to bribe someone. I had nothing, not even my good looks.

The warden at Camp Lejeune's Brig was the type that I absolutely refuse to call a leader. You know someone is awful when their own subordinates have zero respect for them, and unabashedly badmouth their boss in front of others. Her staff and guards would continually talk smack about her, even when they knew that we were listening. The warden reveled in the attention of the prisoners. I have never met a woman who sprayed on such excessive amounts of perfume like our warden did – you smelled her before she even entered GP to make her rounds. We learned to loathe the smell. Typically, she would come to GP when we were in our cells. As she moved in front of your cell, you were required to stand in front of your grated hatch at the position of attention, and declare your name and prisoner number, good morning, Ma'am, Detainee Wilson, number 00128660 Whiskey Delta. She then asked the same two questions, followed by the same statement: 1) How are you doing?; 2) Do you have anything for me?; and, 3) Have a good day. Typically, all of us answered fine and no to the questions, and you too, ma'am to her statement. Now, if you made the mistake of taking her up on her second question, and started listing any issues or problems you were having, she would blast you with did you take this up with your chain-of-command, or your counselor? Well, no, ma'am, I haven't yet. Then take it up with them first, and don't ever jump the chain-of-command again in my Brig, do you understand me? Yes, Ma'am. And that was the end of the conversation. She would quickly move on to the next cell and be gone from GP in less than twenty minutes. She spent less than an hour per month, checking up on her detainees and prisoners. The rest of the time, she was sitting in her office, or over at the battalion brown-nosing her boss. Not a bad gig. How did I know what she was doing and where she was at? From her own guards who were always talking behind her back, not even thinking that we were always listening to what they said. I noticed a trend with Marine wardens in the two Marine Brigs I was in, where I closely evaluated three different Marine wardens. They don't follow a basic principle of good leadership, by leaving your office and circulating, also known as leadership by walking around. As a warden, you should not only be circulating frequently among your staff and guards, but also among your prisoners and detainees. I pondered this trend and came to the conclusion that it is a byproduct of how wardens are selected. In the Marine Corps, they are selected for their technical skills and not their leadership skills. The Navy selects wardens based on proven leadership skills and therefore typically gets an actual leader instead of merely a billet-holder, as we get in the Marine Corps.

I quickly adapted to living in the Brig. I started devouring books, and I chose ones that gave me a healthy perspective from which to evaluate my own experience in prison. I read a World War II book about prisoners in Japanese Prisoner of War (POW) camps, following the brutal Bataan Death March in the Philippines. That any of the POWs actually survived, given what they were put through by the Japanese guards, is a miracle. In one of the POW camps, the Japanese guards forced the remaining POWs into trenches on news of approaching Allied liberation forces. Gasoline was poured on them, and they were set on fire, while still alive. Hundreds were thus incinerated and murdered. Incredibly, a handful were able to escape and alert Allied forces. Their stories made me pause to consider my own situation as a POW. Yes, I felt like I was a POW, the entire time I was confined. But, when considering the physical surroundings of my prison, I realized how good I had it, compared to my POW predecessors. I read another great book about POWs in North Vietnam. It also forced me to step back and appreciate how good I had it, compared to the decrepit conditions and torture the POWs in North Vietnam had endured. And some of them had survived for seven years, before they were repatriated back to the United States. These books led me to understand that no matter how bad you think you have it in life, there is always someone who has had it worse, so be thankful to God for what I do have. It reminded me of the old adage, I walked down the street, feeling sorry for myself, because I had no shoes, until I saw the man with no legs, sitting on the side of the street with a big smile on his face. Shame on me for being so self-centered and selfish!

I listened to many detainees and prisoners tell me their tale of woe. Listening to their stories got me out of my own pity party and put me in a position to help others. They poured out their souls to me, and wanted my advice on what they should do. The detainees wanted to know whether or not to make statements to investigators, and whether they should make a deal to avoid a court martial. The prisoners were upset at the raw deal they'd received from the system. I started to notice trends. For example, during stay at Camp Lejeune's Brig, I was the only one who actually went to a contested court martial. Hundreds of young Marines, and Sailors, had instead accepted either pretrial agreements (PTAs), or Separations in lieu of a Trial (SILTs). I wondered why so many of these young warriors accept a PTA instead of taking their cases to court and fighting the charges. Warriors typically want to fight it out! Hearing story after story, the reason became apparent. A detainee is assigned a defense lawyer, after he is put in confinement and charges have been proffered. When he finally gets to see his assigned lawyer, the military lawyer's first proposal is that his new client accepts a pretrial agreement instead of taking the case to a contested court martial. The defense lawyer does not want to go to court, because that involves a lot of extra work in having to prepare for trial; he would have to burn the midnight oil. Why in the heck would the lawyer want to go to all that extra work, when he still gets the same paycheck with a PTA for his client? For military lawyers, both defense and prosecution, PTAs are a win-win situation, and they literally high-five each other when a client agrees to accept a PTA. The defense lawyer uses the emotion of fear to overcome a young Marine's natural desire to fight instead of flight. He will literally scare the bejesus out of his new client, using maximum sentences and statistics to induce fear. "If we do go to a court martial, and you are convicted of these four specifications of sexual assault, you could be sentenced to more than 100 years in prison: twenty-six and a half years for each specification. Oh, by the way, there is a 99 percent probability of being convicted at a court martial. However, if you authorize me to negotiate a PTA with your convening authority, I'm sure we can get your prison sentence down to three years or less. I've done it with other clients, and they were in and out of the Brig in no time. What do you say?" Put it that way to a young Marine, who doesn't want to spend the rest of his life behind bars, and he'll reach for the pen immediately to sign a PTA, every single time. Usually, they had unwittingly spilled their guts out to an investigator, but if they hadn't, I would encourage them not to. Nothing you say to an investigator is going to help you in any way whatsoever.

Detainees would often ask me if they should take a lie-detector test. Not only no, but hell no, I would tell them. I've always thought of it as junk science, and so do the courts. I have known several men who claim to have easily beat a lie-detector test. A positive lie-detector test result earns you nothing and cannot be introduced in court as exculpatory evidence. More disturbingly is that I have heard first-hand accounts from service members who were intentionally lied to by NCIS agents. A Navy Commander friend of mine, accused of sexually abusing his daughter in a contested divorce case, was lied to by an NCIS agent, while going over the results of his lie-detector test. By falsely claiming my friend had shown signs of deception on a few of his responses, the agent tried to get my friend to admit to things he hadn't done. Lawyers on my defense team had similar stories of deceit involving NCIS agents.

There were far too many young Marines incarcerated for sexual assault, or rape, yet had relatively short sentences. A byproduct of the MeToo movement and bad policies forced on the military by the Obama administration who demanded that military leaders prosecute ALL allegations of sexual assault. A typical example was a young, infantryman Corporal (MOS 0311). He met a married, female Marine, on Camp Lejeune, who started coming to his barracks room for sex. The barracks surveillance videos all show her freely going into, and departing from, his room. However, one day, her husband found out about her secret affair, and she claimed that the Corporal had been raping her. No one really believed her story, but, out of deference to the mandates of the Me Too movement, the Corporal's convening authority directed that he be sent to a court martial. He ended up with a PTA for eight months on charges of rape. Speaking with dozens of prisoners led me to conclude that up to thirty percent of prisoners were wrongfully convicted, or they were convicted of charges unrelated to the main charge.

My lawyers and I had discussed whether or not I would attend the Article 32 hearing, before I was slapped into pretrial confinement. They had recommended that I waive my right to a hearing, and I had agreed. An Article 32 hearing is akin to a Grand Jury hearing, except that it is conducted by an officer, appointed by a military person's convening authority, and his word carries no weight in cases involving sexual assault. In other words, the hearing officer can recommend to the convening authority that there is no evidence, witnesses, or anything to lend credibility to the charges, and the convening authority is still going to direct that the case be adjudicated at a court martial. The convening authority knows that directing legal action is the only safe bet in ensuring he doesn't put his own career in jeopardy. If he does not direct a court martial, he will be second-guessed; either by his own leadership, or by the man-bashing cabal in Congress. If your convening authority happens to be a general officer, as was mine, the Senate can see to it that he never puts another star on his collar should he make the wrong decision about prosecuting a sexual assault case. The list for general officer promotions, goes through the Senate for confirmation, before it goes to the President for his signature. If a general officer does not make the perceived politically correct decision in a legal case, it could terminate his career. The other reason for waiving my right to a hearing was that it would give the prosecution a peek at our defense strategy. Once knowing our strategy, the prosecution would then be able to fine-tune and tailor their case against me. My lead lawyer described it as, "Colonel, sir, it's like playing poker and you inadvertently hold your cards so one of the other players is able to see them." He knows what cards you're holding, and he is going to play his hand accordingly. We cannot reveal our cards to the prosecution. We must keep them hidden. I recommend you waive your right to an Article 32 hearing. Well, put that way, it seemed like a no-brainer decision, and I acceded to his common-sense recommendation.

My first appearance in front of my military judge in February 2017 was to establish that he was going to be my assigned Judge. My defense team had heard that the Judge was friends with the Colonel lawyer who had conducted one of my investigations. They had even served a tour together on Okinawa, working in the same building. The Judge admitted that they were friends, but believed he could be fair, nonetheless. My team recommended we keep him, because who knows what kind of relationship you might get with a new Judge. As usual, I went with my team's recommendation.

That first session was also an arraignment, used to proffer all charges against me, and to record how I pled to each charge. I pled "not guilty" to each of the twenty-seven charges. My defense team also informed me of the way ahead. A motion was going to be heard at the end of March on whether the Judge himself would release me from confinement, prior to the court martial. There would be other motion hearings to do away with one or more charges for different reasons, and for the Judge to consider whether or not questionable evidence would be allowed to be admitted by the prosecution. And my wife and I would be meeting with two of the lawyers to go over the interviews that NCIS had conducted with my accusers and other individuals.

I approached the motion hearing regarding my release with doubt. During one of her weekend visits in March, I told my wife that I doubted the Judge would release me, and not to get her hopes up. He came across as a very cautious individual, and I could sense that he would come down on the side of exercising an abundance of caution by not releasing me. He didn't want to have to explain his decision to the public, or his superiors, if something went wrong, should he release me. My lawyers explained all the mitigation for my release, during the motion hearing at the end of March. It didn't matter to the Judge that he could set boundaries for me, or order that I not even come near the base. Or, that I would wear a GPS ankle-bracelet that would track my every movement, and that I would pay a $400.00 monthly fee for the service, out of my own pocket. Or, that I would be checking in twice-daily with my command, and going no-where without the permission of proper authorities. Essentially, I would be in closely-monitored confinement, but in a different location from the Brig. The Judge studiously heard, and seemed to consider everything my lawyers argued for, but in the end he denied our motion for my release from confinement. I was escorted unceremoniously back to the Brig in handcuffs.

Prior to the Judge's denial of my release from pretrial confinement, my wife informed me at visitation that NCIS agents had raided our home again, spending the entire day tearing it apart. She was seething with anger from the embarrassment of having a squad of NCIS agents with their government vehicles parked in our driveway and along the street in front of our house. The NCIS agents confiscated a thumb drive, which they took back to their headquarters to examine. My wife asked me point blank what was on the thumb drive. "Did you have porn on the drive?" Not at all. The drive contained an unclassified presentation I had given dozens of times to media outlets, members of Congress, and Senators visiting Iraq between 2004 and 2006. I was the operational spokesperson for three of the generals I worked for in Iraq, and they had asked me to be their briefer whenever visitors came out to Camp Fallujah, Iraq. I briefed the likes of Bill Hemmer, G. Gordon Liddy, Senator Biden, Senator McCain, Senator Clinton, Senator Kerry, and numerous congressmen. Senator Clinton's Secret Service Agent gave me a 100-year anniversary commemorative coin as a token of his appreciation. I hadn't used the unclassified presentation on the thumb drive in over a decade. I assured my wife that NCIS agents were not going to glean anything from their forensic examination of my thumb drive.

      In April, I was able to spend three days in a row, reviewing interviews and evidence that the prosecution had been forced to share with my defense team. My defense lawyers, my wife and I sat in a large office, made available to us by the head of the defense section. We reviewed everything, and discussed the legal implications for my case. I was struck by how my original accuser emphasized that her daughter had repeatedly denied in the beginning that I had inappropriately touched her. The depravity of my accuser's mind became apparent, when reviewing her diary entries that she had turned over to the prosecution. Six weeks after her initial allegation that spawned three investigations of me, she wrote in her diary that she had asked her twins that day, whether or not they had ever observed me sticking a finger in my dog's ass. They replied that they had never seen me do any such thing. All I could think was, what mother would intentionally introduce such a disgusting concept to their six-year-old twin daughters? Maybe it's just me, but it seems wholly inappropriate to me that a mother would ask her daughters any such thing. She also suggested to investigators that I was masturbating, every time I went to the bathroom. She claimed that I took longer than normal in the bathroom, and therefore I must have been jerking off. Actually, I was spitting out my dip, and brushing my teeth, while using the bathroom. It disgusts most people when you spit out a wad of tobacco in front of them, and I wanted to be polite about it, so I did it behind closed doors.

      I was very disappointed to review the statement of my accuser's husband. Although, I knew he would side with his wife, because she wore the pants in their relationship, I never imagined that he would actually lie. He lied repeatedly in his statement to NCIS, but it was his narrative regarding his daughter's fall on our hardwood floor that caught my attention. Instead of saying that his daughter running into his leg had caused the accident, it was now her falling off my knee. He intentionally re-wrote the main event of the Dinner Party night to shift the blame for her accident on me. I would never in a million years have believed that he would violate his integrity so intentionally. In fact, throughout the investigation, I actually thought that he would go into NCIS, and admit to them that his wife had made up the whole story, and to stop investigating me. After seeing his written statement, I knew that he was locked into the false narrative his wife had conjured up.

Reviewing the video interview of the other woman accusing me of rape was a peek behind the curtain at how NCIS agents bolster a narrative. A male and female agent have her state her allegations up front, then ask her gently for more details. None of the hard questions that you would expect from investigators actually seeking the truth. In fact, when she is scant on details, the agents blatantly make suggestions to help her fill in the blanks. I was flabbergasted that what they were doing was legally acceptable. The credibility of my second accuser came up at a motions hearing on May 11th, 2017, and whether or not my defense team would be allowed to introduce her previous sexual assault claim against her husband to impeach her character. And, whether my defense team could get access to her prescribed medications for the time period during which she had accused me of raping her. This portion of the transcript from the motion hearing, outlines my defense's attempt to uncover her true motive in making a sexual assault claim against me.

Defense: The issue before this court is sexual assault. And it is clear that she has used sexual assault claims in the past for whatever gains it is. In our case, it's retaliation against Colonel Wilson's wife. The entirety of our case, your Honor, is that Colonel Wilson's accuser was mad at his wife, so she retaliates by bringing a sexual assault claim against somebody who was already in a very vulnerable state, and she knew exactly what she was doing. And, frankly, she has already gotten her way. Colonel Wilson has sat in jail for 100-plus days.
Judge: Do you have evidence that Colonel Wilson's accuser attempted to extort whatever word you want to use – the Wilsons'?
Defense: No, your Honor. But the point is not extortion in this sense for money. Here, it's for retaliation. She wants to get back at Colonel Wilson's wife. But it's the same underlying theme. It's the same bias or prejudice. She knows how to use sexual

assault claims to her advantage. The issue is that she threatened her husband, and she did it knowing that a sexual assault claim would ruin that man's career, and so he was going to pay her whatever she said. In this case, she knows all the background about this since she's friends with Colonel Wilson's wife – knows exactly what a claim like that is going to do. Colonel Wilson's wife pisses her off, for lack of a better word, and all of a sudden, after saying, "Oh, I love you, Colonel Wilson" – blah blah blah – out of nowhere, a sexual assault claim comes. And so, the vehicle to exploit her bias or her motive is the sex assault. So, we believe it is relevant. It is probative. And the fact finder should be allowed to hear about her previous sexual assault claim against her husband in determining whether or not, ultimately, Colonel Wilson's accuser is a credible witness.

The Judge agreed and that he would allow my defense team to bring up the previous sexual assault allegation she had made against her husband that had been officially reported to NCIS. The Judge also authorized an on-camera viewing of her medical records – but only the prescriptions page. A couple of wins for the home team during that hearing.

On May 18th, 2017, I entered the court room for another motion hearing, believing that my court martial was to commence the next month on D-Day, June 6th, 2017. I left the court room, shaking my head and wondering what the hell had just happened. The commencement of the trial date had shifted to the left, by nearly three months. I was condemned to three additional months behind bars, before getting my day in court.

> **Judge**: Defense counsel and I have discussed the tentative trial dates in this case. Based on a number of issues, to include other cases, I have tentatively set the date of 28 August 2017 for this case. That's a Monday, contemplating possibly seating members on that date, with opening statements to commence the following day. Counsel and I

discussed that's Labor Day weekend; however, it's the Court's opinion, based on the seniority of some of the members anticipated, that that actually may work well. The members may be able to concentrate on this case and less on their other military duties. Colonel Wilson, obviously, counsel have indicated to me that they intend to file a continuance. You're in pretrial confinement right now. I'm fully aware of that. It's easy for all of us to sit there and start putting dates months in advance, but I'd like to hear from you regarding this continuance that hasn't been filed yet but is anticipated forthcoming in the next day or so. I want to hear from you, your thoughts, about the Court approving or not approving a continuance and the duration of that continuance.

Colonel Wilson: Well, sir, being a simple infantry officer, I will always defer to the smart guys in the room. I concur with the recommendation of my defense team. They asked me for guidance early on, and I said: "My guidance is whatever it takes. Whenever you're ready to step into the courtroom. Whatever – if I have to stay in pretrial confinement for an additional week, an additional month, an additional two months – I can do that. I'm a resilient Marine, and I will do whatever is required of me." So I defer to them, and I absolutely support their decision, your Honor.

Judge: All right. Thank you, sir.

Several motions were heard during June. At one, the prosecution was arguing to admit as evidence, a declaration from my second wife that she had found a topless picture of a fourteen-year-old girl in my wallet, some thirty years prior, while we were still dating. We had an ugly divorce, two years after marrying, and she stole money from bank account while I was deployed to Saudi Arabia for the First Gulf War. The picture was of a 21-year-old classmate at college whom I had dated briefly before meeting my wife, and she was fully clothed in the picture. The Judge crushed the prosecution's feeble argument with, that is hearsay within hearsay! I am not allowing that in my court room. The prosecution also argued for admission of a hearsay video, from a forensic interview of the alleged victim, the day after the dinner party. The Judge said he would punt his final decision into the court martial itself, and make a determination, after seeing the case laid out by the prosecution.

The prosecution also wanted to introduce the conclusion of a nurse who had conducted a head-to-toe physical examination of the child, thirty-six hours after the dinner party on July 15th, 2016. NCIS agents had recommended the family use this particular nurse, because agents had worked with her previously on other sexual assault cases. Regardless of, and contrary to, the results of her actual physical exam, the nurse was prepared to say that, in her professional opinion, she was convinced that a sexual assault had occurred. My defense team pointed out that everything in her exam indicated the opposite. She had annotated that everything was perfectly normal, and that the child had made zero complaints. The nurse had violated protocol by having the accusing mother in the room when she was asking questions of the "victim." Her answers were thus influenced by the knowledge that her mother was listening in to the conversation. Here is the testimony of the examining nurse at a motion's hearing, discussing her interaction with the child:

> **Nurse**: "I'm a nurse practitioner. I take care of check-ups at TEDI BEAR. Are you having any problems with anything today?" And I made note that I had spoken to her before and during her exam and that she told me she wasn't having any problems with her body that day. Was she having any problems with anything; specifically, those body parts that her family and the NCIS investigator were concerned about. When it came to collecting specimens, I told her I just needed to do it and her mom was with her and she indicated no problem with that.

The Judge ruled that the results of the child's medical exam could be introduced and mentioned at the court martial, but not the upside-down opinion of the nurse that she was convinced a sexual assault had occurred.

> **Prosecution**: The government is not depending on introducing either testimony or

> any type of documentary evidence that actually says the diagnosis of sexual abuse.
> **Judge**: That is my understanding.
> **Prosecution**: Just to be clear is that, no, the nurse is not going to testify that "I made a diagnosis on this child of sexual abuse."
> **Judge**: All right. I don't care if it's for medical treatment or diagnosis. That is called smuggling and inadmissible hearsay. The diagnosis of sexual abuse is not corning in.

Several new lawyers were introduced to help out my two accusers. Each had been immediately assigned a military lawyer who was called a victim's legal counsel (VLC). Each of them was now assigned two additional civilian lawyers from a highfalutin law firm out of Chicago. A law firm trying to make inroads with the military by jumping on the #MeToo bandwagon and offering up their best and brightest pro bono. The prosecution in total had a team of ten lawyers out to scalp me. But I was undaunted by their presence, knowing that I had the truth on my side. Like the classic line from the movie, A Few Good Men, they couldn't handle the truth…of my innocence!

I was ushered into the court room again on June 7th, 2017, for several motions to be settled by the Judge. First up was whether or not a hearsay video conducted by the Children's Advocacy Center (CAC) on July 14th, 2016, the day after the dinner party, would be allowed to be admitted at the trial. My guys did a great job of arguing for exclusion, based on military case law precedent.

> **Defense**: That Knox case that we point to in our defense response is very adamant that the rules don't change just because litigators might prefer a different class of rules for a certain case. Ultimately, the rules are what the rules are. And this case should be based on what the witnesses say in court.
> **Judge**: I completely agree. So you're arguing to the court to hold off on any rulings – defer rulings until after she testifies?
> **Defense**: Yes, your Honor.

The Judge punted the decision on whether or not to allow the hearsay video until after he had heard the prosecution's case during the court martial.

His reasoning being that if the prosecution made a good case without the hearsay video, then he would not allow it. However, if the prosecution's case was weak, he may consider allowing the hearsay video to be used as evidence in the court room.

> **Judge**: With respect to the government's motion requesting a ruling on the controlled phone call. The preliminary ruling of the court is that evidence of the controlled phone call will be admissible provided that the government can establish the necessary foundation at trial.

My defense team scored one for the Gipper by getting the Judge to drop a prosecution charge that I had had too much to drink on one occasion…at a dinner in Darwin, Australia…one of many allegations unrelated to the original charge. I was being charged with violating the standing order that I fell under that only permits drinking in moderation. My guys had made the case that moderation was never defined in the standing order, which prevents the prosecution from proving that I exceeded the standard of moderation that one night in the Land Down Under.

> **Judge**: The Court concurs with the defense that the order vests commanders and other decision makers with unbridled discretion as to whether an individual consumed alcohol in moderation or whether this undefined standard was exceeded. This vague standard will invariably result in moment to moment and individual to individual subjective judgments by commanders who must guess as to the meaning of moderation and differ as to its application. This encourages and results in arbitrary and discriminatory enforcement. Accordingly, defense's motion is granted. Charge III and the sole Specification is dismissed.

I was back in court on July 13th 2017 – exactly one year after the dinner party – for more motions hearings: litigating a defense motion related to remote testimony by children, a defense motion to permit a supplemental questionnaire for all potential members of the jury, a defense brief and supplemental response to the 3 CAC videos, a prosecution motion related to marital privilege and wanting to have the court force my wife to testify, and a prosecution motion wanting to introduce Facebook messages and texts between my wife and her former friend.

The motion related to remote testimony by the children was moot, because the prosecution was certain that the children would be able to testify in court. The Judge ruled the following on the July 2016 CAC videos with the three children.

> **Judge**: With respect to the three July 2016 CAC videos, the court's preliminary ruling is as follows: admitting portions of their statements will serve the purposes of the military rules of evidence, the interest of justice, and support the goal of truth seeking. However, with respect to the necessity requirement, the court finds that the government has not yet met its burden to show that the hearsay statements contained in the three July CAC videos are the most probative evidence available. The court will make a decision regarding whether the necessity prong has been met after the three child witnesses testify at trial.

The Judge was not about to grant the prosecution's motion to compel my wife to testify.

> **Judge**: The law is clear that Mrs. Wilson has a privilege to refuse to testify against Colonel Wilson. The court finds that Mrs. Wilson's decision about whether to invoke her privilege is a trial time decision to be made by Mrs. Wilson. The court lacks the authority to compel a decision via testimony or affidavit pretrial. Even if the court had the authority to compel a decision pretrial, Mrs. Wilson could, ultimately, change her mind during trial and decide to testify or not to testify. As such, the government's request that the court issue a ruling at this time with respect to Mrs. Wilson's spousal incapacity is denied.

As for the prosecution's motion to introduce Facebook messages and texts between my wife and her former friend, the Judge had this to declare:

> **Judge**: The court finds that these Facebook and text messages, on their face, are not very specific, and therefore not admissible. None of the messages clearly demonstrate that the accused physically and/or sexually assaulted his accuser, or that Mrs. Wilson observed any such conduct. Taken as a whole and without the testimony of Mrs. Wilson explaining her messages, their relevance is unclear. Therefore, the probative value, at best, is very low. The court's preliminary ruling is that the probative value of the Facebook and text messages would be substantially outweighed by the dangers of unfair prejudice, confusion of the issues, misleading the members, and waste of court time.

This is how the Judge ruled on the motion for a supplemental questionnaire.

> **Judge**: The nature and scope of the examination of members is within the discretion of the military judge. The purpose of questionnaires before trial is to expedite voir dire and permit more informed exercise of challenges. The court reviewed the defense's proposed supplemental questionnaire. The court will permit several of the proposed questions on the supplemental questionnaire.

The last six weeks prior to my court martial seemed to go by agonizingly slow. The heat index during that long, hot, summer was black flag for those who know, which prevented us numerous times from being able to get our one hour of recreation outside. Our recreation area consisted of a small basketball court, pull-up bar, dip bar, and a few pieces of exercise equipment. Noticeably absent at Camp Lejeune's Brig were any free weights. The warden felt that prisoners might use free weights as weapons.

I strove to be the model prisoner in keeping with my ethos to thrive in prison. Every week, we were assigned performance evaluation scores (PES) by the guards on a scale of 1 to 50. Anyone getting a score of 39 or higher was entitled to extra privileges, like an extra hour of recreation, or being able to stay in the common area after lights out to watch TV for an additional half hour. I dutifully recorded all of my weekly scores in the back of my diary, under the title "Thrive in Here!" My first score on January 21st, 2017, the week after admission, and after I was moved into GP was a dismal 29. The guards typically start all newbies out with a low score, and the comment, "you can only go up from here." I did climb through the next nineteen weeks to a final PES grade of 47. Unheard of for a detainee in pretrial confinement at Camp Lejeune's Brig. It was noticed by Brig leadership, and after the first week of June, my score was re-normed by my counselor with the explanation that the warden wasn't pleased that I kept trending up toward a perfect score. Being dropped back down to a 39 was my new normal. The warden was being pinged by the prosecution lawyers about whether or not she had any dirt on me from my time in the Brig that they could possibly use against me at my court martial...a classic prosecution tactic. My outstanding behavior in the Brig was a disappointment to the prosecution lawyers. Additionally, I had voluntarily been cleaning off the ten dining tables, after every meal, and I had the tightest rack in the Brig, every single day. Guards were writing me up with commendatory chits, highlighting that my rack belonged in a show room display, and other prisoners were constantly asking me for my secrets in making a rack so perfectly tight. I only revealed my secrets to a select few and the rest I promised to come out some day with a YouTube video on how to make a super-tight rack. Spoiler alert...you have to start from scratch each morning.

 Just prior to my court martial commencing at the end of August, I was moved into cell number 13 on the first floor of GP. I took it as a bad omen, given that the dinner party implosion had occurred on July 13th, 2016, and exactly six months later, on Friday, the 13th of January 2017, I had been placed in pretrial confinement. However, after spending many days in court at motions hearings from February through August, I was supremely confident that the jury would definitely find me innocent of the heinous felony charges and let me go free with maybe a slap on the wrist for the minor charges that had been stacked onto the one original charge in my case.

CHAPTER 8
INTO THE ARENA

"If we win the jury, we'll win your freedom."

The morning of August 28th, 2017, I felt like Marcus Aurelius Maximus in the movie Gladiator stepping into the arena except that my battle for survival was taking place in a courtroom on Camp Lejeune, not at the Colosseum in Rome. Marcus was motivated by a promise from his owner prior to stepping into the arena who assured Marcus that "if you win the crowd, you will win your freedom." Ironically, one of my counselors said something that morning echoing a similar sentiment, "if we win the jury, we'll win your freedom."

A gaggle of reporters in the back of the court room soon made the atmosphere feel like a spectacle, more like a circus show. I felt confident that I had the best and the brightest on my defense team, and that they were ready to win my freedom. I was surrounded by a fireteam of four really great lawyers, three Marine lawyers, and a civilian lawyer, who spent his career in the Marines as a lawyer and now had his own practice…General, I called him, the leader of my defense team. I was finally getting my day in court, and confident that we would blow every aspect of the government's case to smithereens. Seated right behind our table was my wife, and our two daughters, as well as one of my brothers. They literally had my back through the entirety of the court martial. They also kept my four lawyers on their toes, during our courtroom breaks, with their insights, ideas, and questions. It was comforting to have them involved in all the discussions I had with my lawyers, because they were my biggest advocates.

Monday was spent by the Judge tying up all the little loose ends. Of particular concern for the Judge was that the jury never see me released from restraints or handcuffed to avoid prejudicial thoughts from creeping into their minds during the course of the court martial. He was even concerned that they not be able to look out of the window of their conference room and ever see me handcuffed or having the handcuffs removed. However, the warden didn't want to play ball, and insisted that I had to enter the courtroom building first before having my handcuffs removed. And, have the handcuffs put back on me, before exiting the building.

Into The Arena (August 2017)

My team had a motion to be able to address my original accuser's previous statement regarding having been date-raped, and how what may have happened to her could have influenced how her line of questioning with her daughter went on the night of the dinner party implosion, the 13th of July 2016. The prosecution did not want my team to bring it up, based on privacy concerns, and they argued it had no bearing on the case at hand. The Judge sided with my team, but established boundaries.

> **Judge**: Based on the reasons articulated by the defense, the Court finds that there is some limited aspects of her past sexual

> assault that is relevant and should not be excluded…that information as it pertains to why she was discussing the matter with her daughter and what motivated her discussion with her daughter.

The Judge ended the session that day with this guidance:

> **Judge**: Counsel, the members will be here at 0900 tomorrow. I know this is going to be a very long and difficult trial for everyone. I think we all have an interest in bringing resolution to this case. The Colonel deserves resolution; the Marine Corps as an institution wants resolution. I'd ask you to work together the best that you can during these next two weeks. Let's litigate the case.

We reconvened in the court room at 0900 on Tuesday, August 29th, 2017. The entire jury pool was sworn in, and the Judge had the Prosecutor announce the case before proceeding with the jury selection. The first task at hand was to select a jury that we believed was the best we could possibly muster from a contaminated jury pool. This was not going to be a jury of my peers. In the military, the jury is called an officer panel, and all the officers must be senior to the defendant. There were Colonels in the jury pool, but their dates-of-rank were prior to mine, making them senior to me. I had calculated that out of approximately 555 Colonels in the Marine Corps on active duty that there were less than 30 who were actually senior to me at that moment in time. Therefore, the rest of the jury pool would be general officers. The government has a huge edge over any defendant at trial, because the very person sending you to a court martial is also the person able to stack the deck against you by hand-picking the jury pool. It would be the equivalent in the civilian judiciary where the District Attorney is able to hand-pick his own jury pool. It is not acceptable on the civilian side, but common practice in the military. Like playing poker in Vegas, where the house is able to pick their own cards. The house would win every time. By the way, the government does win ninety-nine percent of the time. Ninety-nine times out of a hundred that a military defendant walks into a contested general court martial with no pretrial agreement, he leaves with one or more conviction. The conviction may, or may, not be related to the original charge, thanks to the prosecution's tactics of stacking on as many additional charges as possible.

Four years prior, I had been on an officer panel in a sexual assault case involving a Marine recruiter. During deliberations, the senior member of our panel, a Colonel senior to me, had slyly mentioned in the bathroom that he was going to vote guilty since the rest of us were going to acquit the defendant, knowing that only two thirds of the panel is needed to convict or acquit a defendant, and not the full jury as in the civilian judiciary. "You guys have the votes to acquit, but if the general finds out that I voted to acquit, then she is going to be pissed, and it will be the end of my career." He cast his guilty vote to avoid jeopardizing his career. My existential fear regarding my jury was whether or not they would make a just decision in my case or base their decision on personal concerns about their own careers.

I immediately recognized two of the generals in the jury pool. They both worked directly for my boss, the general, who had ordered my court martial. They both knew that our mutual boss wanted my head on a platter, and they were there to do his bidding. The Judge proceeded to instruct the members of the jury pool, as I was thinking that this jury pool is definitely not of my peers, but the senior leadership of the Marine Corps. It dawned on me that I would likely be judged differently by leaders who have to protect the institution from getting a black eye.

Judge: As court members, it is your duty to hear the evidence and determine whether the accused is guilty or not guilty; and if you find him guilty of any of the offenses, to determine an appropriate sentence. Under the law, the accused is presumed to be innocent. The government alone has the burden of proving the accused's guilt by proof beyond a reasonable doubt. If the accused is convicted of any of these offenses, you will also determine a sentence. But before doing so, I'm going to provide you a very brief orientation.
Charge I represents a violation of the UCMJ, Article 120b. There are three specifications under Charge I.

> Charge II represents a violation of the UCMJ, Article 128. There are four specifications under Charge II.
> Charge III represents a violation of the UCMJ, Article 133. There are nine specifications under Charge III.
> The next page, we have Additional Charge I of the UCMJ, Article 120. There are four specifications under Additional Charge I.
> Additional Charge II represents a violation of the UCMJ, Article 128. There are two specifications under Additional Charge II.
> And, finally, Additional Charge III represents a violation of the UCMJ, Article 86, one specification there under.
> Members, at this time, I would like you to spend as much time as you deem necessary to read through and further review these charges.

The Judge then tried to determine any relationships between the jury pool members and the parties in the court to include the potential list of witnesses. Kevin Bacon has proclaimed there is less than six degrees of separation between individuals. I've always maintained that in the Marines it is less than one degree of separation. The Colonel lawyer conducting one of the three investigations on me had been the senior Staff Judge Advocate (SJA) for one of the generals who had worked for my boss. The Judge had served with two of the jury pool members, and multiple members knew Marines on the witness list.

> **Judge**: Anything about your interaction that would cause you to be more or less inclined to believe so-and-so than any other witness?

"No" was the uniform answer by all questioned.

At the end of the voir dire questioning phase of all fourteen jury pool members, my team was calling for the dismissal of eight for bias. The Judge cut loose six of the eight that my team had picked for dismissal but believed that the other two should be retained on the jury. This left seven members on my jury. Three Colonels senior to me in date of rank, and four generals – three one-star generals, and one two-star general who became the defacto senior member of the jury. Noticeably absent were any infantry officers, which was my job in the Marines. For a jury to have been truly of my peers, it would have had to have been comprised solely of fellow Colonels who had my same military occupational specialty of 0302 – infantry officer. The Judge called the court in recess that first day at 1756. I was shackled and taken back to the Brig, where I spent the night in Cell 13 contemplating the day's events.

The next morning, August 30th, 2017, the prosecutor led off with a long, rambling, incoherent, opening statement. It was so long that the Judge declared a court room break, after the prosecutor had finally concluded. Right after the break, my team immediately asked for a mistrial based on things the prosecutor had said thus far in his opening statement.

> **Defense**: We object to portions of the government's opening statement, in particular, the implication to be drawn from the pictures of his second accuser's daughter. They have no bearing to any of the charges in the case. Also, the comment the prosecutor made about his first accuser "knowing all of the weird things." And, most importantly, the government's mention of, "that you may or may or not see the forensic CAC videos from July." And the remedy we're asking for is a mistrial, your Honor. The jury now knows these videos exist, and the defense has no opportunity, really, to un-ring that bell.
> **Judge**: All right. The defense motion for mistrial is denied.

The Judge obviously didn't buy my team's arguments that what the prosecutor brought up in his opening statement was prejudicial to me or undercut our defense. My civilian lawyer gave the opening statement for my team, and he hit all the wickets one would expect. The Judge closed the morning session with this reminder to the jury.

> **Judge**: Members, once again, you're reminded that the opening statements of counsel aren't evidence in this case. Opening statements are made to assist you in understanding the evidence that the counsel anticipate will be presented by the witnesses.

Following the lunch break, the prosecution called its first witness who was the husband of my first accuser. The prosecution had decided to kick off their case with the original allegation from the night of the dinner party implosion on 13 July 2016. Given that my accuser's husband was present with me in the living room for the duration of his family's visit at my house that evening, the prosecution wanted to establish the atmospherics. His only significant testimony, I thought, was that he affirmed what I had said from the start – that I was never alone with any of his three daughters at any time, and that one of the parents was always present during any of my interactions with their daughters. It was then revealed that the phone call he made to my wife's phone to speak with me, the night of 14 July 2016, was an NCIS-inspired recorded call. NCIS agents were hoping that I would beg the father not to go to the authorities and demonstrate a consciousness of guilt that could be used against me at trial.

> **Prosecution**: Over at the Wilsons' house that night, generally, what were people doing?
>
> **Witness**: So my wife had made lasagna. We had a meal. Our Guest and the Colonel and I were talking. The kids were running back and forth. My wife and Colonel Wilson's wife were talking most of the time in the kitchen.
>
> **Prosecution**: That night, did you see Colonel Wilson ever alone your daughter?
>
> **Witness**: No, sir.
>
> **Prosecution**: That night, did you see Colonel Wilson alone with any of your girls?
>
> **Witness**: No, sir, not a second.
>
> He was then asked what he had been doing the entire evening at the dinner party.
>
> **Witness**: That's all I remember doing, just talking to him and Colonel Wilson until my wife came in.

Prosecution: What happened when your wife came out?

Witness: So my wife came out. She looked fired up. She looked like something was wrong. And she was, like, telling the kids to get out – get out of the house. She told me we had to leave. I said, "Why? What's going on?" I was just – I couldn't process everything. I didn't know what was happening. And she's like, "We have to go for your own safety, for everything. We have to go now." I cooperated. I started getting the girls out of the house.

Prosecution: Did you have any other interactions with NCIS?

Witness: I went to NCIS. They had the idea to do a "control call" to the defendant.

Prosecution: And what's a controlled call? I'm sorry.

Witness: A controlled call is – so I call the defendant, and NCIS is actually listening in to the phone conversation.

Prosecution: When you were speaking to Colonel Wilson, do you recall when he said that he was never alone with the children?

Witness: Yes, sir.

Prosecution: You mentioned that you had collected some evidence for NCIS. Do you recall what that was?

Witness: Yes, sir. It was some garments my daughter could have been wearing during the night of disclosure, to include underwear and shorts.

Prosecution: And, collectively, are these all items that you took over to NCIS?

Witness: Yes, sir, they are.

Prosecution: And can you tell the members a little bit about how you got these items and how they got over to NCIS?

Witness: Yes, sir. So NCIS had requested some garments from my daughter to include her underwear, to submit for touch DNA. So my wife went through the laundry, went through her closet where my daughter was throwing her clothes, and handed me the plastic bag that she had put the items in, tied it up, and gave it to me. I handed the bag off to NCIS, where they removed the items from the plastic bags that I had given them and put them in evidence collection bags they pulled for a child.

Prosecution: Were you comfortable having Colonel Wilson around your family and your children at the time?

Witness: Yes. Absolutely.

Prosecution: Why is that?

Witness: Because I trusted him. He – I thought he was a mentor, a father-type figure that I looked up to. And I respected him.

The Judge then allowed my defense team to question the prosecution's first witness.

Defense: Was there drinking going on?

Witness: Yes, sir.

Defense: Were you drinking?

Witness: Yes, sir.

Defense: Was the guest drinking?

Witness: Yes, sir.

Defense: The next morning is when the pretext phone call occurred; is that correct? On the morning of the 14th?

Witness: A pretext? Oh, the controlled call. Yes, sir, the 14th.

Defense: And how did that come about? Did NCIS contact you and say "this is what we need to do."

Witness: NCIS had recommended it, and I didn't know that that capability had existed. So I thought about it. I mean, I figured some spy stuff, but I didn't – I don't know what NCIS has with the wiring and all that stuff, sir. But when they had recommended it, I thought about it for a while. And I made the decision to execute it.

Defense: Did they give you some instructions?

Witness: They did.

Defense: They talked to you about the goal of trying to get Wilson to admit something, though, right?

Witness: Yes, sir.

Defense: And we all heard the phone call. There was no confession of fact, it was denials throughout. Is that the way you remember it?

Witness: Yeah, there were denials.

Defense: You had a little debrief after the phone call. There was a sense of: We didn't hit our target with that.

Witness: Yes, sir.

Defense: And Colonel Wilson never asked

you: Hey, look, let's just drop this; I didn't do it; we don't have to take this any further. He never said anything like that to you?

Witness: He never said, "Let's work this out between us."

Thus ended the testimony of the prosecution's first witness. He had been with me in my living room, the entire evening in question and had seen nothing untoward. The few other occasions he had been over to our home with his family, we had always been within each other's sight or hearing. My bottom line in the recorded phone conversation was that "no" I had never inappropriately touched any of his three daughters and had never even been alone with any of them. However, I advised him that he needed to go with his gut and do what he felt was the right thing – even if that meant reporting me to the authorities.

Prior to ending the court for the day, the Judge reprimanded prosecution lawyers for passing notes from lawyers in the audience up to the lawyers at the prosecution table. There were ten lawyers representing various parties of the prosecution, and they would come up with ideas for questioning, while the witness was on the stand, passing them up to the prosecuting attorneys for immediate action. The Judge put a lid on that activity and directed that such distracting communication be reserved for courtroom breaks. It came across to me that the prosecution came into court with no plan, and the note-passing signaled to me that they were planning on the fly.

The third day of my trial began with my original accuser, the wife of the first witness from the previous day. Things got heated when my lawyer questioned her. So heated, that the Judge kicked the jury out, and warned her that if she had another outburst on the stand that he would dismiss her as a witness, and her testimony stricken from the record. I felt she had subsequent outbursts and expected the Judge to follow through with his threat, but he did not. My accuser studiously avoided looking at me throughout her hours on the stand.

Prosecution: Do you remember your husband going TAD around 2010 to Camp Pendleton?

Witness: Yes, I do.

Prosecution: Can you tell us anything about that?

Witness: He shared with me that he met a great man by the name of Colonel Wilson and that he invited him and some Marines to do a CrossFit workout. And he just spoke very highly of him and enjoyed the workout with him.

Prosecution: When did your family go to Okinawa? In 2013.

Witness: We were there until 2016.

Prosecution: Did your husband work for Colonel Wilson there?

Witness: Yes, he did.

Prosecution: And, generally speaking, did your husband discuss Colonel Wilson and his opinion of Colonel Wilson then?

Witness: Yes. He spoke very highly of him. He became a mentor to my husband and a father figure, and he had nothing but amazing things to say about him.

Prosecution: I want to ask you about interacting with Colonel Wilson and his wife at Camp Lejeune. When did you and your family first go to see Colonel Wilson at Camp Lejeune?

Witness: It was about – I think it was June 13. We stopped by. We just decided to go for a drive and get out of the hotel room. And so we decided just to take a drive. And he said, "Why don't we drive by Colonel Wilson's house and see if he's there?" And so we drove by there and he was outside in his front yard. And we stopped by to say hello. We just stayed outside and chatted for a while. And while we were there his wife pulled up and I was able to meet her for the first time. And they were both very kind to us.

Prosecution: About how long were you at the Wilsons?

Witness: Maybe 45 minutes. Maybe 30 to 45 minutes. Not very long.

Prosecution: Did anyone ever go inside the house?

Witness: No.

Prosecution: Were your children ever alone with Colonel Wilson at that time?

Witness: No.

Prosecution: Okay, we're back to asking questions about Wednesday, July 13th. Did that evening come to an abrupt end?

Witness: Yes, it did.

Prosecution: So on that night, was Colonel Wilson ever alone with your daughter?

Witness: I don't remember a time when he was alone with her that night.

Prosecution: Did your daughter come into the kitchen crying or upset at any time that night?

Witness: She did.

Prosecution: Who was in the kitchen with you?

Witness: Colonel Wilson's wife.

Prosecution: And what happened when your daughter came in?

Witness: I heard a loud thump and I heard my daughter crying. And she came running into me.

Prosecution: Did your husband say anything to you about this?

Witness: He we didn't talk about it at that moment, but he had come and followed my daughter into the kitchen.

Prosecution: I'm going to ask you about your interaction with your daughter in a minute; but first, I want to back up and ask about Colonel Wilson's wife. At this point, how long had you been friends with her?

Witness: About a month.

Prosecution: Had you had personal and private conversations with her?

Witness: Yes, I had.

Prosecution: On how many occasions, roughly?

Witness: I would say two or three.

Prosecution: Had she confided in you things about Colonel Wilson?

Witness: Yes, she had.

Prosecution: Without telling us what these things were, what was your reaction to hearing these things?

Defense: Objection!

Judge: The objection is sustained. I think that's as far as we're going to go. So continue.

Prosecution: So, at this point, you decide you were going to ask your daughter some questions. And, again, without telling us things that she said, what did you ask or what did you say to start off?

Witness: Well, when she first came in, I was holding her in my lap as she cried because she was in pain from falling. And I asked her why she showed her bellybutton to Colonel Wilson.

Prosecution: And then, after you heard her response, did you say or do anything to her?

Witness: I said, "If anyone asks you to see up here you can always say no. You do not need to show them" I said. "This area up here is private to a female, a girl, just like our area down here. We don't show."

Defense: Objection, sir.

Judge: Objection sustained.

Prosecution: She's been warned, sir.

Judge: This line of inquiry is done. So move on.

Prosecution: Your Honor, the government has one additional question asking about, just, if the daughter made any physical movements inside the bathroom to show her mother anything. That's not calling for hearsay. That's not calling for speculation. It is relevant and there's no 403 objection to that question.

Defense: There is, sir, a 403 objection.

Judge: Is that the only objection?

Defense: One moment, sir. And hearsay, sir. There's a statement.

Judge: The question is objectionable. It is hearsay. So the objection is sustained. I will not allow you to ask that question.

Prosecution: What was the – you said that you had pulled down your daughter's pants. What were you looking for?

Witness: I was pulling her pants down to be able to point down towards her vaginal area and ask her if he ever touched her there.

Prosecution: Did you see anything on her when you pulled down her pants and looked at her vaginal area?

Witness: I did not see anything.

Prosecution: You were mentioning that you had talked to her at the end of this. What did you do when you left the bathroom?

Witness: I picked her up and I carried her. And I looked right at my other two daughters, who were in the kitchen, and I said, "Girls. follow mommy. We are leaving." And they did, and then I walked into the living room area, and I looked right at my husband, and I said, "We need to go now." And he said, "What's wrong. babe? Everything okay?" And I said, "We need to go." And then he asked again what was up. And I said, "Trust me when I tell you that we need to go. Trust me for your own personal protection, we need to go." And so we went outside, and I pushed the opener for my van for the passenger door to slide open. The girls both ran ahead and got in. And as we were walking towards the van, I felt this overwhelming…

Defense: Objection. sir. It's a narrative now. It's becoming non-responsive.

Judge: Objection sustained. Restate.

Prosecution: What did you do after you went to the van? I turned around and walked back inside. I walked back in the house, and I looked at Colonel Wilson.

Defense: I'm going to object to this, too, based upon relevance and hearsay.

Judge: Objection sustained.

Prosecution: When you walked back into the house, who did you see?

Witness: Colonel Wilson.

Prosecution: Did you say anything?

Witness: Yes, I did.

Prosecution: What did you say?

Defense: Objection. This is the objection – it's the same.

Judge: Sustained.

Prosecution: Your Honor, is this not an excited utterance? And it's also not being offered for the truth. This is a continuation of – she's describing the basic facts that must be relevant to what she did upon hearing this information.

Judge: I understand. It may not be hearsay, but the probative value is outweighed by 403 concerns. So the objection is sustained. I don't want to hear what you said. I want to hear what you did, not what you said. I understand it's a bit confusing and splitting hairs, but you can testify what you did, not things that you said.

Witness: I said something and then I walked out.

The prosecution finished up their questioning of my accuser, and that ended the morning session. My lawyer commenced with the cross-examination after a break for lunch.

Defense: Good afternoon, ma'am. I'm going to try my best not to dig over the stuff that we went through on direct examination. So it may feel like I'm pecking around a little bit, but I'm going to do my best to, sort of follow it chronologically, okay.

Witness: Nonverbal response.

Defense: So you met Colonel Wilson in Okinawa the first time?

Witness: Yes.

Defense: And I think you said one of the first times, if not the first time, was when your husband brought him over to the house?

Witness: When the flight was delayed.

Defense: And he got to meet your kids; he got to meet you?

Witness: Correct.

Defense: And that was the first time you had heard Uncle Dan – or that he liked to be called "Uncle Dan" by people?

Witness: That's how he introduced himself.

Defense: And did you call him Uncle Dan, too, or did you just call him Dan?

Witness: I called him Dan. I referred to him as Uncle Dan to the girls because that's just the name that they became familiar with.

Defense: Sure. And a term of endearment, right?

Witness: Correct.

Soon thereafter, when the discussion turned to the previous times they had been to our house, things heated up to a boiling point between my lawyer and my first accuser, prompting the Judge to step in and take charge, nearly kicking her out of the court room and striking her testimony from the record.

> **Defense**: The two big ones you talked about were the time that your husband was stuck at the barracks until late because of the incident that happened; and then the other one, he didn't come over to the house, you know, he was working late. You gave us those two, and those were the ones that you spent quite a bit talking about, right?
>
> **Witness**: The two big ones?
>
> **Defense**: Yes.
>
> **Witness**: Why are you referring to them as "big ones?"
>
> **Defense**: Well, you were talking about your daughter sitting on Colonel Wilson's lap.
>
> **Witness**: That was every time.
>
> **Defense**: There were a couple that you talked about your daughter being with him 95 percent of the time. Do you remember that?
>
> **Witness**: You're calling them "big ones" because my husband wasn't there, and there was an obvious opportunity for things to be done to her?
>
> **Defense**: So my question – I'll rephrase it for you, to help. There were two times that you talked about Colonel Wilson spending most of the time with your daughter.
>
> **Witness**: I'm sorry. I have to gather myself

because it's even hitting you as two big opportunities for my daughter to be touched.

Judge: Ma'am, please – we're going to take a recess at this point. Members, if you could please depart to the deliberation room.

Judge: Ma'am, return to your spot on the stand, please. All right. The members have departed the courtroom. Please, everyone, take your seats. Ma'am, please take your seat. You're not excused yet.

Witness: I'm so sorry. I'm very upset. I'm sorry.

Judge: I understand. Please take your seat. I just want to talk to you for a minute.

Witness: Yes, sir.

Judge: I understand this is very stressful for you, okay. But it's very important that you maintain your calm and relax and answer the counsel's questions. If he wants more explanation, he will ask for more, but you can give simple answers, okay. But it's very important that you maintain your composure because if you don't, I'm going to excuse you as a witness and I'm going to strike your entire testimony, okay. So this is the last warning I'm going to give you. So if you can't maintain your composure, I'm going to excuse you as a witness; I'm going to strike your entire testimony. Do you understand?

Witness: I understand.

Judge: If you need a recess, I understand that. If you feel upset, that's a different matter. If you need time to compose yourself, you can ask. Say, "I need a few minutes," and we can take a recess. But it's very important you don't have an outburst like that again.

Witness: Yes, sir.

Judge: The court is called to order. All parties present when the court recessed are again present. All of the members have entered the courtroom. Please, everyone, take your seats. Defense, you may continue.

Defense: Ma'am, you and I have never met before, have we?

Witness: No.

Defense: Before today?

Witness: No.

Prosecution: Objection, your Honor. I think we are about to get outside of the scope. I'm not sure what his question is.

Judge: Let me hear your question first.

Defense: You and I haven't ever met before, but you have done research on me; isn't that true?

Prosecution: Objection, your Honor. That's definitely outside of the scope. And I ask that we have a 39(a) to figure out what this is going to be.

Judge: Members, let me discuss this with the counsel. You don't need to return to 64-2. If you just want to take a seat in the deliberation room. Just let me discuss this with the counsel.

[The members withdrew from the courtroom.]

Judge: Ma'am, if you could also please step outside of the courtroom. You are excused.

[The witness withdrew from the courtroom.]

Judge: Please, everyone else, take your seats.

The witness has departed the witness stand; has left the courtroom. Defense, what is the relevance of this line of questioning?

Defense: It gives us the bias, sir.

Judge: A bias against whom?

Defense: A bias against Colonel Wilson and his defense team, me. She reported me to the U.S. Attorney here, sir. She did research on me and she reported me to the U.S. Attorney for some ridiculousness. Nothing every happened to it, of course, but.

Judge: When did this occur?

Defense: January 21st, 2017.

Judge: You were counsel on the case at that time?

Defense: Me, sir? Yes, sir. Yes. I mean, she specifically said, "Wilson's attorney" in what she reported.

Judge: Without going into the specifics, what was the nature of the complaint?

Defense: She said I hacked – I was trying to hack into her Facebook page and that I had others working for me who were doing dirty work, trying to hack into Facebook pages and things. And she reported it to the U.S. Attorney's office, and she says, "I believe he has someone doing some dirty work for him."

Judge: How many questions do you anticipate asking?

Defense: Maybe two, sir. Maybe three at the topside. I don't know what her answers are going to be. If she says "yes," I would guess probably two or three.

Judge: All right. I believe there is some

relevance, limited. I will allow a few questions in this area. I do believe it can be asked to establish some bias to the defense team at large. I'll allow a few questions.

Defense: Yes, sir.

Judge: Bring the members back. Hold on a second. Let's bring the witness back.

Prosecution: Your Honor, I mean, the Court's already ruled, but the government thinks this is totally improper. 403 is supposed to protect the process, and here it's exactly what we have, is getting to the confusion and the issues misleading the members on the defense team.

Judge: I understand. I'm going to allow just a few questions. It's not going to take a long time.

Prosecution: Which questions, your Honor?

Judge: I'm going to allow: If she's lodged a complaint and the basis for that. She can either answer "yes" or "no." I'm going to allow a few questions in this area.

Prosecution: I don't know that she actually has lodged a complaint.

Judge: She can say, "I never did that" and that will be the end of the inquiry. We're not bringing in extrinsic evidence. We're not going to have a trial within a trial. I trust that the defense counsel has a good-faith basis to ask that question.

Defense: Sir, they turned it over to us in discovery.

Judge: What does the government know about the nature of the complaint?

Prosecution: The government knows that

she was experiencing issues with her cellphone where it appeared that somebody was logging into her Facebook account.

Judge: Did she lodge a complaint with anyone?

Prosecution: She called the FBI tip line.

Judge: Was the complaint lodged against the defense counsel?

Prosecution: She said that someone was hacking her Facebook. She believed it was possibly the defense attorneys or.

Judge: All right. I'll allow a single question or two on the – into that area, whether she made a complaint.

Prosecution: I'm sorry. And, moreover, your Honor, is that if she has a reason for doing this, then, you know, do we get into exploration of why she is doing this and her fear of Colonel Wilson? Major _____'s fear of Colonel Wilson?

Judge: Defense counsel, you are opening some doors here by asking these questions.

Defense: Colonel Wilson was in the brig. How could they be afraid of him?

Judge: All right. I'm going to allow one question. One question is this area: Was a complaint lodged or was an inquiry made regarding the defense counsel potentially trying to get access to her Facebook. And that's it. We're not going to get sidetracked by a whole lot of collateral issues. I'll allow one question.

Prosecution: The Court asks the question, sir?

Judge: I don't plan on asking any questions.

Prosecution: The Special Assistant U.S. Attorney on this base agreed that her reported information didn't substantiate her allegation that Wilson's defense counsel were associated or involved in any unknown device logging into both of her Facebook accounts.

Defense: Now, I don't plan on going into all of that, but she's the one that exploded on the stand for me. I wasn't raising my voice at her or being in any way untoward to her. She's the one that blew up on the stand. And I should be able to examine or explore that bias a little bit. And all I would ask is, "you know you filed a complaint against me. You don't know me, and you believe that somebody from the defense team was trying to hack into your accounts."

Judge: All right let's bring the members back.

[The members entered the courtroom.]

Judge: All right. Ma'am, you can resume your spot on the stand. Defense, you may continue.

Defense: Ma'am, when we left off, I had asked you if you and I had ever met. You said we had not, correct?

Witness: Correct.

Defense: But you had done some research on me, true?

Witness: True.

Defense: In fact, at some point earlier this year, you filed a complaint against me.

Witness: No. Not exactly, directly on you. It was a concern.

Defense: You contacted the Naval Criminal Investigative Service?

Witness: Yes.

Defense: You contacted the prosecution?

Witness: Correct. It wasn't directed at you though, specifically. It was a concern. I was trying – I know exactly where you're going.

Defense: Did you use my name in it?

Witness: I questioned.

Defense: My question is: Did you use my name in the complaint?

Witness: Okay – yes.

Prosecution: Objection, your Honor. I think that's the end of the inquiry.

Defense: Sir, she hasn't –

Judge: It has been asked and answered.

Defense: She hasn't answered the question yet, sir.

Judge: I believe that was an affirmative response: You used defense counsel's name. I'm going to allow another question. Continue.

Defense: Nothing was ever substantiated from that, right?

Witness: No.

Defense: And you heard back from the agent?

Witness: I did.

Defense: There were two evenings that you spent at the Wilson's where you testified earlier that your daughter spent 95 percent of the time with Colonel Wilson. Do you remember that?

Witness: Yes.

Defense: One of those was on July the 8th – correct?

Witness: Yes.

Defense: And the other one was the 9th, correct? Or did I mess that up?

Witness: You messed that up.

Defense: Okay. So tell me the two dates where you had the 95 percent of the time?

Witness: I don't remember. Can I please look?

Defense: And there were two nights that your husband wasn't there?

Witness: Yes.

Defense: Okay. Aren't those the two nights that you said that he spent 95 percent of the time with your daughter?

Witness: Yes.

Defense: And when you're talking about 95 percent of the time, you're talking about they were sitting in the living room?

Witness: Correct.

Defense: Okay. And you were sitting in the kitchen?

Witness: Yes.

Defense: Would you agree with me that you can – if somebody hollered into the kitchen from the living room, you would be able to hear it?

Witness: If you hollered, yes.

Defense: Both of those nights that you were at the Wilson's house and your husband had to work late, after both of those evenings you sent emails to the Wilson's or posted on your Facebook page about what a nice evening it was, true?

Witness: No. I never sent them an email.

Defense: You communicated in some way that it was a nice evening?

Witness: Yes, I did.

Defense: So I'm going to move to the 13th. On the 13th, that's floor plan. I'm going on your screen, ma'am?

Witness: Yes. it is.

Defense: So up until the thud in the living room and your daughter came into the kitchen, up to that point, any issues, concerns, or anything else?

Witness: No.

Defense: Okay. And it's fair to say from that up to when your daughter fell down in the living room, it was a typical night at the Wilsons' house, just like all those other nights, fair?

Witness: Yes.

Defense: So you had talked about some other things where he had kissed you on the neck. He put his arm around you, he gave you, what was it, a wet-willy. He put his finger in your ear. There were some things like that have gone on, but these are the same kind of events that have happened in previous visits to his house, right?

Witness: Yes. I wasn't as brave as my

daughter.

Defense: Sir, I would ask you to instruct her to answer the questions instead of offering commentary and being non-responsive.

Judge: Ma'am, please answer defense counsel's questions. He will give you fairly straightforward questions. You don't need to give a long narrative. You can answer yes or no. If he wants more information, he will get it from you, but please don't volunteer extraneous information. Do you understand?

Witness: Yes, sir.

Defense: When your daughter came into the kitchen and you were having the conversation — I'm just orienting you now. She comes into the kitchen. You're having a conversation about her showing her bellybutton, okay. Do you remember that conversation you had with her?

Witness: Very well.

Defense: Okay. You said to her, "nobody should be asking you to lift up your shirt and show them anything on your body." Isn't that true?

Witness: Can I see the statement, please, before I confirm to everything that I said?

Defense: If you don't remember what you said, I can let you look at it to refresh your recollection. Is that what you're asking for?

Witness: Yes.

Defense: I have marked it as the next appellate exhibit, sir. I'm going to refer you right where you need to look if you want in one second. It's on page 3 of 5 of the last paragraph. The third and fourth line of that last paragraph.

Defense: So I'll ask you the questions again, ma'am. What you said to was, "nobody should be asking you to lift your shirt and show them anything on your body." Is that true?

Witness: Yes.

Defense: And that you just wanted – you just wanted her to know that her belly was still part of her body that we covered, and you don't ever need to show anything on your body and you can always tell someone no.

Witness: Yes.

Defense: Okay. And – but you have had "private part" discussions with her – you and your husband?

Witness: Yes, we have.

Defense: So after you talked to her about "You don't ever need to show anyone anything on your body. You can always tell someone no," you told her that, just like no one should look at or touch her privacy, people should also not ask you to lift up your shirt. Isn't that what you told her?

Witness: That is what I put in my statement. My initial statement –

Defense: I'm just asking you if that's what you told her, ma'am. Did you tell her that or not?

Witness: That's not how I remember it.

Defense: If I showed you a copy of your statement, would that help you remember how you said it?

Witness: Well, I know what's in the statement. I'm just telling you that I don't – I do not recall that moment. I know what I put, but I don't recall at that moment saying "touch." I recall saying "see."

Defense: When you gave the statement to NCIS the next day, you read through it and initialed at the beginning and end of each paragraph, right?

Witness: I did.

Defense: Did you type it or did they?

Witness: I typed it.

Defense: And that piece that I just said – "just like no one should look at or touch her privacy, people should also not ask you to lift up your shirt" – if you typed it, then you're the one that put that in quotes then too; is that right?

Witness: I typed it. I've said that. Yes, I did.

Defense: And you would agree with me that when you put something in quotes, that's the words that you spoke?

Witness: That's what I put in the statement. I understand that.

Defense: Okay. And if I'm looking at the statement that was done just the very next day that you typed yourself, you're the one that introduced into the conversation the word "touch," true?

Witness: Introduced into the conversation – I feel like that is an extremely broad question. And "introduced" can mean a lot of things. And I don't feel comfortable answering that with a yes-or-no answer.

Defense: So I'll narrow it down for you then. The conversation that you typed the very next day – the statement that you typed

the very next day started with you saying to —
or this part of the conversation started with
you saying, "no one should be asking you to
lift your shirt or show them anything on the
body," right?

Witness: Correct.

Defense: Up to that point, there was no
allegation or mention of touch, true?

Witness: I did not mention touch.

Defense: And neither did your daughter,
true?

Witness: We were just starting our
conversation.

Defense: Okay. So up to that point, she had
never said anything about a touch, true?

Witness: She hadn't told me yet.

Defense: So is that true then?

Witness: That's true.

Defense: The next thing you said to her was
"Mommy isn't mad at you, but I want you
know that your belly is still part of your body
that we cover and don't ever need to show
anyone on your body. You can always tell
someone no." That was the next thing you
wrote that you said to her, correct?

Witness: Yes.

Defense: Up to that point, there was no
allegation about touch, true?

Witness: I didn't use the word "touch" in
any of those sentences, that's correct.

Defense: And I was really focused more
towards your daughter had not said anything
about touch, true?

Witness: I was the only one talking at that point – at that moment.

Defense: Well, when your daughter or when you said to your daughter that nobody should be asking you to lift your shirt and show them anything on your body," she answered you. She said something to you, right?

Witness: Further on, yes.

Defense: I mean, right after that, she said something; didn't she?

Witness: She did.

Defense: Okay. It didn't have anything to do about a touch though, right?

Witness: I'm so sorry. I'm not following you very well.

Defense: You asked her the question: "nobody should be asking you to lift your shirt and show them anything on your body" Up to that statement that you made to her, your daughter had never said that anybody touched her, true?

Witness: True.

Defense: And she responded to you when you said that?

Witness: She responded.

Defense: And when she responded – what she immediately responded with had nothing to do with a touch, did it? It had nothing to do with a touch?

Witness: Correct.

Defense: Okay. You didn't tell NCIS that it did though, did you?

Witness: I need to see my statement. I am –

you are.

Defense: Sure. And if you don't remember or you need it to refresh your memory, all you have to do is ask, and I can get the document.

Witness: Okay. Yes, please.

Defense: May I approach, sir?

Judge: You may. This is Appellate Exhibit CXXIII.

Defense: Thank you, sir. So we're still on page 3 of 5, last paragraph. Ma'am, you can't read off of it. All you can do is refresh your recollection with it.

Witness: Where are you at?

Defense: It's the bottom paragraph, starting with the third sentence on page 3. And we already discussed this part. "I said nobody should be asking you to lift your shirt or show them anything on your body." Do you see where it says that?

Witness: I do.

Defense: Okay. So up to the point that you said that to your daughter, she had never said anybody touched her that night, true?

Witness: True.

Defense: Now, she responded to your statement, correct?

Witness: Yes.

Defense: Her response had nothing to do with a touch; isn't that true?

Witness: It had to do with a "see."

Defense: Right. And we're talking about the

belly, right?

Witness: Her outie. Yes.

Defense: Now, the next thing that you said to her was: "Mommy isn't mad at you, but I just wanted you to know that your belly is still part of your body that we always cover and you don't ever need to show anyone anything on your body. And you can always tells someone no." That's the next thing you said, right?

Witness: Correct.

Defense: Up to that point, she's never said anybody touched her, correct?

Witness: She wasn't really talking a lot at that point. She was sitting in my lap and listening.

Defense: What we had just talked about a second ago, when you were talking about "nobody should be asking you to lift your shirt and show them anything on your body," she's talking right after that, correct?

Witness: Very briefly, but that was it.

Defense: And she said something to you that caused you to make that statement to begin with, correct?

Witness: Make what statement?

Defense: The "nobody should be asking you to lift your shirt and show them anything on your body."

Witness: Yes.

Defense: You see you're talking back and forth to one another, true?

Witness: At that moment, she said something and I said something back.

Defense: Okay. And then we went through the issue of the next thing you said to her was: "Mommy isn't mad at you," and she did not respond to that, correct?

Witness: Can I – you keep taking the statement back and you want me to follow along with you.

Defense: It's just a rule, ma'am, that we can only let you look at the statement to refresh your recollection. That's why I keep taking it back.

Witness: Okay.

Defense: It's not that I'm trying to hide something.

Witness: Okay.

Judge: The witness has Appellate Exhibit CXXIII.

Defense: Yes, sir. Thank you. So, again, we're now at the bottom of page 3, on top of page 4. It starts with "I then said."

Witness: Yes.

Defense: So I can't ask you to read it. I can just ask you to refresh your recollection by looking at it and then what immediately follows it.

Witness: Okay.

Defense: Again, I'm sorry. I've got to take it back. So as you're having this discussion with her, the next thing – you know, you tell her, "Mommy isn't mad at you. I just want you to know your belly is still part of your body that we cover. And we don't need to ever show anyone anything on your body. You can always tell someone no." That's what you say next, right?

Witness: Correct.

Defense: And at that point, she doesn't say anybody touched her, correct?

Witness: Correct.

Defense: Then you say, "Just like no one should look at or touch our privacy, people should not ask you to lift up your shirt." That's what you said to her?

Witness: In my statement. I understand that that's what's there.

Defense: Okay. That statement was made not even 24 hours after these allegations came up, right?

Witness: Right.

Defense: And you typed it?

Witness: I did.

Defense: And you put it in the quotes?

Witness: I did.

Defense: Would you agree with me, then, that it's fair to say that that's what you said to her?

Witness: No. What I remember saying to her —

Defense: I just asked you a question whether it was fair, ma'am.

Witness: No.

Defense: But you would agree with me that that's what you typed in your statement.

Witness: Yes.

Defense: Is it fair that your memory of the events that night would be more accurate from back in July 14th of 2016 than they would be today?

Witness: Yes.

Defense: And would you agree with me that your statement on direct examination, that you only talked about private areas, is inconsistent with what you wrote back in July of 2016, on the 14th?

Witness: With what I wrote, yes. But I gave a verbal statement and I did not say "touch."

Defense: So I'm just going to stick with the question that I asked. Would you agree with me that the statement that you typed, that you put in quotes, is different than what you testified to in court today?

Witness: I have "touch" in there. I understand that. I believe it has been well-established and I am trying to explain to you that as I remember it today. And what I initially said before I even wrote anything, I did not say "touch." That was not a focus for me at that moment when I was writing what happened to my child. I wasn't focusing on — I mean, you know, it was a very hard time.

Defense: So my question to you was: Would you agree with me what you typed in there is different then what you testified to on the witness stand today?

Witness: Yes. But it's the same as my initial statement.

Defense: Sir, I'd ask you to just direct her to answer the questions that I've tried to ask three times politely.

Judge: I think that she's asked — that she's answered to the best of her ability. I'm not quite sure you're going to get the answer you're looking for. It has been asked several times. She has answered. Let's move on, please.

Defense: Sir, I guess it's the additional things beyond yes that I'm asking the court to direct. It was a yes-or-no question.

Judge: I don't get the sense that the witness can answer yes or no. Can you answer that question yes or no?

Witness: No.

Defense: I'm going to hand you CXXIII again. I'm going to ask you to look at page 4, on the first paragraph, the second line says "I then stated 'just like no one should look at or touch our privacy, people shouldn't ask you to lift up your shirt…'" "Touch" is in there, correct?

Witness: Will you just – I feel like – I'm so sorry. We just established that we were moving on here, right?

Judge: I'm going to allow the question. The counsel is asking: Is the word "touch" in your written statement?

Witness: It is in the written statement. It was not in my verbal statement. It's before this.

Defense: Your daughter told you that Colonel Wilson didn't touch her; isn't that true? Isn't that the next thing that she said to you?

Witness: I thought we weren't allowed to discuss what –

Prosecution: Objection, your Honor. We should have a 39(a).

Judge: Another 39(a) session isn't necessary.

The defense is free to explore this. This is not hearsay. If defense wants to explore this, they certainly can. Restate the question, please.

Defense: The next thing that she said was "he didn't touch me there," true?

Witness: I will not answer that with a yes or no. I will let that be left alone there. This further –

Judge: Ma'am, the prosecution can ask you some additional questions, so please respond to defense counsel's questions. If there are follow-up questions, prosecution can stand up and ask you follow up questions. So please just answer these questions. It can be yes or no. You don't have to give detailed explanations. Defense, please restate the question.

Defense: So the question I asked was: Immediately after that, your daughter denied that Colonel Wilson touched her?

Witness: Initially, she said no.

Defense: Ma'am –

Witness: She said, "he didn't touch me there" initially.

Defense: And you asked again, true?

Witness: No, I did not. I never asked. She said it willingly. And then she said it – she said, right after I said as soon as I said that: Did she – or she shouldn't let anybody see up her shirt. She said, "he didn't touch me there."

Defense: What you wrote in your NCIS statement – that NCIS statement, you swore to that, right?

Witness: I did.

Defense: Similar to the way you came in and swore in court this morning?

Witness: Yes.

Defense: You discussed the comments with an NCIS Agent?

Witness: Yes, I did.

Defense: And you discussed the contents of that statement with the special agent, correct?

Witness: The contents of the – I don't remember discussing, like I'm so sorry. Like, after I wrote it, we sat down and talked about it. What are you asking?

Defense: Well, the statement that you swore to says this statement, consisting of this 4 page – this page and four other pages – it actually says, "It was typed for me by Agent so and so, and we discussed its contents." Did you type the statement or did the special agent?

Witness: I typed it.

Defense: Okay. And did you discuss the contents in it like it says?

Witness: Well, prior to that, I had given a verbal interview and he was in there.

Defense: It also says that you read and understood the above statement, that statement that I showed you, true?

Witness: Yes.

Defense: And you had the opportunity to make any changes or corrections that you desired to make, correct?

Witness: Yes.

Defense: And it says that you placed your initials over any changes or corrections?

Witness: Yes.

Defense: And it was true to the best of your knowledge and belief?

Witness: Yes.

Defense: Okay. And you swore to it?

Witness: Yes.

Defense: And he had you raise your hand like you did in court today, right?

Witness: Yes.

Defense: The first two times that this issue came up, she denied anybody touched her; is that true?

Witness: What issue?

Defense: The issue that we're here for today, when she came in and she was being counseled for showing her bellybutton and you said – or at least what you wrote was "no one should look at or touch our privacy. People also should not ask you to lift your shirt." She denied anybody touched her, true?

Witness: She said that.

Defense: And you followed up asking where she was touched, right?

Witness: That's not exactly how it went, but I am not at liberty to discuss exactly how it went.

Defense: Wasn't that the next thing that you typed in your NCIS statement?

Witness: That – I don't know. Can you please hand it to me again?

Defense: Sure. It's on page 4, again there of 5, at the top.

Judge: It's Appellate Exhibit CXXIII.

Prosecution: Your Honor, I have an objection to this line of questioning. I think the witness still thinks that she's not allowed to say what her daughter said. I would like some clarification, too, because the Court said that that was not hearsay. It was cross-examination. She went on to say that her daughter said –

Judge: The defense has now put it into issue. So defense counsel will ask the questions and she will answer the questions. And the government will be given an opportunity during redirect to clarify any additional questions.

Prosecution: Does that mean that the witness is allowed to answer with what her daughter said in the conversation, your Honor?

Judge: Depends on defense counsel's question. Let him ask the question.

Prosecution: Yes, your Honor. I don't want to – normally, one would object and say "calls for hearsay."

Judge: All right. Let's have a 39(a). Members, please step out at this point. Gentlemen, I think you can just stay in the court's deliberation room here.

[The members withdrew from the courtroom.]

Judge: At this point, the door has been opened regarding the statement. I wasn't going to allow the government to offer inadmissible hearsay. Defense wants to explore this. I'm going to allow them to explore this. So now all questions are fair game as far as what was said in the bathroom by her daughter.

Prosecution: Thank you. I was just confused.

Judge: So there's no confusion, that was a door for the defense to open. It's been opened. I'll allow defense counsel to ask the questions. The witness can answer. Whatever confusion remains, Prosecution, you can clear it up in redirect. Let's bring the members back in.

VLC: I'm sorry, sir.

Judge: Yes.

VLC: May I have just a moment to consult with my client about the legal implications that she's allowed to discuss.

Judge: What do you mean "the legal implications"?

VLC: Just so it's clear, what was decided and what she can and can't say on the stand.

Judge: I'll explain to her right now.

Judge: Ma'am, the Court's ruling when you couldn't state what your daughter told you — that doesn't apply anymore. All right. So if the question is asked — if they will ask what your daughter stated to you, you may testify to that. Do you understand?

Witness: Yes, sir.

Defense: Sir, I would ask you to also instruct her that she has to answer the questions too. It's not just —

Judge: I will. Ma'am, that doesn't mean you are to volunteer any additional information. Again, the trial counsel is going to have an opportunity to come back and ask you some clarifying questions. So please stick to answering defense counsel's specific question. Don't offer additional information or a narrative. Again, any confusion can be cleared up once the defense counsel is done. Do you understand?

Witness: Yes, sir.

Judge: Let's bring the members back.

[The members entered the courtroom]

Judge: Please, everyone, take your seats. Defense counsel, you may now continue.

Defense: I want to talk to you about your NCIS statement. On the 14th of July, you went to NCIS, correct? It's the day after the dinner party.

Witness: Yes.

Defense: When you went to NCIS, they did an interview with you?

Witness: Yes.

Defense: And it was recorded in some way?

Witness: Yes.

Defense: And that was, sort of, a question and answer – it wasn't sworn, or was it?

Witness: Yes.

Defense: And was it – and it was videotaped?

Witness: Yes.

Defense: And after you got done with that interview, where it was just, kind of, a question and answer and more of a conversation, fair?

Witness: They asked, like, a question maybe. It was kind of – I cannot remember. I just remember telling what happened.

Defense: I'll ask it this way: It wasn't a formal thing like this, like we're in court today?

Witness: It was definitely not like court.

Defense: You were either sitting on a couch or sitting in a chair, and there was an agent in there.

Witness: Yes.

Defense: And it was an interview, but it was really just a conversation between you and the agent. He was asking you questions and you were giving narrative answers, right?

Witness: He asked questions and I answered, yes.

Defense: And after you got done with that, then he asked you to do a sworn statement?

Witness: Yes.

Defense: And that was a statement where you have to sit down in front of a computer, and I'm imagining he probably set up a – Microsoft Word, and probably had a little bit of boilerplate. And then you did all of the paragraphs; is that right?

Witness: Yes.

Defense: And in that room, the agent probably came in and out and gave you as much time as you needed to be as thorough as you wanted to be in giving that statement, true?

Witness: I remember him coming in once.

Defense: I guess my – he gave you as much

time as you wanted though, right?

Witness: Yes, he did.

Defense: And you had the opportunity to reflect on dates, reflect on circumstances, reflect on conversations, correct?

Witness: I had the opportunity, yes.

Defense: And that sworn statement that you provided to NCIS, and your discussion with your daughter about what happened in the living room the night of the dinner party, you were the first person that introduces the word "touch"?

Witness: In the written statement, yes. I understand that that is there.

Defense: And in response to "nobody should touch you there" or "no one should look at or touch our privacy. People shouldn't ask you to also lift your shirt." That is what you asked her, correct? Witness: Yes.

Defense: And she had already gone to this issue of – I mean, we know that she lifted her shirt up because she was being counseled for showing people her bellybutton or talked to.

Witness: She wasn't being counseled.

Defense: And in that statement, the next thing you write is that "He didn't touch me there"?

Witness: That I write?

Defense: Correct.

Witness: Yes. I wrote, "He didn't touch me there." You were correct. That's what she said initially.

Defense: And you said, "Touch you where, baby?" That's what you wrote the conversation was between you and your daughter, correct?

Witness: Yes.

Defense: And she responded: Her privacy.

Witness: Yes.

Defense: And this "privacy," is that your term or her term that she would normally use?

Witness: That's what we call it.

Defense: And you said, "mommy never said he touched you there," right?

Witness: I did. Because it shocked me that she threw that out there.

Defense: And when we're looking at the statement that you typed, in context, you never did say "He touched you there"? did you?

Witness: That he – that I said he touched her there?

Defense: Right. I mean, you never wrote that in your statement that – in other words, nowhere in your statement are you saying, "He touched you there, didn't he?" I mean, that's not in your statement anywhere, right? I'm not being clear. Let me try at this again. When you are asking her these questions, you know, the next thing you…

Witness: Questions? What questions?

Defense: The questions that you are asking your daughter. You're basically describing a conversation that you had with your daughter, correct?

Witness: This is what happened when I found out, yes.

Defense: Okay. And so this thing that I'm going through with you, I mean, this is a – your memory of that conversation, fair?

Witness: Not now. And not in my initial video.

Defense: Okay. The one that I'm talking about, your sworn statement here, this is your memory of that conversation that you had with your daughter the night before?

Witness: I wrote that in my statement. I understand that.

Defense: And at the time that you wrote it, that was your memory of the conversation, correct?

Witness: I can't put myself back in that place.

Defense: Okay. When you sign and say that "the statement is the truth to the best of my knowledge and belief," do you agree with me –

Prosecution: Your Honor, objection; asked and answered. We have been over this and over this and over this.

Judge: Defense counsel, we have covered this a couple of times.

Defense: You said to her "mommy never said he touched you there," and she responded to you that he didn't touch her there. Isn't that true?

Witness: Initially, yes.

Defense: So in the initial discussion, twice she tells you that he did not touch her, correct?

Witness: Yes. She said she – he did not touch her initially, yes.

Defense: When you initially left the Wilson's house that night, was there any discussion at all on the ride home about what the, you know, your belief was as to what happened in the Wilson house?

Witness: No.

Defense: Were you being loud and boisterous?

Witness: No.

Defense: What about after you got home?

Witness: No.

Defense: Did you ever, in front of the girls, tell them that you would like to stab or kill Colonel Wilson?

Witness: After we came out of the house, I was standing outside of my car. And the door was open and I was talking to the dinner guest. And, yes, I said I saw a knife on the counter and I wanted to grab it and wanted to go after him with it. I said that.

Defense: And did your girls hear that?

Witness: Yes, they did.

Defense: Did you get the feeling that that scared them?

Witness: I don't get the feeling that it scared them.

Defense: Did you have any discussions with them at any time prior to getting to the child advocacy center about these allegations?

Witness: Not really. I just told them that we're going there so that – we told them that's where they can go and tell people what happened.

Defense: Was there a time you and your husband were in your eldest daughter's room with all three girls and talked about the allegations?

Witness: I don't remember where we were, but at some point, we definitely spoke to our girls. It had to be discussed, yes.

Defense: And wasn't it right before you went to the child advocacy center?

Witness: I don't remember it being right before we went to the child advocacy center.

Defense: Is it possible that was the case?

Witness: I don't believe so.

Defense: How many times would you guess that you had conversations with her when she came to you?

Witness: Over the past year, several.

Defense: Have you had conversations with your other two daughters about what happened?

Witness: Yes.

Defense: And then you had been with her here at Camp Lejeune talking about the allegations with the prosecutors?

Witness: Been with her? Are you referring to trial prep?

Defense: Correct.

Witness: She had to come in here and get comfortable with the court, and she was in here, yes.

Defense: My question was: You have been with her when she came into Camp Lejeune here to talk about the allegations with the prosecutors, correct?

Witness: Of course I was in here with my daughter.

Defense: The prosecutor asked you about the sex assault nurse exam that your daughter went to, the TEDI BEAR Clinic? Earlier in direct? Were you there in the examination room when it happened or did she just go in there with the examiner by herself?

Witness: I was in there.

Defense: Did she ask your daughter any questions about what happened?

Witness: No – I don't remember.

Defense: Did you provide the information to the nurse about what happened?

Witness: Yes.

Defense: Did you discuss with the sex assault nurse examiner what the allegations were? In another words: Did you give her the information?

Witness: Yes. We sat down and talked.

Defense: And was your daughter there when you sat down and talked?

Witness: No.

Defense: At some point, some of your daughter's clothing is collected from the house and taken to NCIS.

Witness: Yes.

Defense: Did you collect that stuff up put it in a bag and give it to your husband?

Witness: Yes.

Defense: During direct examination, the prosecutor had talked to you about some things that you learned about Colonel Wilson. Do you remember that?

Witness: Can you repeat the question? I'm sorry.

Defense: Yeah. I'm just being careful in the way that I ask it. In the direct examination, the prosecutor asked you about some things that you had learned about Colonel Wilson after you arrived in the Camp Lejeune area? From Colonel Wilson's wife. Do you remember that?

Witness: I do.

Defense: Okay. None of those things that you learned had anything to do with children, correct?

Witness: They did not.

My lead lawyer completed his cross-examination and the tension in the room evaporated, as my original accuser departed the court room. Several big sighs could be heard along with the noisy inhalation of deep breaths. One could have heard a pin drop, as the door closed behind her. My thought was that if someone looked up the definition of a hostile witness in the dictionary, her picture would pop up. Her face was red and contorted with anger – more like hate towards my lawyer. If looks could kill, he would have been dead, particularly when he pointed out the glaring discrepancies between her initial sworn statement to NCIS on July 14th, 2016, and her just-concluded testimony for the prosecution, some fourteen months later. She seemed to resent every question, and insisted on editorializing, rather that just giving a simple "yes" or "no" answer. A few times, I thought the Judge was going to go through with his threat and kick her off the witness stand and strike all of her testimony from the record, but he patiently "talked her off the ledge" after each outburst and got her back to answering my lawyer's questions. We all felt at the break in our conference room that the General had hit a home run with his questioning. My daughters and wife were especially relieved and excited to have that part over.

My lawyer in cross-examination had exposed my accuser up front as a liar, or at least as someone who would readily twist the facts to shape her own narrative. Up front, after she claimed that she didn't know anything about him except that he was my civilian lawyer, he proved that she knew him so well that she had reported him to the FBI, accusing him of hacking into her two Facebook accounts, and tried to get a U.S. Attorney to investigate him. Wisely, the U.S. Attorney had declined her invitation. The General had called her out on significant changes to her current version of what happened, 14 months later, as opposed to what she had initially typed in a sworn statement to NCIS, less than 24 hours after the dinner party implosion on July 13th, 2016. Specifically, that initially, her daughter had repeatedly denied that I had ever touched her in any untoward manner, and that it was she, the mother, who had introduced the topic with her daughter, not the other way around. Significantly, his questioning exposed the truth of the case – that she, the mother, had concocted the whole story, and had then tried to embed it in her daughter's mind. He had also pointed out that it was my accuser who had provided all the information to the nurse practitioner conducting the sexual assault forensic exam on her daughter, and that she had been present in the room during the examination in violation of standard protocol. In spite of all these undue influences by the mother, her child had complained of nothing, and the exam demonstrated that she was a normal, healthy, care-free child, who never even mentioned anything at all about a violent sexual assault having supposedly taken place just prior to the exam.

Here is what our defense expert with thirty years of experience in examining and caring for children had to say about the sexual assault forensic exam conducted on my accuser's daughter:

> **Defense**: In relation to when the accusations were, at least do you know when the SANE exam was conducted?
>
> **Witness**: Oh, yes, I do. It was done 24 hours after the child disclosed whatever happened. The child came in to see the SANE for

examination and evidence collection.

Defense: What were the findings of the examiner?

Witness: The examiner said that there were no findings. It was a normal exam.

Defense: Walk us through, specifically, what was done in that exam, if you know.

Witness: In the exam, the nurse met the mother and the child. It said in the report, NCIS was there. So the nurse and the mom talked a bit before they brought the child back. And the child was told that this was going to be a check-up exam, looking at her body to make sure things were okay. There was not a specific interview or question alone with the child by the medical provider. The mother gave the information to the medical provider as well as NCIS. And I really don't know if information from the interviewer was specifically given to her or NCIS gave her the history of what happened. And that's important because that dictates where the nurse is going to collect the swabs for the evidence collection kit. They started the exam. And the nurse spoke with the girl, asking her about her arms, her legs, her body. And she said that everything was okay. She went on with her report.

Defense: So part of what you said is that there was, essentially, a head-to-toe exam that was done?

Witness: Yes.

Defense: What about swabs that were collected? Do you recall?

Witness: The swabs were collected.

Defense: So in this case, you said the exam was completely normal from, at least, the documents you reviewed?

Witness: Yes, that's correct.

Defense: What about – I think you had mentioned to me previously about issues with the medical history. Can you explain what you mean by that?

Witness: Yes. I noted when I reviewed the document that there was nothing where the nurse and the child spoke alone. Typically, in child abuse cases, it is common for the medical provider to ask the child about what happened so that she can understand what the situation is and get the history from the child. Remember that the forensic interview, which she already had, is completely different than what the medical provider is going to get at because we have different questions.

Defense: What kind of questions would you have asked in this case if you were seeing her?

Witness: I would have wanted her to identify her body parts for me, what the names are that she uses for the genital area, for the butt, and the breasts. I would want to know: Tell me what happened. Tell me more about that. So that once I have that history, that would allow me to know where to collect the swabs, which is important in an acute exam.

Defense: Why is it important to interview the child away from the parent?

Witness: We interview the child away from the parent because often times children want to protect their parents. They don't want to say some things in front of them. And it is more forthcoming. Parents can be very emotional, and the child will feel everything. Even though that parent may be sitting behind them, they can feel them getting upset. And it's just not a good idea usually.

Defense: To your knowledge, did the medical examiner ever attempt to collect a history from the child herself?

Witness: I did not read anything that she talked with the child specifically about this event. The history she had was from the mother, and I believe NCIS or the interviewer.

Next into the courtroom as prosecution witnesses were all three of my accuser's daughters – the seven-year-old twins and their eleven-year-old sister. I felt bad that these kids were forced into testifying in the courtroom. They could have been in a separate room and piped into the courtroom via closed circuit TV, but the prosecution lawyers had insisted on the girls being present in the courtroom. The Judge had directed a small table be positioned, where each of the girls could sit and face the jury and not have to look at me. An attendant accompanied each of the girls into the courtroom and sat with them during their testimony. Their memories of the events that night were sketchy at best. Except that the eleven-year-old said she had never seen anything untoward in my behavior – no touching "that way," no licking, and no spanking, which were separate charges against me. She countermanded her mother's testimony by asserting that her mother had scared the bejesus out of her with her comment about wanting to grab a knife and kill me. Remember, her mother had just testified that she didn't feel like her comment had scared the kids. It not only scared them, but her comment had also scarred them all for life. The elder daughter also clarified that it was the younger twin who had initiated the bellybutton contest by asking me who had the cutest bellybutton, while lifting up her shirt in front of her father and I in the living room. Critically, the elder daughter confirmed that the mother had indeed corralled all three of the girls into her room, to get their stories on the same sheet of music, before going off to the Child Advocacy Center for interviews. Something the mother had vehemently denied doing.

The prosecution then brought in our dinner guest from the night of July 13th 2016. My lawyers elicited some interesting tidbits, after establishing that he had been close friends for years with my accuser and her husband whereas he and I were just meeting for the first time that explosive night. Ironically, he was of no help to the prosecution, and merely confirmed that he had not witnessed any inappropriate behavior on my part except my accuser sitting on my lap, which she never actually did. She came and sat next to me on the couch for a spell, before returning into the kitchen to continue drinking cocktails with my wife and carrying on with their gossip session. None of their salacious gossip included any mention of me ever acting inappropriately towards children.

> **Defense**: And I think you also said on direct that Colonel Wilson was rough housing with the kids.
>
> **Witness**: Yeah. I mean, playing with the kids.
>
> **Defense**: Do you recall Colonel Wilson playing "Marine" with the kids?
>
> **Witness**: Yes.
>
> **Defense**: And it seemed like they were enjoying it?
>
> **Witness**: Yes.
>
> **Defense**: It seemed like the kids really seemed to like Colonel Wilson quite a bit?
>
> **Witness**: It seemed so.
>
> **Defense**: And they were climbing all over him?
>
> **Witness**: Yes.
>
> **Defense**: You never saw any licking that night, did you?
>
> **Witness**: I don't recall that.
>
> **Defense**: You didn't see anything inappropriate that night?
>
> **Witness**: Nothing inappropriate.
>
> **Defense**: So one of the parents was in the

room when that bellybutton conversation took place?

Witness: The girls' father was sitting to the right of me on that couch where I was sitting.

Defense: So do you recall her saying to Colonel Wilson, "I don't give a fuck that you're a Colonel. I'm going to take you down"?

Witness: Something to that extent.

Defense: And Colonel Wilson looked dumbfounded?

Witness: Yes. I think we were – all of us was quite stunned.

Defense: And do you recall telling NCIS that Colonel Wilson was dumbfounded?

Witness: Stunned, dumbfounded, amazed, shocked – yeah.

Defense: And when you were speaking to NCIS, you were actually texting with the husband and wife; isn't that right?

Witness: No. Not when I was speaking with them. Right before I spoke to them, I texted them and said that I was going to speak to them.

Defense: You said, "I'm talking to NCIS right now. Wish me luck."

Witness: I said – I texted them, if I recall, that NCIS is coming to see me. Wish me luck. I forget whatever I said to them.

Defense: And you told them that you wanted to be as supportive as possible to them.

Witness: Yes.

Defense: And that you would even be willing to talk to the Commandant to support them.

Witness: I would.

Defense: And even after this point, you have been in communication with them?

Witness: I have.

The prosecution's DNA analyst was very circumspect about the DNA found on the underwear of my accuser's daughter. My lawyer pointed out that the DNA was an exact match for the girl's father, while the analyst insisted that there was not enough quantity in the sample to identify an exact profile. Their lab's data also indicated that there were 3.2 trillion more likely male matches to the discovered DNA than to my DNA.

Defense: The genetic marker that registered at a high enough level in that second column on the underwear is consistent with the Major and not consistent with Colonel Wilson, correct?

Witness: I can't make any comparisons between the question sample and the known reference.

Defense: So you gave us a definition about the number of times it repeats on the Y-chromosome. On that sample, the number of repeats on the underwear matched the Major and not Colonel Wilson; is that correct?

Witness: I can't make any inclusionary or exclusionary statements.

Defense: So I'm not asking you to include or exclude one or the other. I'm just talking about the genetic marker that's reflected on this printout that your machine printed out. If we're looking at the data in these two columns, they both match the Major and they don't match Colonel Wilson. That's what it reflects, correct?

Witness: Yes.

The prosecution brought in a second DNA analyst from another government lab, but she also insisted that the sample quantity was insufficient to produce a consistent DNA profile, albeit that half of the key genetic markers proved that it was 100 percent the father's DNA that was found on his daughter's underwear. The parents had even submitted separate sworn statements to NCIS agents, insisting that they never mixed their laundry loads, eliminating the possibility of DNA transfer through laundry. Following this huge red flag revelation, NCIS never did any further investigation as to why the father's DNA was the only male DNA found on his daughter's underwear. NCIS agents consciously chose to ignore that fact

Every time the child I was alleged to have assaulted was asked about the alleged sexual assault by child psychologists, forensic examiners, and by lawyers, she responded with a different version of what had allegedly happened to her. There was no consistent narrative in any of the retellings that would indicate something bad had actually happened to her. The only consistent memory in her mind was that whatever had happened to her had occurred on July 13th, 2016, in the living room of my home with her father, her two sisters, and a dinner guest present throughout, along with both wives coming and going randomly between the kitchen and the living room.

The case was so pathetically weak that in the end, before resting his case pertaining to the child rape charges on Saturday, September 2nd, the prosecutor pleaded with the Judge to allow the hearsay video from the child advocacy center to be played for the jury; "So if we're going to be stuck with 'this happened on disclosure night,' that's going to be a significant impediment for the government to prove its case." The Judge agreed, with limitations on what would be shown in court, and a redacted version was played for the court when the court convened again on Labor Day, September 4th, 2017. My impression as I watched the CAC video was that the questioner was asking questions of the child in a way that led the child down a certain path, like breadcrumbs marking the trail. Instead of eliciting a narrative from the child in her own words, she was asked yes/no questions, leading questions, true-false questions, and even confusing compound questions. Questions so confusing that the heads' of all the adults in the courtroom were spinning.

Our defense expert, a practicing child psychologist with decades of experience, destroyed the credibility of the CAC video with her testimony. The prosecution had literally brought in "country bumpkins" as their expert witnesses, which is why their testimony was disingenuous and disjointed. Both admitted that their in-court testimony provided income for the places they worked at, and one revealed that his annual salary was tied to how well he did at generating income for his university. Turns out the guy was a frequent prosecution witness in military courtrooms for sexual assault cases. Our defense expert was a prominent child psychologist with decades of experience. She was brilliant on the witness stand and patiently explained why this outrageous allegation was a concoction from the mother's sick mind, and not from her child. Also, that the mother had done a poor job of embedding the dubious story in her daughter's memory.

> **Defense**: Can you explain the concept of contamination?
>
> **Witness**: I think the best analogy I can tell you is when you have a glass of clear water, if you drop one ink drop in it, it starts to muddy the water. If you drop two drops, it gets muddier still and so on. So if you are interviewing a child, and you use X amount of close-ended questions in the beginning of the interview, you're starting to muddy the water. If you now use suggestible questions, more muddying occurs. Repetitive questions increase the probability of the child acquiescing and answering suggestible questions. So repeated questions increase the probability of the child acquiescing to suggestible questions – more drops muddying the water. It gets more

contaminated, darker. And at some point, you can't rehabilitate it, and the opportunity to maintain competent, reliable information may be lost.

Defense: Even a parent, for instance, might contaminate in some way the child's story, correct?

Witness: One of the factors in an interview is that you have to understand all previous conversations to the interview.

Defense: Can you explain the concept of negative stereotype induction and why that's important in this case?

Witness: We want to know the child's emotional tone, what she's bringing into the interview. What are her preconceived notions? In this case, we know that the night before, the girl's mother calls the Colonel a "fucking bastard." We've had testimony that the child heard this all the children in the car. Her mother says, "If I had a knife, I'd stab him in the neck"; and then later tells the children, "Don't repeat this."

Defense: Can you explain some more issues with that interview?

Witness: I have some problems with the fact that interviewer introduces the word "lap." And we have to work on the children's words. So it's like interviewing a piece of evidence that she hasn't talked about yet.

Defense: Is there anything else?

Witness: Yes. There are several confusing questions. The quality of the questions posed will affect the quality of the answer you get. If you ask an ambiguous question, you will get an ambiguous answer. If you ask a confusing question, you will get a confusing answer.

Defense: Would you say that her response was somewhat ambiguous?

Witness: She didn't answer the question.

Defense: Just so we don't have to go line-by-line for everything, if you could just now explain the takeaways of what you believe to be confusing from that interview.

Witness: What's confusing is what does "push" mean? What's confusing is over or under. I think it was such a leading question and suggestible. I don't believe we have enough detail. We have all the statements that it didn't happen under her underwear. And right at the end, interviewer comes back into the room. That's a real problem. We have a problem with that there's no active listening. Repetitive questions increase the probability that the child's going to acquiesce. I really think a big part that's missing is the parental reactions and the preinterview conversations.

Defense: Can you explain the concept of indoctrination and give an example?

Witness: If I say to a child - a lot of times, I'll do this with custody evaluations and small children, especially if there's some allegations that might have a criminal tone. I'll say, "Did your dad use any curse words?"

"No."

"Did your dad sometimes raise his voice?"

"No."

"Did your dad say the F word?"

"No."

"Did he ever say "fuck you" to anybody?"

"Yes."

"He said 'fuck you' to other people. How many times did he say fuck you to other people?"

"Oh, a lot of times."

The research on this is: You can indoctrinate, you could get children to believe horrendous things have happened that actually did not happen. You can easily plant a memory. And, you know, we know that with the Salem Witch Trials, we saw that in the 1980s, when the questions were asked, a lot of people who went to jail, their cases were overturned because the questioning indoctrinated the child into believing things that happened that were incredulous. So research is very clear, that you can implant a memory. A child can be indoctrinated into thinking things happened that have just never happened.

Defense: Can those types of false memories involve touching or private parts or sexual misconduct?

Witness: Absolutely. That's why we started coming out with protocols. Because in the 1980s, there was an important case, New Jersey v. Kelly Michaels. In Kelly Michaels, they got the children to say that she was playing the piano naked in the basement of the church where the day school was. Now, in a church, where anybody could walk in at any time, a nursery schoolteacher was playing naked. They got the children to say that. And this is where this experiment is very important. Because it's not just a neutral behavior; it's not just a bland behavior. In another experiment, they took children at preschool age: 4, 5, 6 – and they told them that their finger had been bitten by a mousetrap. And they repeated this to the child several times – that their finger got caught in a mousetrap. And, after 10 days, they wanted to deprogram the child because the children actually believed that their finger was caught in a mousetrap because an adult said it a couple of times. They could not deprogram three of the kids. The kids stuck to their story – that their finger was caught in that mousetrap. That shows indoctrination – that something pretty telltale happened, and the children had stories about something that never happened.

Defense: Do you believe, based on the testimony and evidence you've reviewed, that it would be your opinion that it is difficult to determine if the allegations were sexually motivated or not?

Witness: Yes. And that is the question.

Back in our conference room afterwards, my family and lawyer team were ecstatic that the prosecution had failed miserably to prove that anything untoward had occurred the night of the dinner party. Furthermore, our expert had hit the nail on the head. It was a concocted story by the mother, but poorly implanted in her daughter's mind. Our groupthink was that all of the original charges were blown out of the courtroom from the testimony of my accuser. We merely had to wait for the jury to confirm what we all knew in a matter of days – that I would be set free.

CHAPTER 9
HELL HATH NO FURY

The next phase of the prosecution's case was to bring in my #MeToo accuser on Labor Day and have her describe what happened to her. The prosecution attempted to have the Judge remove my wife from the courtroom, since my second accuser had a "no contact" order in place against my wife. The Judge refused to kick my wife from his courtroom, and even asked her if she wished to remain in the courtroom, during her former friend's testimony – she did. My second accuser's testimony finished off the day with her needing to come back the following day for more. We concluded that session with a concern by my team about her condition – she seemed heavily medicated or intoxicated.

Defense: Sir, I have a concern. And I don't know what – but I have a concern that the witness was under the influence of something just based upon her twice – not going catatonic but shutting down. And I also noticed that she seemed to be slurring a little bit. She did go through a litany of medications. I'm asking that the issue be addressed.
Judge: I'm willing to bring her back and ask the questions because that would be a fair line of cross-examination.

[The witness re-entered the courtroom.]
Judge: If you could, just please resume your seat. I don't mean to embarrass you, but I'd rather ask these questions – please take your seat – outside of the presence of the members. Are you currently, right now, taking any type of medication?
Witness: Am I taking any medication?
Judge: Are you under the influence of anything right now? Did you take any type of prescription medication or over the counter medication?
Witness: Well, I took a couple of Advil earlier.
Judge: All right. I assume you hadn't been drinking before today's testimony?
Witness: No.
[The witness withdrew from the courtroom.]
Judge: Court is in recess. (The court-martial recessed at 1618 on 4 September 2017.)

She returned to the stand the next day and seemed in even worse shape – slurring, excessively long pauses, etc. My lawyers got a chance to cross-exam her, and it became ugly real fast with everyone in the courtroom straining on the edge of our seats to hear her subdued responses.

Defense: And in your interaction, at least initially with Colonel Wilson's wife, she was trying to give you some advice and counsel based upon her years of experience with the spouses' club, true?
Witness: Yes.
Defense: And the conversation that you had between one another was, sort of, how to navigate the politics of the Officer's Spouses Club, true?
Witness: True.
Defense: After your, sort of, initial lunch with Mrs. Wilson, you engaged in, over the next several months, thousands of Facebook messages back and forth. Would you agree with that?
Witness: Yes.
Defense: Over 6,000. Would you agree with that?

Witness: I'm sure you have all of the exact numbers, sir.
Defense: The relationship, say, between October 19 and when you first made contact with one another, let's just call it the 19th up until the Thanksgiving dinner. Was it a mutual relationship where you both would confide in one another?
Witness: Yes.
Defense: And for you, some of that piece was the problems you were starting to have with your marriage; is that fair?
Witness: Sure.
Defense: And part of that issue was that you and your husband were talking about divorcing, and you had concerns about money; is that fair?
Witness: Sure.
Defense: Mrs. X who is part of the Officer's Spouses Club. Were you particularly angry at her?
Witness: I don't remember being angry at her.
Defense: You know who she is though?
Witness: Yes, I do know who she is.
Defense: Isn't it true that you were so angry with her interaction with you that you took shaving cream, and you drew a gigantic penis on her car – her husband's car, and also used shaving cream to deface the two flags they had on their house with penises?
Witness: That is absolutely not true.
Defense: Do you know what I'm talking about?
Witness: Yes.
Defense: So I'm going to move forward to, sort of, the Thanksgiving timeframe. Your family was invited to come over to the Wilson's, true?
Witness: True.
Defense: You spent Thanksgiving there – at least you did?
Witness: With my daughter, yes.

Defense: And that was the first time you had met Colonel Wilson?
Witness: Do you have documentation saying otherwise?
Defense: Sir, would you ask her to answer the question?
Judge: Ma'am, it's just a simple yes or no question. If you can't remember, say – I don't know.
Defense: Was it the first time you had been at his house when Colonel Wilson was there?
Witness: I think so.
Defense: Is it fair to say that he was friendly with you while you were at the house?
Witness: That would be fair to say.
Defense: And after that visit on Thanksgiving, you and Colonel Wilson connected on Facebook as well; is that fair?
Witness: Yes.
Defense: Would you also agree with me that between the end of November, before Thursday, Thanksgiving so from that timeframe forward until the early parts of January, that you and Colonel Wilson engaged in a lot of private messages on Facebook?
Witness: Yes.
Defense: Over 2,000?
Witness: You probably have the exact number. So probably.
Defense: Now, when you were talking to us earlier, you talked to us about a surgery that you had soon after Thanksgiving?
Witness: Yes.
Defense: And you had mentioned that you had titanium in some place. Was that at the C5, C6 – I think that you described that yesterday. C4, C5?
Witness: Yes.
Judge: I believe the witness is pointing to her neck.
Defense: Neck area? Thank you.
Defense: I don't need to see the scar.
Witness: No! Let me show you!

Judge: No one has asked to see the scar, so please put your jacket back on. If the counsel wants to see it, they'll ask.

Defense: And it was for that, that Mrs. Wilson had offered to drive you up to the Virginia Beach/Portsmouth area; is that right?

Witness: To surgery, yes.

Defense: And, sort of, that first interaction that you had with Colonel Wilson on Facebook was that, you know, that they would help take care of the room – or they would take care of the room when you went up to have your surgery?

Witness: Do you have that Facebook message?

Defense: I'm going to hand you what's been marked as Appellate Exhibit CXXXIII and ask you to take a look at that. And I've highlighted some parts that might help you.

Witness: Okay.

Defense: So the first interaction that you had with Colonel Wilson was that they would pay for your – for the room when you guys went to Portsmouth; is that fair?

Witness: Well, it wasn't like he sent me a message before.

Defense: Perhaps not the first, but one of the first messages that you guys exchanged back and forth was him saying that they would take care of the room?

Witness: Yes.

Defense: And, sort of, from that exchange forward – and let's say, you know, through the first several weeks up into the Christmas timeframe – you had joking messages back and forth with Colonel Wilson, more serious conversations back and forth with Colonel Wilson, kind of both; is that fair?

Witness: Yes.

Defense: So, ma'am, it was at least at that point, on December 9, you're making appointments and such to go talk to lawyers

about the divorce and what your rights would be, true?
Witness: It's a confusing question.
Defense: Okay. So you knew if you are divorced you might have certain rights available to you for settlements as a result of the divorce. You're aware of that, right?
Witness: I guess you could, yes. Sure.
Defense: You want to get the most you can from alimony from your husband at this point; is that true?
Witness: I think that's your opinion, sir.
Defense: Well, don't you tell Colonel Wilson in a private message that you're going to stop the messaging back and forth because you're going to?
Prosecution: Objection, your Honor. It's calling for hearsay. It's not for the truth of the matter asserted, sir.
Judge: The objection is overruled.
Defense: So you tell Colonel Wilson you'll be right back because you're calling an attorney to "butt fuck" your husband?
Witness: I would like to explain.
Defense: Isn't that what you said to Colonel Wilson?
Witness: I would like to explain.
Defense: Sir, would you direct her to answer the question, please?
Judge: Ma'am, the trial counsel can follow-up with more detailed information. You can answer it – again, short and simple. The trial counsel will follow up as necessary.
Witness: Yes, I did say that. And I did read that I did say that. I would like to be able to explain that.
Defense: And the context of that is that you were trying to make sure that you get the most that you had for yourself as a result of the divorce; isn't that true? I'm not saying there is anything wrong with it, but, I mean, that's what you're trying to accomplish, right?

Witness: I feel that that's your explanation, sir. I feel that you're putting words in my mouth, sir.
Judge: Ma'am, it's either a yes or no or I don't know.
Defense: Didn't you ask Colonel Wilson to help you come up with some questions to take to the lawyer so you could, I guess, speak more intelligently to the lawyer about how to best help yourself? And you asked him for help?
Witness: I did ask Colonel Wilson for help.
Defense: And, in fact, you asked him to go with you to the lawyer's office? So after the, you know, again, my point is: After the Thanksgiving weekend – or the past Thanksgiving holiday, you and he became friends?
Witness: I did ask him to go with me to the lawyer's office, yes.

I'm fast-forwarding now to the part about my wife and I taking her down to Beaufort, South Carolina, to go house-hunting. We stayed in the General Officer Quarters room of the Temporary Lodging Facility for officers aboard Marine Corps Air Station, Beaufort from Monday, December 26th 2016 till Friday morning, December 30th 2016 when we returned to our home on Camp Lejeune, North Carolina. The ladies slept together in the bedroom with our dog, and I slept on the pull-out couch in the living room. I had passed out on the couch late that evening, while watching TV. My wife's friend decided to draw a penis on my face with mascara.

Defense: Can we agree that that was your idea to do that, that you brought it up?
Witness: I think that I did bring it up, and I think I said – and then his wife dared me. I said, like, "don't dare me," and she dared. Like, we laughed about it.
Defense: Right. Yesterday, you just brought that Colonel Wilson's wife had dared you to do it, but the whole idea was yours to begin with, true?
Witness: You know, I'm not sure if she dared me or I dared her. I know – I don't

really remember who – we were drinking; we were laughing.
Defense: And so the story that you told her was, "This is the kind of stuff we used to do back in school when we get back at somebody. We'd draw a penis and balls on his face," something like that?
Witness: Yeah, if I – sure.
Defense: Does that bring back anything to the question I was asking you earlier about defacing the car with a penis?
Witness: I mean, it sounds exactly like you're – if you're going to tie it all together.

My wife's friend claimed to NCIS that I had raped her repeatedly – three times – on the Wednesday night of our stay in Beaufort, while she was lying in bed with my wife and our dog. This was the exchange between my civilian lawyer and the lady, formerly my wife's friend.

Defense: So those first two nights, the 26th and the 27th of December 2016, do you – on those two nights – have a routine with respect to taking your Tramadol, taking your Lunesta, taking your Release, taking your Diazepam?
Witness: I have a – we all have our routines of what we do, yes, sir.
Defense: So let me fast forward then. On the 28th, you talked to us on direct examination that you took Topamax, that you took Release, that you took Valium – right?
Witness: I mean, I could say – it's fair to say – I mean, I can tell you right now that it's fair to say that I took my medicine.
Defense: Now, did I understand correctly that you talked to your doctor and that your doctor said it was okay that you drink alcohol while you were taking all four of those medications?
Witness: Sure. Yes. He knew.
Defense: Would you agree with me that taking Topamax, Release, Valium, and Lunesta along with alcohol could cause very lucid dreams?

Witness: I would agree with that.
Defense: Could you agree with me that it could cause hallucinations – all four of those with alcohol could cause hallucinations?
Witness: That might be your perception.
Defense: When you go down to the BOQ – Bachelor Officer Quarters – the night of the 26th, the dog slept with you and Susan?
Witness: When they snuck the dog into the BOQ, yes.
Defense: Right. I didn't ask you about sneaking anything I'm sorry.
Witness: I thought you did, sorry.
Defense: I asked you – yeah. If you don't understand the question, you can ask me and I'll break it down for you as much as I can. I apologize. I'm sorry. The dog slept with you and Susan in the bed?
Witness: Yes.
Defense: You described this first incident where you were asleep, laying on your side, and you said that he came in and jumped on top of you?
Witness: Yes.
Defense: The dog was in the bed with you, as well as Susan, correct?
Witness: I don't remember where the dog was, sir.
Defense: You said that Colonel Wilson jumped on you, and you don't know if it was from the side or from the end, but it was, like, a Mack truck?
Witness: Mack truck, yes.
Defense: And could you get the feeling like he was up in the air and then he came down on top of you? Is that the feeling that you had?
Witness: It felt like a Mack truck – tank. He's a big man, sir.
Defense: And I think you told us that it was after a little bit that his wife woke up?
Witness: Yes, sir.

Defense: Now, after he got off the bed and left the room, at that point, you had the ability to leave if you wanted to, true?
Witness: Yes.
Defense: And you made the decision not to?
Witness: I was scared, sir.
Defense: I understand you were scared, but you made the decision not to leave, true?
Witness: True.
Defense: Do you have your cell phone with you?
Witness: Yes.
Defense: Okay. Did you call anybody, text anybody, or let anybody know what was going on?
Witness: No, I did not.
Defense: Did you ever get out of bed?
Witness: No, I did not.
Defense: Was there a bathroom connected to the bedroom?
Witness: Yes, there was.
Defense: Now, certainly, you knew that you could have got out of bed and at least locked the door?
Witness: Yes, I could have.
Defense: But your memory is that you went back to sleep?
Witness: Yes, sir. I went back to sleep.
Defense: And then the exact same thing. I know you were laying in a different position; you described that the exact same thing happens again, the only difference being – is you said that his hand went under your pajamas this time.
Witness: Yes, sir.
Defense: So the same kind of questions: You could have got up and locked the door after he left?
Witness: Yes, sir, I could have.
Defense: And you didn't get out of bed?
Witness: No, sir, I did not.
Defense: And your memory is that you went back to sleep? Yes, sir, I went back to sleep. Now, during these first two instances that

you talked about, did his wife ever get out of the bed?
Witness: Whatever I stated yesterday is what I remember happening.
Defense: I'm asking you today, though: Do you remember Colonel Wilson's wife getting out of bed one time?
Witness: I remember her hitting him. I remember her screaming at him, remember her rubbing my head, sir, and telling me it was going to be okay, sir.
Defense: And, like you said, it happened a third time and you were laying on your side?
Witness: Yes, sir.
Defense: Now, all three of these times, you, kind of, described him jumping on top of you. Is that fair?
Witness: Yes, sir, that is fair. Yes, sir.
Defense: So this third time, you told us yesterday that Colonel Wilson's wife started hitting him with a frying pan – or some kind of a pan?
Witness: No, I did not. No, I did not. Yes, there was. Yes, I could have.
Defense: And during that third meeting on the 20th of January, NCIS started showing you frying pans, didn't they?
Witness: Yes, sir.
Defense: And in that interview with NCIS, as you're talking about the frying pan, you tell them words to the effect of she said – or you say, "I remember her hitting him with something." And that Colonel Wilson's wife told you, "I was hitting him with a frying pan." Is that a memory you have today?
Witness: Yes, sir.
Defense: But you told them, "It feels like a dream." Do you remember that?
Witness: Yes.
Defense: Did that whole night feel like a dream?
Witness: Oh, no.
Defense: Just the frying pan part?
Witness: May I explain?

Defense: I'm just asking about the frying pan part. Is that what you were talking about to NCIS that felt like a dream? I'm just asking a yes or no question, ma'am. Is that what you were talking about when you told NCIS "it felt like a dream"? Well was it the frying pan part?

Witness: That's a confusing question, sir.

Defense: So on the 20th of January 2017, you were talking to NCIS about the frying pan as they were showing you frying pans, right?

Witness: I understand. I'm just saying that that part that you're asking me – that you're saying that I'm saying that the – I mean, no. Then – I mean, that's "no" because it's – because it's crazy that somebody is hitting somebody with a frying pan. It's like a cartoon is what I'm saying and that it sounds like a dream. Because who hits somebody with a frying pan? That's what I meant.

Defense: The agent said, "So it's not a lucid memory?" Do you remember him asking you that right after you started talking about it feeling like a dream? You said, "It's not a lucid memory," and he said, "Thank you. That's perfect." Isn't that what you told him?

Witness: If that's what you have, sir. I would like to explain it, sir.

Defense: I'm just asking if thats what you told him, ma'am.

Witness: If that's what you have, then that's what I said, sir. But I would like to explain it. Yes, sir.

Defense: It then went on to say you, "Do you dreamishly recall?" And you said…

Prosecution: Objection, your Honor!

Judge: Defense counsel? This is all hearsay.

Defense: It's not being offered for the truth of the matter, sir. Sir, it's also testing memory. It's a prior inconsistent statement which she said yesterday as well.

Judge: I'll allow it for that purpose.

Defense: The agent said to you, "You dreamishly recall," and you said, "Right." Do you remember that?
Prosecution: We still object on hearsay, your Honor, assertion.
Judge: The objection is overruled.
Defense: Is that correct? If you can, answer the question please.
Witness: I'm sorry. Could you repeat the question?
Defense: And I would like a chance to explain that.
Judge: Ma'am, if there is any follow-up, the trial counsel can ask the question. So answer defense counsel's question. We understand you may want to amplify that, and you will be given an opportunity.
Witness: Yes, sir.
Defense: Earlier, I was talking to you about Lunesta and any other substances that you took and the alcohol that you consumed. Would you agree with me that maybe all of this is something that you remember dreamishly?
Witness: No.
Defense: When you got up on the morning of the 29th, did you all go eat breakfast together at The Red Rooster in Beaufort?
Witness: I don't believe that's the day that went to breakfast. I'm not sure. I don't think so.
Defense: By the next day then, on the 29th, is that when you and Colonel Wilson's wife went to look at more houses?
Witness: I believe so, sir.
Defense: And was the realtor with you when you looked at more houses or were you just doing drive-bys?
Witness: We met the realtor at one point.
Defense: During that day with Colonel Wilson's wife, you collected – like I said, you look at some houses; you did some shopping; and had something to eat as well?
Witness: I believe so, sir.

Defense: Okay. You and Colonel Wilson's wife slept in the same room that night, on the 29th?
Witness: Yes, sir.
Defense: And got up the next morning, and that's the morning of the 30th, that you've got to come back to Camp Lejeune?
Witness: I believe so, sir.
Defense: Now, at this point, would you agree with me that you are not scared of Colonel Wilson?
Witness: I would not agree.
Defense: Would you agree with me that you wanted to show him a house, and on your way home out of Beaufort to go back to Jacksonville – or Camp Lejeune – you took him past the house that you put an offer on?
Witness: I did take both of them to see the house, yes.
Defense: So if your contract was accepted, he would know right where you lived. Would you agree with that?
Witness: I – that would be correct.
Defense: When you – so – and then let's just talk about at the time that you're starting to leave Beaufort, at that point, you haven't called home to tell your husband what happened?
Witness: No, I did not.
Defense: You haven't called the police in any way?
Witness: No, I did not.
Defense: You didn't go down to get your own room at the BOQ from the desk manager?
Witness: No, I did not.
Defense: When you get back to Camp Lejeune on the 30th, you, on the 30th, don't report any of this to anybody?
Witness: Not right away, sir.
Defense: And you don't disclose it to anyone?
Witness: I may have told a few close people, sir.

Judge: Ma'am, I can't hear your responses. You're going to need to talk up, please.
Witness: Okay. I'm sorry. I'm not sure who I told.
Defense: In between the 30th, that night when you get back to Camp Lejeune – between then and around the 9th, you and Colonel Wilson exchanged hundreds of private messages. Would you agree with that?
Witness: I don't remember, sir.
Defense: And I misspoke, but would you agree with me that from the time you got back on the 30th until around the 4th of January or so that you and Colonel Wilson engaged in a hundred or so private messages back and forth on Facebook?
Witness: [Nonverbal response.]
Defense: I said several hundred, and it's why I'm clarifying, over a hundred, would you agree with that?
Witness: Yes.
Defense: And it was over 700 with Colonel Wilson's wife.
Witness: Yes.
Defense: Now, you told us yesterday that you were familiar with the allegations Colonel Wilson was facing from the summer of 2016?
Witness: Yes.
Defense: So and there had been some discussions about his case with you and Colonel Wilson's wife and you and Colonel Wilson both?
Witness: Yes.
Defense: And you were interested in helping them out with the defense of their case?
Witness: Yes.
Defense: Even after you got back from South Carolina, you still wanted to help them out with the case, true?
Witness: Help Colonel Wilson's wife.
Defense: Sure. Helping Colonel Wilson's wife helped Colonel Wilson – it helps Colonel Wilson; you would agree with that though, right?

Witness: I think that's kind of confusing, sir.
Defense: If you help Colonel Wilson's wife help Colonel Wilson, that, in fact, helps Colonel Wilson, correct?
Witness: I guess, yes.
Defense: You were giving them strategies?
Witness: I guess, yes. I guess.
Defense: So, "I guess, yes," is a little confusing to me. Would you agree that you were giving them strategies to help defend against his original accuser's allegations?
Witness: Yes.
Defense: And this was after you got back from South Carolina?
Witness: Right.
Defense: In that timeframe, you found out that the contract was rejected on the house – true? Witness: Yes.
Defense: And you were continuing to try to find some place that you could live that you could afford to?
Witness: Yeah.
Defense: And there were things like a condo on the water that required a substantial down payment that was above what you would be able to do, fair?
Witness: Yes.
Defense: You would agree with me that there was also banter going back and forth between you and Colonel Wilson as well, wouldn't you?
Witness: Okay.
Defense: Would you agree with that?
Witness: I don't remember, but okay.
Defense: So here's my question Okay. And I'll try to be more clear. Okay. You made this allegation that Colonel Wilson sexually assaulted you on the 28th of December. And at the end December, the 30th into the 4th and 5th of January, you are engaging in sexual banter with him. Would you agree with that?
Witness: I am trying to act – I'm trying to be like I had always been. I was very fearful of Colonel Wilson, sir.

Defense: So you've had an opportunity to review your text messages?
Witness: Yes.
Defense: You're engaging in sexual banter with him about meeting a doctor down in Wilmington and having sex with him?
Witness: Yes.
Defense: And that you were trying to get with him for the amount of money that he makes?
Witness: Yes.
Defense: You're going – you're talking to Colonel Wilson about going down and seeing a doctor for a lunch date, right?
Witness: Yes.
Defense: And your daughter is sick at the time?
Witness: Sure.
Defense: And I'm sure it's, sort of – you use a term in there called "cock blocker." Do you remember that?
Witness: [Nonverbal response.]
Defense: And that's because she is getting in the way of you going down to engage in sex with that doctor, true?
Prosecution: Relevance, your Honor. That's misstatement of the evidence.
Judge: The objection is sustained.
Defense: Would you agree with me that there was a sexual connotation to the word "cock blocker"?
Witness: I would agree. It's a joke.
Defense: Sure. I agree that it's a joke. But you would agree with it, then, that there's a sexual connotation to it?
Witness: Yes.
Defense: Okay. And these are the conversations that you're having with Colonel Wilson after you say that he sexually assaulted you – because you were scared?
Witness: Yes.
Defense: And while you say you were afraid, weren't you in communication on around the 30th of December – I mean, just right when

you got back – with the Wilson's about taking another trip down to Beaufort – in fact, to Parris Island – with Colonel Wilson and his wife?
Witness: Yes.
Defense: And you were talking about the Colonel getting VIP tickets so that you guys could go to a boot camp graduation, right?
Witness: Yes.
Defense: And you were talking about how you would get rooms – that you would get two rooms? And that those would be adjoining rooms?
Witness: Yes.
Defense: And you were, you know, talking to Colonel Wilson's wife about, you know, how many that you wanted and that you wanted six seats because you were having some other people come as well, right?
Witness: Yes.
Defense: You, in the past, while sending Facebook messages back and forth with Colonel Wilson, have sent him, probably, a dozen different listings of houses that you have looked at?
Witness: Yes.
Defense: Okay. And you could have sent him a picture of the house that way instead of showing him exactly where you were potentially going to be living, true?
Witness: True.
Defense: That's all of the questions I have, sir.

The prosecution brought in a Marine who had stopped by for a visit on our last evening in Beaufort with my second accuser, Thursday, December 29th 2016. A few years earlier, he and I had served together at Parris Island. He had since left the Marines and was in nursing school. I can't imagine why the prosecution decided to bring him in, other than to demonstrate their utter incompetence. My Marine's testimony only confirmed from another person that my wife's friend in no way appeared like she had recently been violently, and repeatedly raped, by a "Mack truck," or "tank."

Defense: Good afternoon, Sir. I just have a couple of questions for you and we'll get you out of here. When you went into Colonel Wilson's BOQ room on the 29th, you said nothing was out of the ordinary, correct?
Witness: Yes.
Defense: Everybody seemed in a good mood, correct?
Witness: Yes.
Defense: And as to their guest specifically: Did anything about your conversation with her stick out, specifically, in your mind or in your memory? Did she appear happy about something in particular to your knowledge or to your memory?
Witness: Yes. She had just put an offer down on a house down in Beaufort.
Defense: And she was talking about that offer?
Witness: Yes.
Defense: And she was excited about that?
Witness: Yes.
Defense: And you – so you said you spoke to her and Colonel Wilson's wife about nursing programs over Facebook in the past? Or in some messenger?
Witness: It was a cell phone conversation.
Defense: Okay. But you also talked to her in person about nursing programs on the 29th of December?
Witness: We – that is very – it's highly likely that we had approached that subject. I don't – I would see it be natural that we would talk about the nursing program. But, again, that specifically, I don't remember.
Defense: She didn't appear fearful to you?
Witness: Absolutely not.
Defense: Distressed about anything?
Witness: [Nonverbal response.]
Defense: Colonel Wilson's wife didn't appear distressed about anything?
Witness: [Nonverbal response.]
Defense: Colonel Wilson didn't appear distressed about anything?

Witness: No.
Defense: Did you see any visible signs of, you know, blunt-force trauma or bruises on Colonel Wilson?
Witness: No.
Defense: No scratches or any – any sign of violence whatsoever on Colonel Wilson?
Witness: No, sir.
Defense: No further questions, sir.

The prosecution brought in the manager of the place we stayed at on base in Beaufort, and I was pleased they did so, as I was listening to his interaction with my lawyer:

Defense: Pertaining to Colonel Wilson specifically, nothing out of the ordinary stood out to you with regard to his stay, correct?
Witness: No, sir.
Defense: No noise complaints?
Witness: No, sir.
Defense: And I believe you testified on direct, Colonel Wilson did not reserve the DV suite, correct?
Witness: He did not.
Defense: He reserved two rooms?
Witness: Yes, he did.
Defense: And when he arrived by himself to check-in, he requested – he was requesting two rooms?
Witness: Yes.
Defense: And, per your policy, you saw that he was an 0-6, so you said, "You actually rate the DV suite, and you can save some money. It's got a pullout couch."
Witness: Yes, sir.
Defense: Right. So had, you know, you just not realized he was an 0-6 or you just not advised him that he rated the DV suite, he would have gotten two rooms?
Witness: Yes, sir.
Defense: And two key cards for each room?
Witness: That is correct, sir.

Speaking of Beaufort, the prosecution brought in the Executive Officer of the Headquarters Battalion that I was officially assigned to, regarding the government's charge of unauthorized absence. It came up after my wife's former friend had reported our trip to NCIS, and said that is where I had raped her. The prosecution, tipped off by NCIS, filed a charge of unauthorized absence even though I had no reporting instructions…could come and go as I pleased, and it was in between Christmas and New Year's when most of the Marines on base are on leave, or on basket leave – gratuitous time off. On the witness stand the Executive Officer confirmed that he was unaware of any special reporting instructions regarding me, or that I was required to check in daily with either him or his boss, the Commanding Officer. They had never even discussed my accountability procedures. Here is what his Boss subsequently testified to, the Commanding Officer of Headquarters Battalion about my unique situation:

> **Defense**: Did you ever run Colonel Wilson UA (Unauthorized Absence) or not present on the morning report?
> **Witness**: No.
> **Defense**: Who was in charge of him?
> **Witness**: At the time, he was working for my headquarters.
> **Defense**: Did you ever see him run UA on a morning report, not accounted for?
> **Witness**: Not to my recollection, no.
> **Defense**: And his duties were to work on his defense?
> **Witness**: Yes.
> **Defense**: And did anybody ever give you any feedback that they had trouble getting ahold of him – phone calls, emails, text messages, anything at all?
> **Witness**: No, no. I personally, when I needed to contact Colonel Wilson, never had any trouble reaching him via text messages, cell phone, or anything like that.

The Judge on his own – *sua sponte* - brought up that the UA charge was so weak that it should be scrubbed from consideration, but in the end acceded to the prosecution's plea to keep it in the mix. The consensus in our conference room was that the jury would find me innocent of all the rape charges by the woman who had befriended my wife during the investigation, but then had become resentful toward my wife, after my wife had ended their friendship, shortly after returning from our Beaufort trip. She knew she could exact revenge by making a false claim of rape against her friend's husband – me. She was right. My Boss, upon being briefed by the NCIS agents, had immediately ordered my pre-trial confinement.

CHAPTER 10
LAND DOWN UNDER

For the final tranche of charges by the prosecution, which predated all the above charges from my two accusers, I must back up a bit and take you to the "Land Down Under" of Australia in February of 2016 to describe what I did to get myself recalled, and that resulted in multiple charges for "Conduct Unbecoming an Officer" at my court martial in September 2017.

I had planned to retire from the Marine Corps at the end of my tour on Okinawa, as the Chief-of-Staff of 3rd Marine Division. In January 2015 my retirement papers had been submitted and approved by Headquarters, Marine Corps. I was to finish up my duties in August and commence terminal leave in September of 2015 with 1 January 2016 to be my actual retirement date.

The second Friday afternoon of 2015 (9 January), I was enjoying the camaraderie of fellow warriors at Traditions Officers' Club on Camp Courtney, Okinawa. I lived just above the club in a cottage for the past year and a half, as a geographical bachelor. I went down to the club almost every Friday afternoon, because I could make a dinner out of the finger foods, while socializing with fellow officers. On that particular afternoon, we were still celebrating the dawn of a new year, which for me meant retirement, after 34 years of active-duty service. I distinctly recall being approached by my counterpart at III MEF. A fellow Colonel, he was the MEF Chief-of-Staff, and I had known him for decades. He had been my assignments monitor on two occasions and was a fellow infantry officer. I considered him a good friend. Years earlier, when I had been selected to attend "top-level school," he had ensured that I was vectored to the most prestigious war college of them all, The National War College at Fort McNair, Washington, DC.

He took me aside, and acknowledged my desire to retire, but had a proposal for me. He wanted me to consider pulling my retirement papers and taking over as the Officer-in-Charge of III MEF's Special Operations and Training Group (SOTG), headquartered just up the road at Camp Hansen, Okinawa. He believed that as an infantry officer, I would be the best choice to lead that special team of warriors. In less than a split-second, I spat out "yes, I accept!" Within the split-second, I had had two quick visions. The first scene was me sitting on my back porch as a retiree, smoking a cigar, and forever wondering what it would have been like to lead the warriors of SOTG. The second scene was of me helo-rappelling, fast-roping, firing cool weapons, all side-by-side with students going through SOTG's various courses. Obviously, the second scene was more compelling, and I instantly agreed to accept the assignment.

I took over on June 4th, 2015, as the Officer-In-Charge of III MEF's SOTG. I really was sad about leaving 3rd Marine Division, my beloved Team CALTRAP, but very excited at seizing this new opportunity to lead "special" warriors. What self-respecting infantry officer would not want to lead a team with the nickname of "The Society of Tough Guys"? Well, I did, and I have to tell you that it was the "funnest" 8 months of my career. I fired sniper rifles with the sniper course students, to include at targets from a moving helicopter. I fired various weapons on ranges with students going through our special weapons and tactics course. I jumped out of a helicopter into the Pacific Ocean off White Beach, swam to a rubber boat with other students, conducting a mock amphibious attack on a small island. I fast-roped from The Osprey, tilt-rotor aircraft, with other students in our Helicopter, Rope, Suspension Training Course, and conducted SPIE (Special Insertion & Extraction) operations with them, dangling from a rope beneath a Super-Stallion, CH-53 helicopter, 1,000 feet above the lush, verdant jungles of Okinawa. I travelled several times to the islands of Guam and Palau to facilitate operations we wanted to conduct there to evaluate the skills of our students.

Just when you think things are too good to be true, they are. Apparently, I had done such a great job of leading SOTG, that before a year was up, the MEF Chief-of-Staff now believed I could turn over leadership to my Executive Officer and go off to Australia to lead another important mission.

He wanted me to be the new Officer-In-Charge of MarForPac's Forward Coordination Element in Darwin, Australia. My mission was to support the Marines scheduled to deploy there in April through October of 2016, during Darwin's "dry season." I was to lead a team of 30 Marines, flown in from MarForPac. We would arrange for all the logistical and training support required by the inbound Marines of Marine Rotational Force, Darwin (MRF-D), expected to be about 1,200 Marines. My team would be co-located with a team of our Australian counterparts at Darwin's Larrakeya Naval Base. The rotational force Marines would be housed at Robertson's Barracks, a few miles east of Darwin. From there, MRF-D Marines would be training at several sites in Australia with Australian Army soldiers.

Before going to Australia, I was asked to travel to Hawaii to meet the staff who would be supporting me and get guidance from my new General. I spent a week there and met the Colonel I would be replacing and stayed at the home of my old Sergeant Major friend from 3rd Marine Division. It was a fun and productive visit, and I departed on Saturday for Australia. I arrived in Darwin Sunday evening, February 14th 2016. Two Marines I knew were planning to meet me at the airport, and take me to my new quarters, aboard Larrakeyah Naval Base. I had served with them at Parris Island. They both informed me via Blackberry messages that I received during a layover that they would not be at the airport in Darwin to meet me. Turns out that my soon-to-be counterpart had contacted each of them and ordered them not to go to the airport. Instead, he would meet me and take me to the base. I thought that was really odd, but instead of sending up a huge red flag about his behavior, I didn't think twice about it. You sometimes encounter foreign officers who have strange mannerisms, and that's what I chalked it up to.

The next morning, he showed me around the base, and we ended up at his office spaces, which were in a large section of a very secure building. The Marine Colonel I was replacing in the billet was at the office, and the three of us sat down for a chat. The Marine's turnover with me consisted of just letting me know to go to my counterpart for anything and everything. He quickly took off, so as not to be late for a Crocodile tour with his wife who had flown in with him from Hawaii thanks to the fat per diem check he had been receiving while on temporary duty to Australia.

My Australian counterpart began to regale me as to what an important person he was. He had been called out of retirement by none other than the Australian Army's Chief of Staff, and he was their senior guy to coordinate training and logistics for the Marines arriving every year in the dry season to train with the Australian Armed Forces. He assured me that he would handle all the contracting, and that all I had to do was sign on the dotted line, as the senior American military representative. I started to get the feeling that he was running a rigged system. He was bragging about owning five companies, and worth millions of dollars. He mentioned how he was going to "hook up" the Marine Colonel that I was replacing with a plum retirement job in Australia. He gave me an example of how much wasta he carried with the Army's Chief of Staff, when he told me about being the guy responsible for my friend, an Australian General, getting firing from his post in Darwin. The Australian General and I had served together in the Pentagon, and he had been the Commanding General of the Australian Army Brigade at Robertson Barracks, when I had visited previously in November 2014. The General had angered my counterpart, according to my counterpart, by not giving him the building he'd wanted for an armory. My counterpart had presented the matter to the Chief, as if the General was trying to sabotage the relationship with the American Marines. Nothing could have been further from the truth, but my counterpart prevailed, and the General was transferred out of Darwin to Army headquarters in Canberra, where he was given a second star and made the General in charge of Army training. My counterpart relished in the telling of this story, because he wanted me to appreciate how influential he was. He went on to tell me that he had the "goods' on another American Marine Colonel, who was the senior liaison officer with the Australian military, stationed in Canberra. This Colonel was an aviator and was a geographical bachelor. My counterpart claimed that he had proof that said Marine Colonel was having adulterous affairs with Australian ladies. I took everything in my counterpart said without much thought, when it should have been activating alarm bells in my head.

The next day, my counterpart informed me that I would be expected to participate in a ceremony to commemorate the sinking of the USS Pearcy in World War II. It occurred shortly after the Japanese attack on Pearl Harbor, and the Australians considered it as their "Pearl Harbor." The American Ambassador was flying in for the ceremony, and her and I would be laying wreaths to commemorate the Americans and Australians killed in the attack. Immediately following the wreath-laying ceremony, a local TV reporter asked if I would talk to her on camera. When I returned from the ceremony, my counterpart had already viewed the clip on local TV, and seemed to be green with envy at the media attention I had received. "You've gotten more media attention in less than a week, than I've gotten in the two years I've done this job." He was genuinely jealous of me, even though he had been the one to thrust me into the ceremony. I think that was the turning point in his mind when he realized that he had to get rid of me. I was drawing more public attention than he was, and more importantly, he sensed that I was not going to be the "patsy" that my predecessor was, and just sign my name to every logistic contract he put in front of me. I was already beginning to suspect that many of the contracts were in some way going to line his own pockets, or the pockets of his business partners.

Toward the end of my first week, my counterpart hosted a farewell dinner for my predecessor and his wife. It was a nice restaurant, and we were all enjoying ourselves. After the dinner, we were walking to the parking lot, when the wife of the Marine Colonel I was replacing remarked that her thighs were sore from walking all around Darwin that afternoon, during their site-seeing. I remarked under my breath that maybe her thighs were sore from having too much sex in their hotel room. I immediately followed it up with, "just kidding." Her and my counterpart were the only two who heard my crude remark. She laughed and awkwardly slapped my shoulder, and said, "stop."

I was the only member of my Marine team on deck, as the rest weren't flying in for several more days. I was thoroughly enjoying myself on base, getting to know many awesome members of the Australian military and interacting with them, while enjoying meals at their dining facility for officers. I became fast friends with the head Chef, Anthony, who would literally call me before meals to ask what I wanted to eat from their menu and how I would like it cooked. He then had it waiting for me when I walked in the dining facility. Anthony spoiled me like I was one of his own Australian military guys and had even invited me out to his home to sample the dozens of varieties of whiskeys that he had collected through the years.

I took to getting out of my corner office, and roaming around the larger office, interacting with the Australian military and civilian members of my counterpart's team. I quickly sensed that there was a stifling atmosphere in the office, and I was determined to change that. My counterpart had zero sense of humor and was an annoying micro-manager. He reminded me of the prototypical old British gentry; stiff upper lip, aristocratic, and always exuding an attitude of belonging to a higher class and being more intelligent than everyone else. The kind look down on everyone over their glasses. I spent hours chatting with a female Australian Major and a female civilian office worker. I was going to be interacting with them for many months, so I wanted to establish great relationships with everyone from the get-go. They were both sociable and seemed to like talking with me, asking me all kinds of questions about my personal and professional life.

My third or fourth day there, I was in the main office area, kicking back, and chatting with the civilian secretary, when she excused herself to go to the bathroom. I had a mischievous thought and rolled up to her computer. I would "prank" my counterpart to evaluate what kind of a sense of humor he actually had. In the Pentagon, I had "pranked" several of my co-workers, when they had left their computers unattended, and it had provided me, and others, with hilarious belly-laughs. I sent off an email to my counterpart from the civilian secretary's computer that said, "We should go out for dinner some time." An hour later, my counterpart called her to his office and read her the riot act. He must have put two and two together, because shortly thereafter he asked me if I would mind stepping into his office, and made a big show of closing the door, and sitting down with a solemn look on his face. He didn't think my prank email was funny at all and told me that my American humor was not appreciated. I essentially told the junior officer that he needed to pull the stick out of his ass and get a sense of humor. The next week he reported the prank email to his higher headquarters, as being on the level of having hacked into the heart of the Australian's National Security Agency.

I stayed late in the office that evening, and after I realized that everyone had left, I texted the Australian Major, asking her why everyone had taken off so early. I then sent her a silly text that there was a body in the "boot" of my car, and did she know anything about that? She didn't respond at all, but the next day she reported my text to my counterpart, since he had by then instructed all of his subordinates to inform him of any interaction with with the American Colonel.

My counterpart invited me to his apartment in Darwin for dinner my first weekend in Australia. He picked me up at the Naval base around 1800 and drove us to his complex. He has a family but was living as a geographical bachelor for the duration of his temporary gig in Darwin. At this point, I had no clue as to his Machiavellian plan to get rid of me. He genuinely seemed like he was wanting to bond with me. He was showing me pictures of his family on his iPhone, and I was showing him pictures of mine. He swiped the wrong way on my iPhone and up popped a picture of a friend's wife. My Marine friend and I had been swapping pictures on Facebook Messenger, and I had asked him for a picture of his wife. I had returned the favor by sending him a sexy picture of my wife. He had sent me a picture of his wife posing in lingerie. What Marine's call a "deployment picture," intended to show off to your closest buddies, so they know that you have a hot wife, and for you to constantly remind yourself what awaits you back in the land of milk and honey. My Marine friend had also sent me several nude pictures of other women whom he bragged about having extra-marital affairs with. I had then asked him – in jest – if he could send me a pair of his wife's panties to which he replied "LOL," and that was the end of our private conversation on Messenger regarding panties. My counterpart inadvertently saw the picture of my friend's wife and exclaimed, "Wow, she's hot. Can you please send this picture to me, Colonel?" A combination of trying to bond with my counterpart, and the whiskey I'd consumed, led me to forward him the picture without giving it any thought.

My counterpart demonstrated his contempt for a senior foreign officer at the end of my evening at his apartment, by asking me if I would mind finding my own way home. He claimed that he had consumed too much whiskey and wasn't able to drive me. Had our roles been reversed, I would have at least called a cab for a foreign officer, new to the city of Darwin. Instead, I walked back, spoke briefly with the Australian gate guard, and made my own way to my quarters. Imagine my shock and disdain for my counterpart then, when a few days later, he was accusing me to his superiors of excessive consumption of alcohol. The very guy who couldn't give me a ride home, because of his excessive consumption of alcohol.

Thursday morning of my second, and final, week, I took a frantic call from the Marine Colonel, down at the Australian Armed Forces Headquarters in Canberra, Australia. His call was my first indication that my counterpart was making a serious bid to get me fired. He breathlessly related a few of the allegations that my counterpart had made to his superiors. My counterpart had told them that I had been drinking excessively, to include the night he had me over for dinner. He also told his superiors that I had sent him a naked picture of a subordinate's wife. He went on to allege that I had sent text messages to the Australian female Major, trying to lure her into a sexual relationship, and that I had perpetrated a huge breech of Australia's national security with my prank email. The Marine Colonel told me that I needed to check myself. I told him that he needed to watch himself, because my counterpart had bragged to me about having significant dirt on him. The kind of dirt that could easily be used to blackmail someone in most any foreign country. He seemed taken aback by that news, and our conversation ended, soon thereafter. Thursday afternoon, I got the call from III MEF's Chief of Staff, my friend, asking me to return to Okinawa immediately. Two three-star Marine Generals had discussed the matter, after being contacted by a senior Australian General, and had decided that it was best to recall me in the interests of maintaining a good military partnership with the Australian Armed Forces.

I emailed the III MEF Chief-of-Staff and my assignments monitor at Quantico that night, expressing my anger at being relieved without an investigation, and asking that they both expedite my retirement from the Marine Corps. Later that Friday afternoon, my neighbor on base, an Australian Navy Lieutenant Commander, invited me over to his place for cigars and whiskey. He was dumbfounded when I told him that I was being recalled and leaving in the morning. My neighbor was so incensed by how my counterpart had stabbed me in the back that he got on the phone, and chewed my counterpart's ass, while I was sitting there listening. My counterpart at that point had flown the coup, two thousand miles to the south, to meet with his superiors in Canberra, and also to avoid me. My neighbor shouted at him on the phone that doing what he did to me was disgraceful, and no way to treat a visiting foreign officer. Shortly after the scathing phone call, I got a message from my counterpart on Facebook Messenger. He said that he hoped I would give him a chance some day to explain himself. I wrote back, telling him to never contact me again, and that if I ever saw him again in life, it would be too soon.

On my 13th day in Australia, I flew back to Okinawa, where I met with my Boss, the three-star General the next week. I was angry about being recalled and asked him to have me investigated in order to clear my name. He assured me that he had only recalled me to me protect me and to preserve the Marine Corps' relationship with the Australian military. He was not going to have me investigated, because no official complaint had been filed against me, and the level of the allegations didn't rise to the level of "officer misconduct." He believed that all the allegations mentioned to him by the Australian General were nothing more than "guy talk," or at worst, boorish behavior. I asked him to expedite my retirement, and he asked me to take one more tour for the team. That the Marine Corps could still use a senior Marine Infantry Colonel with my experience. I told him I would do just that and my monitor arranged for me to go to II MEF, based at Camp Lejeune, North Carolina.

Nineteen months later, and we are in the final few days of my general court martial. Of course, the prosecution had posed questions to the Australians in such a way as to make me look like the proverbial "Ugly American." This is how the cross-examination went down with the prosecution's witnesses – all flown in from Australia on our taxpayers' dime. Starting with my counterpart:

> **Defense**: Well, I'm just referring to in general at the office. There was an avenue for service members or civilian workers to make formal complaints.
> **Witness**: Oh, absolutely. There is a complaint process.
> **Defense**: Okay. And you didn't make a complaint about Colonel Wilson about his behavior, correct? You didn't utilize that form?
> **Witness**: No.
> **Defense**: And your Major and Secretary did not make formal complaints against Colonel Wilson, correct?
> **Witness**: Not to my knowledge.
> **Defense**: And being the supervisor, you would've had knowledge of that?
> **Witness**: Correct.
> **Defense**: Okay. And the email incident with your Secretary, I think you agree with me that that, at the end of the day, what was, in fact, a prank – or you took it as a prank?
> **Witness**: Yes, absolutely.

Defense: The prosecutor showed you this document, sir. This is the record of the SMS, I believe you called it –
Witness: Yes.
Defense: The messages to your Major. I'm just wondering about the third message from the colonel. "You pinched all my cash and left a dead body in the boot of my renty."
Witness: Yeah. That doesn't look – I'm not certain I've seen that before.
Defense: Sir, may I approach?
Judge: You may.
Witness: You know, I can't remember. It's written in a report, which I specifically provided. And it's –
Defense: I'm talking about this message here.
Witness: Yeah.
Defense: The third message from Colonel Wilson.
Witness: I honestly can't remember seeing that before.
Defense: Okay. I'm not trying to attack foundation or anything like that.
Witness: That particular message, I don't recall. I mean, the messages that I transcribed from her phone, I don't recall that one being there.
Defense: Okay. Sir, I'm going to remove the – or retrieve the evidence. Thank you, sir. I was just wondering if you know what that means. Does that have any context to you.
Witness: Sorry. Can I just have a look?
Defense: Sir, I'll return it again.
Witness: Do you want me to interpret it then?
Defense: I don't know if interpret is the right word. I want to know what it is or if you know. If you don't know, that's – is that like a movie quote or a TV quote? Is that a running joke that you all had in the office?
Witness: It's gibberish to me.

Defense: Okay. So to your knowledge, that's not like somebody had made a joke earlier in the day or anything like that?
Witness: Nope.
Defense: Isn't it fair to say that Colonel Wilson had to walk home because you were unable to drive him home?
Witness: No.
Defense: Is that what happened? Did he walk home?
Witness: Yes.
Defense: And you got a text before that message that – before the picture arrived in your – I'm going to call it an inbox. I don't know if that's what you –
Witness: My iPad messenger? Correct.
Defense: And wasn't there a text that came ahead of it with language in the text that said, "Here you go, my friend"?
Witness: I don't recall that.
Defense: Might you not recall that because of the wine that you had?
Prosecution: Your Honor, counsel's testifying on facts not in evidence.
Judge: Is there an objection?
Defense: I'm trying to put them in evidence, sir.
Judge: Is there an objection?
Prosecution: Yes, sir. Counsel's testifying. It's a leading question.
Judge: The objection – it's been asked and answered. Okay. So the objection's sustained. I'm going to sustain it for a different reason.
Defense: That's all I have.

Next into the courtroom was the Marine Colonel's wife – the wife of the guy I was replacing in Australia, back in February of 2016. The lady I had made a crude comment to, as we were walking to the parking area following our dinner.

Prosecution: And when you left the restaurant to go out to the car did anything happen?
Witness: Yes. As we were walking to the car, I had worn high-heel sandals and I made the

comment, "I picked the wrong shoes to wear. My thighs are very sore from doing this workout in Darwin." And when I made that comment, Colonel Wilson made a comment – I don't remember the exact words but alluding to – that my thighs were sore from having sex with my husband.
Prosecution: What was your reaction to that?
Witness: I, kind of, like swatted him on the shoulder.
Prosecution: How well did you know Colonel Wilson at that time?
Witness: I had met him about a week before that on Super Bowl Sunday in Hawaii before we went to Australia. I had about a ten-minute conversation with him about Australia and how much I enjoyed the opportunity to travel to Australia and kind of telling him the things that he should try and get to see while he was there. And I did not see or talk to him again until dinner that night.
Prosecution: Did you see your husband react to what Colonel Wilson said?
Witness: I don't believe my husband heard him.
Prosecution: Why do you say that ma'am?
Witness: Because he didn't respond or say anything.
Prosecution: That's all the questions I have, ma'am. That's all the questions I have, sir.
Judge: Defense Counsel, any cross-examination?
Defense: Yes, sir. The comment that was made to you, you didn't find that it threatening at all did you?
Witness: Not threatening, no.
Defense: You didn't think that he was hitting in any way?
Witness: No.
Defense: Okay. And you didn't tell your husband about this or you all didn't talk about it until you all got back to Hawaii?

Witness: Yes.
Defense: That's all I got, sir.

    The prosecution then brought in my former Marine friend to talk about the picture he had sent me of his wife. He thought that when he had deleted our conversations on Messenger that no one would be able to ever see what we had actually said. It came as a shock and surprise to him that my lawyer had the entire text of what had transpired in our Messenger conversation. I had not deleted it, and one of my daughters was in administrative control of my Facebook account, after I was sent into pretrial confinement. She had provided the Messenger conversation to my defense team, per my authorization. I wish my former friend's facial expressions could have been captured when it dawned on him that he couldn't BS my lawyer about our conversation on Messenger, because my guys had the actual transcript. This is how the cross-examination went:

> **Defense**: And is it fair to say that you guys would communicate a lot on private messenger?
> **Witness**: Yes, sir.
> **Defense**: And do you – when the investigation started into these allegations pertaining to you, did you turn over all of your Facebook messenger account information pertaining to you and Colonel Wilson to the investigator?
> **Witness**: I offered it to the prosecution and then nothing materialized.
> **Defense**: Okay. So just so I'm tracking – I just want to make sure I got this right. You had the entire string of messages?
> **Witness**: Oh, no. They wanted to search my phone and hook it up to some high-speed computer thing to see if it could extract that information, but that never happened.
> **Defense**: They never hooked it up to a phone – excuse me. They never hooked it up to the machine to extract the information from your phone?
> **Witness**: Correct, sir. It never happened.
> **Defense**: The first time you said you gave a picture to Colonel Wilson, can we agree that it was through Facebook Messenger?

Witness: Yes, sir.

Defense: Do you remember what the conversation was leading up to you providing that picture? Because it sounds like you're almost under duress. Do you remember how the conversation went between you and the Colonel?

Witness: I do not remember exactly. I – word for word what was stated?

Defense: I felt like you were intimating that he was pressuring you into sending the picture? Did you feel like you were being pressured?

Witness: In part, yes.

Defense: So if I showed you a copy of that exchange. Do you think that that would refresh your recollection as to the content of the messages? Does that help refresh your recollection?

Witness: Yes, it does.

Defense: So the conversation that you were having with Colonel Wilson when you sent the picture to him was – it really just started the day before you had text messaged about going for a run together, right?

Witness: Can you say that again?

Defense: So the 19th – February 19, you guys had chatted back and forth about going for run, correct?

Witness: Yes.

Defense: So then the next day you sent him a message and said: Did you just get an iMessage from me?

Witness: Well, I wanted to see if he had wifi.

Defense: And he responded back to you, "No. Did you send a dirty picture? Awesome!" Isn't that what he responded to your question?

Witness: That's what he responded in text, yes.

Defense: And then you said, "What's your number. I might have some." Isn't that what you said?

Witness: I would have to look at that again.

Defense: So would you agree with me that your next message was, "What's your number?" And then followed by, "Yes. I might have some"?
Witness: Yes. "I might have some." But that doesn't mean that I was going to give it to him.
Defense: And then he came back with, "Send pic, bro," right? You can look at it if that'll help refresh your recollection.
Witness: Yes.
Defense: Sound right. Does that sound right?
Witness: Again, yes.
Defense: And then that prosecutor showed you that picture of your wife. Is that your wife?
Witness: Yes.
Defense: And then you asked Colonel Wilson if that was good enough?
Witness: Yes, I did.
Defense: So after you sent what you said that he wanted you to send, you asked if that was good enough for him; is that fair?
Witness: Yes.
Defense: Can we agree that that conversation that I just went over with you, he wasn't ordering you to do anything?
Witness: I never stated he ordered me.
Defense: And up at that point, your relationship has been very friendly with him?
Witness: To a certain extent, yes.
Defense: And it continues to be a very friendly relationship. You'll agree with that, right?
Witness: Yes.
Defense: On that same day, you guys continued talking about sending pictures, and you say to him in that same line of conversations: "You haven't shared anything." Didn't you say that to him?
Witness: I didn't – I do remember that.

Defense: If I show you a continuation of that conversation, would that help refresh your recollection?
Witness: Yes, sir, it would.
Defense: Does that refresh your memory, sort of, what the continuation of the conversation was?
Witness: Yes.
Defense: And reviewing your conversation, what you remember now, he's asking for more pictures; you're, kind of, pushing him off. And then you tell him he hasn't shared anything yet, true?
Witness: Yes, sir.
Defense: And then he sends you a picture of his wife that's maybe not a boudoir shot, sort of a glamour shot, but a little risqué. Would you agree?
Witness: Yes, sir.
Defense: And you remember what that picture is, right?
Witness: Yes, sir.
Defense: She's wearing, like, a white blouse, fair?
Witness: Yes, sir.
Defense: From this point forward, your relationship is full of banter back and forth about women, true?
Witness: At times, yes, sir.
Defense: You're sending him pictures of women not your wife, correct?
Witness: Correct, sir.
Defense: And you are talking to him about the relationships you have with these women that you're sending him pictures of, true?
Witness: I haven't had relationship with any other women.
Defense: Do you believe that your messages back and forth with him signify that you're having relationships with the women that you're sending him pictures of?
Witness: I made those statements, but they were false though.

Defense: My question to you was: In the conversation that you're having back and forth over the next couple of weeks with Colonel Wilson – and I get that it may be an overly familiar relationship – both of you were sending pictures back and forth of woman that are either scantily clad or some of them are naked, true?
Witness: Yes, sir.
Defense: And is it also fair to say that in your relationship with him, that after you sent this one picture of your wife to him on February the 20th, and you and he started sending pictures back and forth of other women, he doesn't ask you for any more pictures of your wife. Isn't that true?
Witness: Yes, sir.
Defense: From there forward, you continued to engage with him in, we can call it "locker room talk" or back and forth. Is that fair?
Witness: Yes, sir.
Defense: And you would send him messages with scantily clad or unclothed woman and he would send you some pictures back and forth?
Witness: Yes, sir.

    The other charge involving this former Marine friend was that I had asked him in jest to send me a pair of his wife's panties on Facebook Messenger, while I was in Australia, and he was back on Okinawa. When the prosecution had him, they had presented it that I had asked him for his wife's panties, after I had returned to Okinawa and was at his apartment for breakfast. Again, prior to coming into the courtroom, he thought that no record existed of our conversation on Facebook Messenger, but it did. I had, jokingly, made the request, then said "Share more you selfish bastard." He came back with LOL, and that was the end of it. Merely "guy talk" in a private conversation.

Defense: Okay. So I feel like we're struggling in communicating. After he says, "Share more you selfish bastard." It say's "LOL," doesn't it?
Witness: Oh, I'm sorry.
Defense: Isn't that what it say?

Witness: Yes.
Defense: Laugh out loud, right?
Witness: Yes. I'm sorry.
Defense: So it's not like this is — it's not like he is yelling at you and really being condescending. This is like: Share some more, you selfish bastard, ha, ha, ha. Isn't that what he's doing?
Witness: I wasn't trying to not say what was written on the text.
Defense: But you did though, right?
Witness: It was a mistake.
Defense: That's all the questions I have, sir.

The prosecution had the female Australian Army Major on the stand to talk about the innocuous three text messages that I had sent her one evening, after everyone had departed the shared offices we occupied at Larrakeyah Naval Base:

Defense: The first time you had gone to the Commander to complain about Colonel Wilson distracting the computer workspace, as far as Colonel Wilson being in the computer workspace, what he talking about, it wasn't demeaning in any way?
Witness: Demeaning to me personally? No. I don't believe I was mentioned in his discussions and the like, and I don't believe he was being demeaning to me.
Defense: He wasn't talking about work and it was distracting you from work?
Witness: Yeah.
Defense: Now, with the Facebook message that Colonel Wilson sent you, you saw the first message that he sent, correct?
Witness: Yes.
Defense: And you briefly responded to that message?
Witness: Yes.
Defense: And based off your experience with Colonel Wilson in the past, you were concerned for his health and well-being?
Witness: Yes.
Defense: And that's why you told your Commander about the facebook

conversation – because of your concern for Colonel Wilson, primarily?
Witness: Well, that was one of a couple of reasons. His health and well-being, yes.
Defense: Ma'am, my question was – and I was just mirroring what you said on direct examination and what you testified in direct examination – the reason you talked to your supervisor is because of your concern for Colonel Wilson's health and well-being. That's what you said?
Witness: That right. I did say that.

And the final witness from our shared office in Australia was the civilian secretary from whom's computer I had sent the prank email. Flown in by the prosecution all the way from Australia to attest to my prank email:

Defense: So when you sat down at your computer and you saw this email, what did you do?
Witness: I got straight up and went straight into my boss's office and said. "I didn't send that. That was not from me." And he had no idea what I was talking about because he hadn't opened the email.
Defense: Why did you go straight into his office?
Witness: I had only known him for seven days. I had no relationship with him at all. I didn't want him to think that that email had come from me, that I was in any way going to do anything like that. And he just said, "Yup, okay." And sent me off back to my office.
Defense: Did you interpret this as a prank?
Witness: I don't think Colonel Wilson meant anything bad by it.
Defense: Did Colonel Wilson say anything to you before he left Darwin?
Witness: Yup. The next morning I was coming into the office and Colonel Wilson was leaving. And he asked could he speak to me, and I said, "Yeah, of course." And he apologized for what he had done and he told me he was leaving the country.

CHAPTER 11
CLOSING ACT
"It ain't over until the fat lady sings!"

September 8th is my younger brother's birthday, and on that morning in 2017, he was seated right behind me in a courtroom. I hadn't been around for many of his birthdays, but he was there for me on his special day. His presence was a present, but I was supposed to be the one giving him a present. The prosecution had finished with their case, and all the defense could do was cross-examine prosecution witnesses. We were only allowed two expert witnesses to come in and opine for the jury members on the clean bill of health SAFE exam, and the hearsay video from the Child Advocacy Center. Due to a bad policy forced on the military in 2014 by Congress and the Presidential administration at the time, we were specifically prohibited from putting on a "good character" defense. In violation of the Fourteenth Amendment, which specifies equal protection under the law, the policy prohibits anyone accused of sexual assault from using "good character" as a defense. A defendant can be accused of murder, or any other crime, and still use their "good character" as a defense, but no longer if you've been accused of sexual assault. Instead of walking into the courtroom and being presumed innocent, this policy implies a presumption of guilt for any defendant in a sexual assault case. Consequently, I was forbidden from getting my stepdaughter and daughter on the stand to tell the jury what a great Dad I had been and that I had never even made an off-color comment in their presence. My defense team assured me that their mere presence in the courtroom, seated right behind me, along with my wife and brother was good enough. I felt my daughters should be allowed to testify on my behalf. In a he said, she said case, with no facts, no hard evidence, and DNA being introduced that is not even yours, then "good character" is all you really to rely on.

I had wanted to take the stand in my own trial, and my civilian lawyer had promised to make that happen. For months he had told me he was sending an expert to spend time with me in going over with me how I needed to behave on the stand and preparing me with hardball questions for my testimony. That expert never showed up, and my defense team was concerned that the prosecution had so many potential landmines that I might go off on their lawyers, like the Colonel did in the movie A Few Good Men, played by the actor Jack Nicholson. They had a point there, because I don't tolerate disrespect from anyone, and I may have gone off on the prosecutor whom I considered the biggest pogue of the bunch. I could well have ended up a hostile witness myself, having the Judge kick me off the stand, as he nearly did to my two accusers. My defense team assured me that the rack of ribbons on my chest spoke volumes about my credibility and good character, as well as my family having my back. Once again, I acceded to their greater experience in these matters, and stifled my pride.

We were starting the eleventh day of my General Court Martial, it was a Friday, and I could sense that the jury, and everyone in the courtroom were "smelling the barn" and eager to be done with it already. I was excited beyond description, because I just knew that this jury was going to fully exonerate me of all the felony charges and see that the UA and Australian charges were so petty that they shouldn't have been added to the case in the first place. The Judge wrapped things up with instructions to the jury and reviewed all the charges they needed to determine verdicts. A few of the charges were scrubbed by the Judge during the course of the court martial, which is why it may appear at first glance that I missed including all of the charges in this summary.

[The court-martial was called to order at 0832 on 8 September 2017.]

> **Judge**: Court is called to order. All parties present when the court recessed are again present. The members are absent. Bailiff, can you please call the members.
> [The members of the court-martial entered the courtroom.]
> **Judge**: Bailiff, if you could publish to the members Court Exhibit 1. That's the consolidated exhibit list, as requested by the

members. Bailiff, could you also publish Appellate Exhibit CLVI.

[The bailiff did as directed.]

Judge: Members, I will now discuss the various offenses:

In Specification 1 of Charge I, the accused is charged with the offense of rape of a child, in violation of Article 120b, UCMJ.

In Specification 2 of Charge I, the accused is charged with the offense of sexual abuse of a child, in violation of Article 120b, UCMJ.

In Specification 1 of Charge II, the accused is charged with the offense of assault consummated by a battery upon a child, in violation of Article 128, UCMJ.

In Specification 4 of Charge II, the accused is charged with the offense of assault consummated by a battery upon a child, in violation of Article 128, UCMJ.

In Specification 1 of Charge III, the accused is charged with conduct unbecoming an officer and gentleman, in violation of Article 133, UCMJ.

Specification 2 of Charge III also alleges conduct unbecoming of an officer and gentleman, in violation of Article 133, UCMJ.

Specification 3 of Charge III alleges conduct unbecoming of an officer and gentleman, also in violation of Article 133, UCMJ.

Specification 4 of Charge III alleges conduct unbecoming of an officer and gentleman, in violation of Article 133, UCMJ.

Specification 5 of Charge III alleges conduct unbecoming of an officer and gentleman, in violation of Article 133, UCMJ.

Specification 6 of Charge III alleges conduct unbecoming of an officer and gentleman, in violation of Article 133, UCMJ.

Specification 7 of Charge III alleges conduct unbecoming of an officer and gentleman, in violation of Article 133, UCMJ.

Specification 8 of Charge III alleges conduct unbecoming of an officer and gentleman, in violation of Article 133, UCMJ.

Specification 9 of Charge III alleges conduct unbecoming of an officer and gentleman, in violation of Article 133, UCMJ. Members, at this time, you will hear the arguments by counsel:

Prosecution: The government has proven its case beyond a reasonable doubt with legal and competent evidence. You've heard that over the last couple of weeks. And the purpose of the closing argument is to walk the members through not only just what the evidence was, the purpose of the closing argument is also to explore all of the logical possibilities and show that the only reasonable possibility that remains is the one of guilt of Colonel Wilson. That's exactly what we're going to do. We're going to talk, also, a little bit about spillover. We are confident that the members will decide on this issue and all of the charges and specifications against Colonel Wilson, for everything, that he is guilty on all charges.

Judge: Defense Counsel, you may argue on findings.

Defense: This is Colonel Wilson's, probably, I would guess without any doubt, the most important day of his life. And I'll tell you right now as I'm standing in front of you, I'm probably the most biased person in the courtroom because I'm going to ask you and plead with you to go back into that deliberation room and find Colonel Wilson not guilty. I have a vested interest in this case – my client. But I am asking you: Don't look to us for an answer. The burden never shifts. And the reason we make decisions based upon reasonable doubt, I think, is twofold. One, it is for the greater good. So the allegations involving the girl. It could have happened just like she says in one of her statements. But I think it's also important that you listen to the words that she said in this courtroom. Because this is the sworn testimony here. Now, we've provided you Defense Exhibit B, I believe, that lays out this spreadsheet that I talked to both of the DNA examiners about. And they've got it, right? I mean, there's either not enough DNA or there's not enough targets. But the two labs refused to talk with one another. The United States Army Criminal Investigation Lab will report a low side at a level of 50. That's what she said from the stand. And if you go back and look at what the prosecutors put in immediately afterwards and it's the graph that has all the lines going up and down – and you look at the four that crest over 50, and what they reported a reportable number of at so – I mean, that's a valid number. You understand what prior consistent statements are. If they were consistent, would they be in? What corroborates anything that the girl said? I'm not saying she doesn't believe something happened to her, but what corroborates anything that she said? And I'll talk a little bit about implanting memories, implanting suggestives, and how suggestive kids are. And if you've been around kids that have and still believe in the Easter Bunny and Santa Claus and the Tooth Fairy, ask yourself if kids can be implanted with memories and beliefs. There's nothing that corroborates anything that the girl said except for the fact that she was at Colonel Wilson's house. They tried to take her not to the hospital or to the base, but they took her to the TEDI BEAR Clinic. And it should't be lost on you that these are child advocacy centers. These are advocacy centers where they're taking these kids. And that creates issues with respect to confirmation bias. Think about what happened at that TEDI BEAR Clinic. There's nothing about that medical exam that corroborates anything that the girl said. I mean, you have to ask yourself, and ask yourself hard, that if those four numbers matched Colonel Wilson, the government would be standing on top of the bar right here screaming about the four numbers matching Colonel Wilson. But the DNA doesn't corroborate the girl saying Colonel Wilson did anything to her. They tried to get Colonel Wilson to confess to something or make an admission to something. They took the Major in and he got briefed by NCIS on how to ask the questions. I think it's fair to say they're not just going to hook his phone up to a recorder and let him just go willy-nilly trying to get Colonel Wilson to make an admission, that they gave him ideas on how to try to do that. The government came in in opening statements and they said, "Whatever it is, it didn't happen on the 13th of July." Whatever it is, it didn't happen on the 13th of July. That's what they told you. And they spent a lot of their closing argument a minute ago going through how they were poking holes in their own theory. I mean, they're really poking holes in their own witness is what's happening. And there's no evidence that he was ever alone with her on the 13th of July. That's what the evidence, if you're looking at the timeline, if you're looking the date it's supposed to have, thats the evidence in the case. You have two denials. Two denials, and she asks again. It's important because this is a sworn statement that she typed to NCIS the day after the allegations came up. Her mind is going to be much more in-touch with the conversation that she had with her daughter that night before, on the 14th, then from more than a year later. But what you do know is that she typed her own statement on July 14th, that she swore to it. And in that statement, she mentions "touch" first, her daughter denies it. She mentions "touch" again, and her daughter denies it again. That's as close to a contemporaneous recording that you have in this case as to what happened in that bathroom. And now you're left to wonder, what else were they told not to say? I submit to you, like I said, I'm a biased participant in this process. And I submit that so is the mother.

So moving on to the other accuser. And what's her reaction after she says he left the room – lock the door? Call the police? Text somebody? Anything at all? Nothing. What possible explanation is it for – I mean, her explanation, apparently, is: I took Trazadone. I took Valium. I took Lunesta. And I took Release. All four of those and drank cocktails at the same time. Because why? Why does she think she can do that? Because her doctor said it was okay – does anybody believe that, that her doctor said it was okay to drink cocktails and take those four kinds of medications? So she gets back into the relative safety of Camp Lejeune and her husband – what happens? He texts her and asks, "Hey, are you okay?" She's got something going on at home. She's lost the contract on a house that she's put in, and now she's screwed because she doesn't have any place to go. She's texting Colonel Wilson: "I'm out of here on April 1. What do I do?" "Maid quarters open April 1. Whatever you need. We're here for you." There is no difference in the conversation that they're having after New Year's than it was before New Year's. None at all. Does that make any sense if the allegations she has said happened during the Christmas/New Year's break are true? I submit to you, it makes no sense. She's still messaging Colonel Wilson, "I love you." Does that make sense? If something traumatic happened to you in South Carolina, why would you be referring back to the person who assaulted you about good times had in South Carolina. That makes no sense at all. If you look at the content of these text messages before and after the trip to South Carolina, you compare that to her demeanor on the witness stand and the words that she spoke when she was speaking, and the fact that she won't let us know what was said to that reporter that she won't sign a release – that has reasonable doubt. It has got to be. The burden is: Could you believe it? You know, the doubt is: It might be true. I've told you about the super serious decisions that we make every single day in our life that are made with reasonable doubt. And that doesn't get to happen here. The government has the burden. Colonel Wilson, as he sits right there right now, even as we're finishing up these arguments, as you get ready to go and hear all the evidence that you believe – he's an innocent man sitting right there. The responsibility now passes to you to hold the government to their burden, to challenge: Could it be something else? And return findings of not guilty on all of these charges. Thank you.

The fat lady had sung and had rendered a magnificent closing act. The Judge called a break and we quickly exited the courtroom to huddle in our conference room. The General, my lead civilian lawyer, had knocked the closing out of the park. We were all elated. I just knew that I was going to be set free on my brother's birthday of all days. How cool would that be? Everyone was hugging each other and high-five'ing the four lawyers on the defense team. Toward the end of the break, one of my captain lawyers returned from the bathroom and excitingly related how he had encountered a prosecution lawyer in the bathroom who had extended his hand and had congratulated him on winning the case for Colonel Wilson. It seemed that even the government lawyers had conceded to our victory. This was Cloud Nine stuff.

The Judge then issued his final guidance to the jury members:
Judge: The concurrence of at least two-thirds of the members is required for any finding of guilty. Since we have seven members, that means that five members

must concur in any finding of guilty. If you have five votes of guilty with regard to the offense, then that will result in a finding of guilty for that offense. If fewer than five members vote for a finding of guilty, then your ballot resulted in a finding of not guilty.
Judge: General, it's my understanding that the members would like an overnight recess.
Senior Jury Member: Yes.
Judge: General. what time would you like everyone back tomorrow?
Senior Jury Member: 0800.
Judge: Yes. sir. Members, we've talked with the counsel. We have no objection if the individual members – if you want to take your personal notes with you tonight to review them, that should facilitate your deliberations. Once again, you can't show your notes to any other member, but if you want to take your notes and review them, the court has no objection, nor does the counsel. Thank you. We'll be back at 0800 tomorrow. Court's in recess.
[The court-martial recessed at 1820 on 8 September 2017.]

The jury members were not going to burn the midnight oil and complete their deliberations, so my hopes of going free on my brother's birthday were dashed – but I can take a licking and keep on ticking. I would just get right back up out of the rack tomorrow morning in Cell #13 and be prepared to fight one more round. I can do all things through Him who strengthens me! Suck it up, Buttercup! I was quickly shackled by my entourage of guards and hauled back to Camp Lejeune's Brig for the night, leaving my daughters and wife somewhat dejected and teary-eyed in our conference room.

CHAPTER 12
A JURY OF COWARDS

We were back in court first thing in the morning on September 9th, 2017, and the Judge immediately dismissed the jury to deliberate. Throughout the day, the Judge reconvened all parties in the courtroom to answer questions from the jury, like what does "divers" mean? It was from the senior general on the jury, and my first thought was "what a dumbass." The Judge had explained that word ad nauseam throughout the trial...had the general been in la-la land and not paying attention, or was he just that stupid? The longer the jury deliberated, the more I had a sinking feeling. I thought they would quickly find me innocent, "not guilty", of all the allegations from my two female accusers, but find me "guilty" of most of the minor boorish behavior from my thirteen days in Australia, earlier in 2016. Hopefully, the jury had gotten the memo that we all got that I was innocent of the awful felonious charges, and to set me free. Finally, we got word to get back into the courtroom for the verdicts. I have to admit that my heart was pounding, while it was all being read off by the senior member of the jury, a two-star general.

[The court-martial opened at 1614 on 9 September 2017.]

>**Judge**: Court is called to order. All parties present when the court last recessed are again present. The members have reentered the courtroom. Please, everyone, take your seats.

General, has the court reached findings in this case?

Senior Jury Member: Yes, your Honor.

Judge: Are the findings reflected on the findings worksheet?

Senior Jury Member: Yes, your Honor.

Judge: General, have you signed the findings worksheet at the last page and dated it?

Senior Jury Member: Yes.

Judge: Have you crossed out everything that doesn't apply?

Senior Jury Member: Yes, we have.

Judge: General, please start reading from Colonel Daniel H. Wilson, U.S. Marine Corps. You can remain seated.

Senior Jury Member: Colonel Daniel H. Wilson, United States Marine Corps, this court-martial finds you:

Of Spec 1 of Charge I: **Not Guilty**

Of Spec 2 Of Charge I: **Guilty**

Of Charge I: **Guilty**

Of Spec 1 of Charge II: **Not Guilty**

Of Spec 3: **Not Guilty**

Of Spec 4: **Not Guilty**

Of Charge II: **Not Guilty**

Of Spec 1 of Charge III: **Guilty**

Of Spec 2 of Charge III: **Guilty**

Of Spec 3 of Charge III: **Guilty**

Of Spec 4 of Charge III: **Guilty**

Of Spec 5 of Charge III: **Guilty**

Of Spec 6 of Charge III: **Guilty**

Of Spec 7 of Charge III: **Not Guilty**

Of Spec 8 of Charge III: **Not Guilty**

Of Spec 9 of Charge III: **Not Guilty**

Of Charge III: **Guilty**

Of Spec 1 Additional Charge I: **Not Guilty**

Of Spec 2 Additional Charge I: **Not Guilty**

Of Spec 3 Additional Charge I: **Not Guilty**

Of Spec 4 Additional Charge I: **Not Guilty**

Of Additional Charge I: **Not Guilty**

Of Spec 1 Add Charge II: **Not Guilty**

Of Spec 2 Add Charge II: **Not Guilty**

Of Additional Charge II: **Not Guilty**

Of Sole Spec Add Charge III: **Guilty**

Of Additional Charge III: **Guilty**

Judge: Members, obviously, you have found Colonel Wilson guilty of a number of the offenses. There will be sentencing proceedings in this case. I would like to talk with the counsel, but I suspect they would like to start that tomorrow if the members are amenable, not today.

General, when would you like to start sentencing proceedings?

Senior Jury Member: We will go tomorrow.

I was seriously deflated, as the verdicts were being read. I had no clue what I was "guilty" or "not guilty" of, because I was just hearing a bunch of confusing numbers. I was quickly given the details by my lawyers when we sat down. I was found "guilty" of only one of the ten allegations from my original accuser – "not guilty" on the other nine charges, stemming from her dinner party explosion on July 13th, 2016. I was found "not guilty" of all the charges – six – from my #MeToo accuser. I was further found "guilty" of the UA charge and all of the other minor charges from my adventures in the land down under. The jury had not gotten the memo, and I was not to go free.

Back in the conference room prior to my trip back to the Brig for the night, my lawyers informed me that I had been found "guilty" of touching the child in a way to gratify my sexual desires. I was now going to "tarred and feathered" with the label of "child molester" for life, yet I knew that I wasn't that monster. That single charge carried a sentence of 26 and a half years in prison. I was having a hard time coming to grips with the thought of going to prison as a convicted child molester, the worst possible crime to be convicted of in the United States. I knew that I was going to have to watch my back for any prisoner who might want to become an instant hero in taking out prisoner Wilson, former Marine full bird Colonel. I also knew that just the stigma of that one conviction would put a scarlet letter around my neck for life. A heavy burden to bear. Yet, I believed that it would be fixed at the Appellate Court when my due process rights had run their course. I confidently reassured my distraught wife and daughters that it was just a matter of "when" my conviction would be overturned, not "if" it would be.

I returned to Cell #13 at Camp Lejeune's Brig that night knowing that I was going to be spending thousands more nights in prison. I quickly calculated that I had already been incarcerated for 239 days since January 13th, and I could do all things through Him who strengthens me. I would have to simply take it one day at a time, the same way I had climbed up the tallest mountain in Africa as a teenage kid, Mount Kilimanjaro – one step at a time. I also knew by then that while my body might be in prison, my mind was free to escape and roam around the world at any time I desired. Not even "the sky's the limit…the infinite universe is open for exploration." My thoughts and thinking were always free, and no physical structure could imprison them. I had even taken a few fanciful trips on my Harley motorcycle, while behind bars, and I would be able to take many more. I might even plan a trip to Sturgis in my mind and take it while in prison. My prayer that night was simply that God's will be done, whatever that may be, and have faith that He his plan for my life is always way better than anything I can dream up. My thought to self, closing my eyes that night on my steel rack was, "keep the faith, Colonel Wilson, if God is for you, no one can stand against you!"

We came back into the courtroom the next morning for sentencing. I was thinking that "tomorrow is 9/11 when our country was attacked by terrorists in 2001 using commercial airliners as weapons, and I should never forget the thousands who were murdered." I was also thinking that my personal 9/11 had occurred on 9/9 of 2017 – also, my very own "Pearl Harbor" – a date that will live in infamy. I entered the courtroom as a convicted felon, and I was prepared to get the maximum sentence. I know if I was on a jury, and I really believed that a defendant was guilty and had convicted him of molesting a child, I'd be asking the Judge for the maximum sentence and then some. The Judge had a period for both the prosecution and defense to make appeals to the jury for sentencing. First up for the prosecution was to be my original accuser with her victim's impact statement, but the Judge had already reviewed her statement, and immediately lectured the woman's VLC lawyer, then decided to scrap her statement entirely that contained offensive language toward my wife and I.

My civilian counsel then brought up how a civilian lawyer from the prosecution team had violated his "gag" order and had talked to the press the previous evening.

> **Defense**: The victim legal counsel in this case, one of the counsel, from Arnold Porter, gave statements to the press that was published last night. It has been seen by thousands of people. Statements that impeached the jury verdict – or the members' verdict in this case – calls into question their decision making. It provides additional information that we may or may not put into evidence during sentencing. And, I mean, this is violation of this court's order.

The Judge wasn't too concerned about it because he had ordered the jury not to watch any TV news or read any news reports. The sentencing proceedings continued with the girl's father starting to read a victim's impact statement from his seven-year-old daughter, although it sounded more like a statement drafted by an angry mother. The Judge quickly shut down the Major. The prosecution rested their side of the sentencing hearing, and my team took over, putting my younger brother first on the witness stand:

> **Defense**: You had said something previously about this bringing your family closer together. Can you explain what you mean?
>
> **Witness**: Absolutely. And, of course, Dan always optimist, he looks at the glass half-full rather than half-empty. And he's the one that says, "You know, I've come to the Brig. I've learned some things there. I've learned some humility. And some other lessons there that I wouldn't have learned otherwise."
>
> **Defense**: You had also mentioned to me something about Colonel Wilson being very generous. Can you?
>
> **Witness**: Whenever I come to his home, "Mi casa es su casa," is what he says. He makes

me sleep in the master bedroom with my wife, and Dan and his wife go sleep in a small room. He is very gregarious, fun-loving and protective of the people in his family. And his family includes all Marines, and that's the way he views things.

Defense: You mentioned Colonel Wilson was protective of you when you were growing up together in Africa.

Witness: Absolutely. I was being bullied at the missionary boarding school we both attended in Kijabe, Kenya. One day, the bullying stopped abruptly. Apparently, Dan had heard about it and told the bully that he would beat the living daylights out of him, if he ever so much as looked at me again.

Defense: If you had to describe Colonel Wilson with one character trait, what would you say?

Witness: I mean, the words that come to mind are, "Semper Fi." Dan is always faithful to his family, his country and his Marine Corps. But he's also courageous and I think in these last two weeks, I would have to replace Semper Fi with courageous or undaunted. Just because through adversity and through seeing these things, he is always the one that tries to rally and get us back together and get focused on where we should go from here.

Defense: Do you love your brother?

Witness: Yes. Of course I love my brother, very much.

Defense: And you are committed to helping

> him through whatever happens?
>
> **Witness**: Absolutely. You know, there's an apocryphal African story of elephants. When one elephant is injured, the other elephants in the herd come alongside and help out the injured elephant, you know, like shoulder to shoulder. And that is what we are doing in our family with Colonel Dan, my brother – trying to help him by having our herd surround him with love and support.

I was getting choked up listening to my younger brother. I had been thinking back to our childhood in Africa when I had bullied him a lot since I was five years older. It was heartening to hear he didn't resent me, but still loved me, and his encouragement throughout my court martial was inspiring. Next up was my stepdaughter, and she was amazing. I kept thinking how if this jury had been able to hear from her during my trial, there is no way they would have found me guilty of that one child molestation charge. After hearing her defend my "good character" the jury would have found me "not guilty" of all sixteen of the charges from my original accusers:

> **Defense**: Can you tell us briefly how you know Colonel Wilson?
>
> **Witness**: I met Colonel Wilson when I was eight. My mom had just gone through a divorce and we had moved into a new home. As it turns out, he was in the home next to ours. My mom would frequently ask my brother and I to go next door and get "Dan the Man" to come over and help out with the household duties. Anything that she couldn't do – car repairs and things like that – whatever needed to be handled by a man. And Dan would always come right over and take care of whatever needed to be done.

Defense: And, eventually, he became your stepfather?

Witness: Yes. Eventually, my mom actually proposed to him. She knew that she had a good catch and that Dan was the love of her life. So she proposed to him, and shortly after they got married.

Defense: You mentioned stability. Could you mention a little more about stability – about the school tuition issue?

Witness: So we had gone to private school since kindergarten, and I believe we were in the seventh grade around the time of this incident. But my mom couldn't afford tuition. And so everyday when she dropped us off, she was scared that she would get a call that we got turned away from the classroom. I know that the debt was getting pretty high. So one night, and before they were even married – I don't even know if they were dating. I imagine they were. My mom cried to Dan about it, and the next day my mom showed up at the school and the secretary said, you have a great financier. So they must have dating, and they were not engaged at that point. And she's like, "Financier? What are you talking about?" And the secretary said – "This man came with a $2000 check to pay your tuition, and I told him it wasn't enough. And he said that he was going to go home and sell stock and come with the rest of the money tomorrow." So he made sure that we could stay in the school that we had been going to since kindergarten.

Defense: Tell the members a little bit about

the house fire incident.

Witness: So after my freshman year at the University of California of Riverside, I had moved home. I was about to go to bed one night, and I heard shouting and screaming in the house. I thought that was usual. I was concerned. And then I heard Dan say, "Get out. Get out." We all jumped out the window. Dan was pounding on the neighbors door – or the side of the mobile homes next to ours – screaming, "Get out. Get your kids out." And then Dan went back into the house looking for my brother and he came out covered in soot, and said, "I can't find him. Where was he? What room was he in?" And he went back in there again and put his life on the line to save my brother who isn't even his biological kid.

Defense: You had a health issue that Colonel Wilson was there for you?

Witness: I would say it was the worst day of my life. And I don't like crying in front of people. I don't like being vulnerable. So I remember that night, and it's probably the most meaningful night of my life with what he did. I sat outside on the patio table, and I just was staring at the stars. And he just sat with me. He didn't need to say anything. He knew that. He knew I just needed him there because he's my father figure. I've lived in that house with him, you know, since I was eight. And he just sat there and just let me cry and bawl and maintain my dignity. And I grieved, while he was there with me, making sure I was okay.

Defense: Tell the members just a little bit

about your childhood and growing up in the household?

Witness: So it was great. It was my first experience of being around the military. So I obviously had a lot of questions and stuff. But Dan always took care of us. He was driving us to school, picking us up, helping with homework, washing dishes. Dan is also a very generous man. He bought me my first car when I turned sixteen and did the same for my brother and stepsister. He bought my mom a new car before they were even married. He's a great father.

Defense: Let's fast-forward up now to the present day. How has this court-martial impacted your family life?

Witness: In trying times like these, you really realize how much you love your family. And I now realize how much I love Dan because of this. In some ways, these difficult times make you much stronger.

I was moved to tears, hearing my stepdaughter say such loving things about me. I had been her stepdad for twenty years and had never heard such kindness coming from her about how she really felt about me. The next person in was a good friend of my wife and stepdaughter who had lived with us for long periods of time. Again, I was moved to tears by the nice things she had to say about me. I had no idea she felt that way about me. I had to secretly scold myself to "stop being such a crybaby…big boys don't cry." Here was her testimony:

Defense: Why are you here today in support of Colonel Wilson?

Witness: I am here today because I love his family like they are my own family. And my interaction with Colonel Wilson has been, like, a father that I have never had in my life. I have never really had that kind of guidance and genuine love from somebody. And he didn't even know me, but he welcomed me with open arms, and it was just very warm. And I'm here to support him, and I will always support him and love him like a father.

Defense: Tell us about yourself.

Witness: When I was younger, was taken away from my family. I was physically abused by my mother. And my father abandoned me when I was 12. He left me at a birthday party and never came and picked me up. I just never really had a stable upbringing. So I hold Colonel Wilson very near and dear in my heart.

Defense: Have you been living with Mrs. Wilson?

Witness: I have. And I came here initially because I was in Texas. And I was, sort of, seeing somebody and I felt unsafe. It got to a point where I actually felt not – I wasn't sure what was happening and I panicked. And I – the first person that I could think of to call was Colonel Dan Wilson. And he told me straight up – he was like, "Do I need to come out there?" And I said, "No, no. Don't come out here." But he said, "Anything you need you know you can always come here like if you feel unsafe with your family. No questions asked." And I said, "I'm going to fly out tomorrow," And that's exactly what I did. And when I arrived, he gave me a big hug, a big bear hug. And I just felt safe.

> **Defense**: Can you explain how Colonel Wilson has treated you, and how he is a father to you?
>
> **Witness**: He is just always giving advice. The most random things ever, like, I can just call and he'll just make me feel better. He just boosts my moral. It's – his favorite thing to say is, you know, "I'm boosting the morale. I'm just being positive," and, like, "You can do whatever you want. I believe in you." Just, like, constant – and I'm not even used to that. And it's just, like, an overwhelming sense of just, like, love. And not even coming from a place, like, what can you do for me, or anything. It's just genuine, like, a selfless love.

The final witness was my daughter who, once again, had me choked up hearing her responses. At times I wondered if she was really talking about me, but reassured myself that she definitely was. I also couldn't help thinking again that had we been allowed to put her on the stand during my court martial, there is no way the jury would have convicted me of anything at all. My daughter and stepdaughter would have stolen their hearts and they would have know for sure, hearing from the both of them, that I was an innocent man. Listening to my daughter, inspired me to want to be a better father for such an awesome human being like her:

> **Defense**: Can you tell us how Colonel Wilson has been as a father?
>
> **Witness**: Incredible. He's been a Marine my whole life, and he has been all over the world. But whenever we could make it happen which was as frequently as possible. I spent time with him, and he came up to my place as often as he could. The time that we spent together was profitable to me in the sense that I learned key lessons about life. He

bought me my first car. He bought my mom a car when he returned from Desert Storm because she needed one. He gave me my first computer. And one of the things he had me do was disassemble it so I could know how to reassemble it when I brought it home. He taught me how to drive a stick shift. He taught me how to change the oil in my car. And so despite those distances and where the Marine Corps took him for work, he still made such a huge effort to be that father in my life. Everyone in my family knows and respects my dad. They know him as a Marine, an honorable Marine. And that's how I know my dad. I was able to be raised by two parents who were very friendly and cordial with each other. And there was never any hostility between the two. And my mom has the utmost respect and regard for my dad. She would be here today to speak on his behalf, if she had been allowed to.

Defense: Based on your interactions with Colonel Wilson, can you share how you view your father and what he is like as a person?

Witness: He's a natural born leader. So I take tips from him in how he interacts with people. An example would be – he tries to make everyone feel comfortable, and so I've tried to figure out, in my life, how I can apply that to people I meet. And I know I think he's funny, and he is intelligent. He knows so much about everything, and it challenges me to want to learn. And, you know, I've been able to know so much about the military through my conversations with him. I know so much about his life growing up in Africa because of all of the stories he shares. So

> we're able to talk. I can call him. Obviously, not the last eight months, but I used to be able to call or contact him and just call to talk about whatever was going on in my life.

I was blown away by my daughter. Wow – incredible! Then it was my turn to address the jury members. I had thought long and hard the previous night in my cell about this moment. I wanted to blast them, reminiscent of the Colonel in the courtroom scene in the movie A Few Good Men.

> "You can't handle the truth!"

> "The truth is that I am an innocent man, and you got it right with 15 of the 16 serious charges being findings of 'not guilty', but then you 'f'd' it up royally by finding me 'guilty' of one charge, after finding me 'not guilty' of two similar charges.

> WTF, over! 'Leave no Marine behind?' Well, you just shot one of your own Marines in the back and have left him to bleed out on the legal battlefield. You have just condemned an innocent man, and his entire family, to a lifetime of shame. I'm a tough guy and will survive this. You, on the other hand, have condemned yourselves as being guilty of moral cowardice.

> You truly are a jury of cowards!"

Instead, I calmed myself down, picked up the statement my civilian lawyer had prepared for me, stood up, approached the jury box, stopped six paces away and centered, came to the position of modified parade rest, and read this to the jury:

> **Me, Myself, and I**: General, members, I'm embarrassed to be standing before you here today, not just because of the charges, but also of the need for the commanding general to have you here for the last two weeks away from your family's, commands, and Marines. I hope you do believe that I never intended to cause anyone pain, or to cause anyone to think poorly of me or the Marine Corps to which I have dedicated my entire life. I've been a Marine for over 36 years. I have deployed eleven times as a Marine, and I have held numerous leadership positions. My highest honor was leading Marines into combat and bringing every one of them home with me. I planned on retiring, but I was offered the II MEF, G-3 position, and I thought it would be my retirement tour. When the investigation began, I went off the deep end with my drinking. I was consuming nearly a handle of whiskey a day. In early January of this year, I began a five-day detox stage at Bryan Mawr prior to attending a treatment center in Virginia. I was taken from Bryn Mawr and placed in the Brig two days after my second accuser spoke to NCIS. From the beginning of my career, I would probably be described as a rough and tumble, politically incorrect, hard-headed, tobacco-chewing, cigar smoking, whiskey-drinking infantryman. I used to wear that as a badge of honor, but no more. I have had time to

reflect on all the people that I've hurt by my selfish consumption of alcohol. Perhaps, the most emotional hurt that I have caused is to my lovely bride. She has been with me for 20 years and has seen me at my worst. She has remained with me during the investigations and trial. As a side note, in the eight months that I've been in the Brig, she's never missed a single visitation opportunity. The thought of her being alone and not being able to support her because of my conduct is painful. I know that the responsibility you now have is to sentence me. I've considered myself a protector of people my entire life. I have never been in trouble before that wasn't handled by counseling in my entire career. I know that you may feel that some punishment is required. I only ask that you consider the confinement that I have already served. If I am allowed to remain a Marine, my retirement is imminent, and I know that the Secretary of the Navy must do a retirement grade determination. I ask that you consider my service, my record of performance as a Marine, and my family, if you can do so.

The jury exited to their deliberation room to arrive at a sentence, per the judge's instructions. The child sexual assault charge had twenty-six and a half years as the maximum sentence. Furthermore, the jury could give me up to a year for any of the six convictions of conduct unbecoming of an officer. I fully expected the jury would throw the book at me. Imagine my surprise, then, when the jury came back fairly quickly with a sentence of five and a half years and dismissal from the Marine Corps. I believe that they knew I was innocent, but also knew that if they let me go free without a serious conviction, they would never see a star, or another star, on their collars. They all knew that any Senator, disagreeing with their decision to let Colonel

Wilson go free, could have held up their future promotions or advancement. They had literally thrown me under the bus to protect their careers. They had also, as senior leaders protecting the institution they served, had wanted to protect the Marine Corps from getting a black eye by finding me guilty of at least one of the serious charges. They soothed over their guilty consciences by giving me a relatively light sentence…20 percent, or about one fifth of the maximum. "Shameful, cowardly," I thought, but I had seen that exact same thing happen in a different courtroom, four years prior to my court martial. Finding guilt in a defendant to protect one's own career. My existential fear, prior to and during the court martial, had played out in real life. I also felt that they found me guilty of most of the charges stemming from my thirteen days in Australia to "throw a bone" to the Australian military. Finding me guilty sent a message to the Aussies that "Marines take care of our own bad actors," and we value our relationship with your military.

I said goodbye to my family and thanked my lawyers for defending me in court. My guard entourage shackled me and returned me unceremoniously to Camp Lejeune's Brig, where I was issued a post-trial suit of orange. I immediately transitioned from blue to orange, and would now be known as Colonel Dan, Prisoner Number 00128660 Whisky Delta. I did go back to Cell #13 in General Population, where I remained for the next six weeks.

CHAPTER 13
CASE #22

I was transferred to the Brig at Miramar, California, on November 2nd 2017. A guard at Camp Lejeune's Brig had asked me on Halloween what I would like for "trick or treat". I told him I'd love a pouch of Copenhagen. The next morning, I was pleasantly surprised to spot a single pouch just inside my cell – Cell #13. I secretly enjoyed the nicotine buzz throughout the day of November 1st, hoping my cell wouldn't have a shake down by the guards that day. I had just flushed it down the toilet when the guards came to escort me to solitary confinement. At first I thought that I had been caught, and my transfer to solitary was the prelude to disciplinary action for the contraband that had been smuggled into me. Maybe I had been setup and double-crossed by the guard. But no such worry. My counselor paid me a visit to inform me that I was being transferred to Miramar's Brig the next morning. The reason I was given was that Miramar's Brig has a two-year sexual assault offender rehabilitation program, and given my conviction, I was required to attend it. Although run by the Navy, all of the various military services provide staff and guards, as well as any prisoners convicted of sexual assault offenses.

I was transported on a military VIP plane from coast to coast, one of two prisoner passengers, with four guards constantly staring at us. We were shackled hand and foot for the eleven-hour trip across country with two refueling stops. I thought that it would make a good little clip for a story on America's Most Wanted TV series, and it wouldn't have surprised me if video cameras were trained on us, recording our move and facial expressions. As an infantryman traveling to Iraq, or Afghanistan, I had experienced many longer flights, or lengthy waits to get on military aircraft, so it didn't bother me at all. In fact, one flight from Andrews Air Force Base near DC in General Petraeus's C-17 aircraft took nearly eighteen hours non-stop to Kabul, Afghanistan. We had an areal refueling over Turkey so we didn't have to land and refuel.

We weren't allowed any reading material on the flight to the West Coast, so I just contemplated the next steps I needed to take in the appellate process. The biggest step was being assigned a military appellate attorney. Miramar's Brig was more like a Gentlemen's Club compared with the prisoner-of-war camp I had just spent nine and a half months in at Camp Lejeune. Marines always have to take everything a step further than the rest of the military. We like to think that we give you more for your tax dollar. That mentality affects the guards to where they think that they have to make things harder on prisoners than the other services. It leads to an attitude of disdain towards anyone incarcerated, and you are treated like a piece of shit by most of the guards. I just experienced that treatment at Camp Lejeune's Brig, and the move to Miramar was a welcome change. Prisoners at Miramar get to wear their service utility uniforms, which for me was my green camouflage fatigues instead of an orange suit, like at Marine Brigs. No rank insignia are worn on your uniform, but everyone knows your rank, and typically uses it.

Most of the prisoners and guards called me Colonel Wilson, during my stay at Miramar. One Marine guard, whom I will call Lance Corporal Benatz, would repeatedly ask me if I was going to write a book about my case, and if I did, would I be so kind as to mention him in the book. I duly promised Lance Corporal Benatz that I would mention him in a book, if I ever got around to writing one. Another Marine guard at Miramar quickly took a liking to me and wanted to know what contraband he could get me. I mentioned how it would be nice to enjoy a pouch of Copenhagen from time to time. He started providing me with pouches when he was on duty, and throughout my five months stay at Miramar's Brig.

I got myself into the Barber Shop as a barber, but that didn't last too long because too many of the prisoner's complained that I had given them a high and tight haircut. I would ask them when they sat in the chair how they'd like their hair styled, but then I would proceed to give each of them a good old Marine Corps high and tight cut, all the while thinking in my head, "you're getting my style of trim, young man – my style fits all." I had started cutting my own hair as Lieutenant Dan and could whip on myself a high and tight in five minutes. In less than two weeks, the female staff member who supervised the barber shop prisoners confronted me before we opened up one morning and begged me not to come back to work. She was getting too many complaints from the prisoners, and it was her job to keep them happy with their hair. I returned to my pod and volunteered to be a groundskeeper. I really enjoyed that job because it got me out of the pod for a couple hours every morning to enjoy sunlight, and I was even authorized to wear a cool-looking black boonie cover to protect my face from the sun – something no other prisoner got to wear.

We had a ping pong table and chess boards in our pod, but we were only allowed to play ping pong in the pod after evening chow, prior to the final count and lights out. I played hours of ping pong with Air Force Major Clarence Anderson, and we became fast friends. He won the preponderance of our games until just before Christmas when I started winning the majority of games. The way it worked was that whoever won a game owned the table for the next game. Clarence dominated board time before Christmas, and I dominated the board after Christmas – BC and AC. I got to hear Clarence's story of betrayal by his ex-wife, and how he was convicted of sexual assault with his wife's boyfriend being bribed with cash for his testimony. Clarence's case is a true travesty of justice, replete with outright lies by senior Air Force officials in response to Congressional Inquiries. This is where I really began to believe that God had put me in a military prison for a reason. The reason being that God expected me to be an agent of change when I was out. "You can't fix City Hall from inside of City Hall." Clearly there were so many injustices and inequities in the military's legal system that it needed to be fixed so that future patriots joining the military will have a fairer system of justice. I also had fun playing chess, particularly with an incarcerated Air Force Chaplain who hailed from the West Coast of Africa. We constantly swapped stories about growing up in Africa, while playing chess. He was pretty good at ping pong too, but not nearly as good as my friend Clarence Anderson. "Army," the Marine Master Sergeant in the cell adjacent to mine became a fast friend and we were constantly playing chess. He was really good though, like the level of good approaching "grand master" status. Yet again, he was another service member shafted by a corrupt military legal system in conjunction with the MeToo movement. "You always have to believe the 'victim', and never the accused."

In January of 2018, I was informed at Miramar that my court martial case had been sent to the first level of appeals, the Navy-Marine Corps Court of Criminal Appeals (NMCCA), and that a panel of three judges had eighteen months to review my case and make their decision. I needed to call the defense section at the court ASAP and talk to my assigned military appellate lawyer. I called up and spoke to a Navy Lieutenant with exactly one three-year tour of duty under his belt at Norfolk Naval Base prior to being assigned to the defense section of the NMCCA. I became very concerned when I heard the following on the phone from the kid, "Sir, looking over your case, I don't see much there for us to appeal, but write me a letter and let me know what you think are the appellate issues. Take your time because we have eighteen months and the judges typically go out to the deadline before rendering their opinion, if they even decide to look at your case in the first place. They typically rubber stamp the result of a general court martial. It's unlikely the judge panel will decide anything before the end of July 2019. By the way, I'm swamped with cases so I'm putting yours on the 'back burner' for now. I hope you understand and that I have to get back to work now. Goodbye Prisoner Wilson." He then hung up the phone on me and I'm left staring at the phone and shaking my head in disbelief. What the "f" was that? My bevy of lawyers at the court martial had assured me at the end that I would be assigned the highest-ranking member in the defense section when my case went to the NMCCA. The kid I had just talked to was definitely the lowest ranking member of the defense section. I was being set up for failure by the system. I would need to hire a civilian appellate attorney and ditch this useless kid.

The silver lining in my phone conversation was when the young lawyer at NMCCA casually mentioned that my assigned case number was twenty-two for the calendar year 2018. Therefore, 201800022. I was overwhelmed with an instant feeling of relief. I knew in that moment that I was to be exonerated by the NMCCA. Twenty-two had always been a good number for me, like my winning lottery ticket number. I have so many fantastic associations with the number 22 that I could literally write a book about it. Just three quick examples: I was commissioned from Staff Sergeant to Second Lieutenant and became a "Mustang" Marine Officer on 22 December 1988. I graduated as the top performing officer from the Infantry

Officers Course on 22 November 1989, and I took over what was a successful command tour as a Colonel – Weapons & Field Training Battalion, Parris Island, South Carolina – on 22 July 2011. It was a "God" moment for me hearing that my appellate case number was 22, and from that day on, I never wavered in my belief that I was going to be exonerated by the NMCCA. Again, not a matter of "if", but only "when". And I now knew that it would be some day before the end of July in 2019. That sign from God gave me a peace of mind and serenity like I had never experienced. I mentioned it frequently to my wife and daughters during the next eighteen months. I made sure to annotate it in my Diary that I was adding to daily in a religious manner.

    A big obstacle, however, was that I couldn't afford an appellate attorney and how do I go about finding a good one from inside prison? My paycheck was cut off immediately following my court martial and my wife had been given exactly two weeks to vacate our home on base, or else. I had already been forced to max out all of my credit cards to pay my civilian attorney and I still owed him $70,000.00, although I assured him that scout's honor, I would make full restitution some how, some way, some day. My wife and I were now paupers and destitute. She had been forced to move in with her stepdad in California, so she would have a place to stay and some food to eat. Well, my father the preacher used to tell me, "When you need a teacher, God will put a teacher in your path." I now believe that from this experience at Miramar in January 2018.

    I was going to the postal room one day to retrieve a book that had been sent me. Passing by another pod, the counselor from that pod came out and asked to have some words with me. He handed me a note with a name and number on it, "Katie Cherkasky….867-5309" the note had written on it. The gentleman then goes on to say "I figured you might need a good civilian appellate attorney, and Katie, of Golden Law, has done good by several of the prisoners in my pod, making great things happen in their cases. I've been tracking your case for a while now, and when I heard about your bullshit conviction, Colonel, I thought you might need a lawyer of Katie's caliber. I sincerely hope things work out for you, sir." I was so overcome by the moment that I didn't know what to say, but I blurted out a "thank you, sir, and I greatly appreciate your recommendation. I just happen to be looking for a good civilian appellate attorney. I will definitely be giving Katie a call ASAP. Thank you very much." It was another "God" moment, and I felt like I was on top of the world, and I breathed a "thank you" prayer to my Higher Power, although I wanted to yell it out from the mountaintops.

I got on the phone with my wife that evening and relayed the conversation with my appellate attorney. She then got on the phone with my stepdaughter who volunteered to pay for a civilian appellate attorney from her purse. My wife let me know in our next phone conversation so I called my stepdaughter to thank her. I also told her about Katie, and my stepdaughter said, "well, give me Katie's number and we can both call her then compare notes, like both get a feel for her." I gave her the number – 867-5309. I then decided to try calling it myself. I got Katie on the prison phone with the third ring and felt an instant connection. Her being my civilian appellate attorney was just meant to be and I knew it in our first conversation on the phone. I called my stepdaughter back the very next day and she had also spoken with Katie and had a good feeling about her. That was significant for me, because my stepdaughter and I have the exact same personality profile on the Myers-Briggs Personality test. We get each other. Hearing about my stepdaughter getting a good vibe from Katie reinforced in me that it was right move to make. I called Katie right up and hired her. My stepdaughter followed right up by giving Katie a retainer fee to get her started. Here was a post my daughter put up on my Facebook page on 28 February 2018, right before we officially hired Katie to defend me at the appellate court:

Well, it can't always be good news...

Dan was assigned a military appeals lawyer recently. Since then we have noticed he seems much more stressed and anxious about the appeals process. Don't get me wrong, the assigned military lawyer is nice and seems smart. But he is young and openly stated Dan's case is on the back burner right now. Could you imagine being incarcerated and losing everything over a false allegation only to be told by the one person who can really help you out that you are on the back burner for now?

I've offered to pay for Dan's appeals lawyer so we are currently interviewing private attorneys. Our hope is that the private attorney can work in tandem with the military attorney like we had during the original trial. At this point the more help we have the better. While the 'evidence' (or lack there of) makes it seem like it would be easy to get the verdict overturned, the lawyers actually do have to read through the extremely long court martial transcript. It's a lot to process.

Dan asked me this weekend to begin to highlight other cases of injustice similar to his. I'll begin using his Facebook to educate our friends and families of how common this issue is. I will also begin to share more of our struggles because in all honesty we need help. Until then, please continue to write Dan and/or visit him. There is nothing in the world better than hearing Dan's excitement over letters he receives from friends or surprise visitors that have him in tears.

Thanks again for your love and support!

Dan's Daughter

In January, I was officially given a letter by the Miramar Brig's chief psychologist informing me that she was recommending that I not attend the two-year sexual assault offender rehabilitation course. She had conducted several screening interviews with and told me that I had scored the lowest of anyone on her exam in the two years that she had served at the Brig. She did not believe that I was a sexual assault offender in spite of my conviction and was therefore recommending to the Brig Staff that I not be placed in their rehab course. She gave me a signed copy of her letter and told me that she believed it would be counterproductive for me to go through the course. I was happy to hear the news, because I had heard all kinds of nonsense about having your penis hooked up to sensors that detect whenever you get sexually excited, after viewing certain porn pictures. I wouldn't have subjected myself to that anyway and would never have attended their outlandish course from the feedback I was getting from other prisoners enrolled in the course. This now meant that the Brig Staff would be searching to move me to another facility in order to free up another bed space for their treatment program.

A few weeks later at the end of March, I was whisked away to solitary confinement and told I was being transferred the next day to another facility.

An entourage of guards transported me the following day about forty miles up the road to Camp Pendleton's Brig. "Oh, man," I thought, "not back to another Brig run by Marine guards. Here we go again, back to a prisoner-of-war camp!" I reminded myself on the drive up that I wasn't just going to "survive", I was going to "thrive". I had previously served with the Warden of the Brig and his wife at Parris Island. We developed a good relationship, and he would have me come to his office from time to time to chat. His big concern was that I get into an argument with one of his young guards that might escalate into a physical confrontation. I assured him that I was just there to stamp my timecard and move on with life. I expressed an interest in the dog training program and he had me enrolled. I was moved to a special squad-bay in the prison, where we lived and trained with the dogs who would eventually be adopted out to military veterans in need of a service dog. I was paired up with a young female puppy named Jade, and instantly fell in love with her. I only lasted a few months in the program when I had a disagreement with the female guard Corporal running the program. She had us together one morning to brief us prisoners in the program that she had unilaterally decided to take away one of our benefits. At the end of her speech, she asked if anyone had any questions or comments. I let her know that what she was taking away was going to have a negative impact on our morale. She felt like I was undermining her authority and had her Gunnery Sergeant supervisor fire me from the program. It was heartbreaking saying goodbye to Jade, and I think I saw tears in her eyes knowing I was leaving. I believe she had fallen in love with me, as I had with her.

Soon thereafter I got into a program teaching us at an off-site location to be Air Conditioning technicians. The guy contracted to teach it was a retired Navy Chief who treated us like shit. I became so incensed by this goon who was a horrible instructor that we all loathed, that I didn't learn a lick about air conditioning even though I graduated with a certificate from the course. He was such an asshole that I completely tuned him out through three months of twice-weekly classes.

Katie's first visit to me in prison was after I had transferred to Camp Pendleton's Brig. I was instantly impressed with her knowledge about my court martial and case. She already had numerous issues identified for the appellate judges to consider. I was taken aback by her brilliance and depth of knowledge. No wonder she was the top of her class at law school, I thought. She had also been a superstar Air Force lawyer, and a Federal Prosecutor –

impressive credentials. Katie and her husband, Andy, had left the Air Force to start their own law firm, Golden Law. She laid out her plan of action and I couldn't find any fault, and I'm typically a super-skeptical individual. She needed to get a copy of my record of trial, then go through it with a fine-tooth comb, looking for the errors. She would then prepare an Appellant's Brief on my behalf for the judges at the NMCCA to consider. She hoped that the judge panel would allow for an open hearing so that she could personally appear in front of them and present my case. After filing the Appellant's Brief, the government would be given an opportunity to respond, and then the judges would take it for action. She emphasized that it would be a long road ahead, but she was very optimistic at our chances of success.

My daughter started sending me copies of opinions from the NMCCA judges so I could get inside their heads and see how they think about issues. In all, she sent me two dozen opinions over the course of the year prior to the judges making their decision in my case. The more I read, the more convinced I became that they would overturn my conviction. My daughter was also writing me highly motivating and inspirational card and letters. I would get three to five each week but reread each of the over dozens of times. "She is such a terrific writer," I would think. "I can't wait to read her book."

My stepdaughter had administrative control over my Facebook account and would frequently post updates about me or my case. She also posted my address at the Brig, and I was flooded weekly with letters from Marines and other friends, encouraging me and expressing their outrage about the conviction. She also started a website (TeamFreeWilson.com) where she would post updates, and post my written updates from prison. She also started posting the book reports my daughter asked me to do for every book she sent me. I would send my book report to my daughter who would give it to my stepdaughter to post on the website. My stepdaughter also had a Special Power-of-Attorney from me, and she was contacted by Marine officials wondering how to dispose of my household goods. They informed her that she either needed to come pick them up or takeover payments to the storage facility where our household goods were stored. She elected to pay the storage fee, over $700.00 per month, for the remainder of my confinement at Camp Pendleton's Brig.

My daughter sent me the finest books she could think of. Mostly from Pulitzer-prize winning authors, like Ron Chernow's biography of Alexander Hamilton. Eventually, my daughter sent me nearly every book written at the time by Ron Chernow. I still remember reading Grant and the famous quote that Chernow puts in there about General William Tecumseh Sherman answering a reporter who asked Sherman about Grant being a drunk. "He stood by me when I was crazy and I stood by him when he was drunk, and now, sir, we stand by each other always." I would also call my daughter the most frequently during the week. She became my best friend, advisor, confidant, and cheerleader. I always got off the phone with her elated from our fantastic conversation. I hated the annoying announcement towards the end of our ten-minute time limit, informing us that we had just one minute to win it. We would start talking really fast back and forth to each other to try and get out everything that we wanted to say before the next call.

During one visit in the spring of 2018 my stepdaughter brought a script of remarks made by my original accuser to a Congressional Committee on sexual assaults in the military. She had expanded her web of lies by declaring to the committee that I had sexually assaulted both of her twins and that she had known about it six weeks after the dinner party incident. She didn't tell the committee why she had never reported that allegation to NCIS to investigate. She stuck with that story when she filed a tort claim against the Department of the Navy in the summer of 2018 for the damages that Colonel Wilson had inflicted on her daughter. My stepdaughter, through the Freedom of Information Act, had obtained a copy of her tort claim, which she brought to the Brig to show me during a visitation. She wanted $10 million for both twins on account of my allegedly sexually assaulting each of them, and she demanded $5 million for the eldest daughter for my allegedly "plying her with alcohol," based on my joke about drinking apple juice. Of course, she had a retired military lawyer sign off on her bogus tort claims, as if he had been witness to it all. He unwittingly signed off on false official statements. Ironically, on the tort filing form, there is a dire warning of penalties for anyone making false claims. If the Marine Corps failed to pay her $25 million dollar tort claim within a year, she was prepared to sue the Marine Corps in a Federal Court. My thought at the time was that maybe her motive all along was to become a cash-money millionaire.

In mid-September of 2018, I met with Katie again to go over her draft Appellant's Brief. She went through each of the 82 pages with me. I was highly impressed. It was spot on in every regard. Every word and sentence had meaning. One could simply look at the Table of Contents page and know exactly what each of the issues were that Katie was presenting to the court for consideration. Here's a portion of the very first one regarding factual and legal insufficiency, or Assignment of Error as they are known in legalese:

> I. THIS COURT MAY ONLY APPROVE FINDINGS OF GUILTY THAT ARE CORRECT IN LAW AND FACT. IN CHARGE I, SPECIFICATION II, THE GOVERNMENT CHARGED COLONEL WILSON WITH TOUCHING THE GENITALIA OF A CHILD WITH THE INTENT TO SATISFY HIS SEXUAL DESIRES. BUT THE GOVERNMENT DID NOT PROVE BEYOND A REASONABLE DOUBT THAT HE HAD THIS REQUIRED SPECIFIC INTENT. COLONEL WILSON'S CONVICTION FOR CHILD SEXUAL ABUSE WAS NOT FACTUALLY AND LEGALLY SUFFICIENT.
>
> <u>Law and Analysis</u>
> This Court's powers under Article 66 serve as a powerful prophylactic against Government abuse and ensure that service members are convicted by proof beyond a reasonable doubt. This authority provides "a source of structural integrity to ensure the protection of service members' rights within a system of military discipline and justice where commanders themselves retain awesome and plenary responsibility." This Court's Article 66 powers extend even to full-bird colonels accused of offenses against children and is particularly critical in the kind of high-visibility and highly emotional case at bar. NCIS' exhaustive investigation yielded no physical evidence or corroborating eyewitness testimony that Colonel Wilson ever touched the child's genitalia; let alone any evidence whatsoever that he did so with criminal intent. All the government presented were equivocal claims by the girl, mostly in videos made long after the alleged events,

and encouraged by her mother. Colonel Wilson did not touch the child inappropriately, and she was never clear about when Colonel Wilson allegedly touched her. Law-enforcement officials observed the child forensic interview on 14 July. Apparently concerned about her insistence that Colonel Wilson had touched her inappropriately only once and that it had happened on 13 July, these officials directed the child forensic interviewer to get the child to provide alternate dates for the purported abuse. At trial, the Government theorized Colonel Wilson did not touch her genitalia on 13 July, but rather had possibly done so on other dates. But just as Colonel Wilson was not alone with the child on 13 July, he was not alone with her on any of the other occasions. Compounding this is the complete lack of physical evidence in this case. There were no findings of any disturbance from the sexual assault forensic exam. Not only were there no anomalous physical findings from the extensive head-to-toe exam, there was no DNA evidence presented establishing that Colonel Wilson had touched the girl's genitalia. Due to the absence of physical evidence, the Government's case rested almost entirely on the girl's in-court testimony, and the erroneously admitted video interview. Despite an exhaustive investigation, the Government did not present any evidence that Colonel Wilson was aroused, that he had any history of abusing children, that he had any predilection or sexual interest in children (e.g. in child pornography), or that he engaged in other pseudo-romantic behavior such as by kissing. Nor was there any physical evidence—such as semen—that would have allowed a fact finder to conclude beyond a reasonable doubt that Colonel Wilson possessed the requisite mens rea to be guilty of sexual abuse of a child. The government's "grooming" expert testimony is circular reasoning insufficient to prove any sexual intent. During its findings' argument, other than referencing Colonel Wilson's supposed "grooming" behavior, the Government never argued he had touched the girl with the intent to arouse his sexual desire. Not only did trial counsel never mention the words "sexual," "desire," or "intent" as it relates to the girl, but trial counsel never even advanced the theory that Colonel Wilson must have had the requisite mens rea simply by virtue of purportedly touching her genitalia. This Court should set aside the finding of guilty to Charge I, Specification 2; and order a sentence rehearing.

Katie submitted my Appellant's Brief to the NMCCA on 24 September 2018, more than a year after my court martial. I got a printed copy that I was allowed to keep in my possession. Ninety-nine percent of the time, I was convinced that the Department of the Navy's Appellate Court would overturn my conviction and free me from prison, but there was that one percent when the debate committee in my head would pose the question, "what if they don't?" I would then reach for my Appellant's Brief and reread it from the beginning to the end – every single page. This always reassured and left me thinking afterwards, "there is no way those judges are not going to overturn my case."

On 27 November 2018, I decided to write an article, projecting myself into the future as if I was a reporter for USA Today, reporting on the action taken by the NCAA judges to overturn my conviction. I dated it for 2 July 2019, as if the NMCCA had released their Opinion on 1 July 2019, the day prior:

Shocking reversal in the case of The United States v. Colonel Daniel H. Wilson, USMC!

In a stunning reversal, the Navy and Marine Corps Criminal Court of Appeals unanimously overturned Colonel Dan Wilson's, September 2017 conviction of sexual assault of a

child on July 1st, 2019. A panel of appellate court judges voted 3 to 0, overturning Wilson's case "with prejudice". In the written opinion of the panel, they declared that "Colonel Wilson's case was a travesty of justice. The panel's harshest criticism was reserved for the judge who presided over Wilson's court martial. "He made numerous bad decisions throughout the court martial and demonstrated an unabashed partiality in favor of the prosecution. The jury, comprised predominantly of general officers, did not escape the judges' uncharacteristic criticism "it is apparent to this court that the officer panel (jury) was more concerned about their own careers and potentially damaging publicity for the Marine Corps than it was about true justice for Colonel Dan Wilson. Colonel Wilson was an acceptable casualty on the legal battlefield; collateral damage to protect the institution of the Marine Corps, and their own careers. They shot their own Marine in the back and left him on the battlefield to bleed out. There were simply no relevant facts to substantiate Wilson's conviction of sexual assault. The other charges of officer misconduct should never have been included in his case. They had nothing to do with the original charges and were merely used by the prosecution to convince the jury of Wilson's propensity to commit the charges of sexual assault and aggravated assault. Case law has previously struck down cases where the prosecution has used propensity to commit as a legal argument to convict a defendant. Attempts to reach Colonel Wilson for his reaction to the announcement were obstructed by prison officials at Camp Pendleton, who stated that prisoners are not allowed to speak to the press while incarcerated. They refused to confirm when Colonel Wilson will be released; however, anonymous sources at Headquarters Marine Corps confirmed that Wilson's release is imminent – anticipated within the next few days. A Marine Corps Public affairs spokesman said that the appellate court's decision demonstrates their independence from any unlawful command influences. We will continue to follow this breaking story as further developments occur.

I wrote out the entire article in my diary and in a separate diary entry I wrote, "I had fun writing it. Now if only it becomes a self-fulfilling prophecy! One must keep the flame of hope eternally lit!"

I got a call from Katie in April of 2019. She was disappointed that the NMCCA had rejected her request for oral arguments. She was not going to get an opportunity to present my case to the judges. They would merely review it on their own. My response was, "Katie, I see this as a positive development. The Appellant's Brief you prepared for me is so crystal clear that they have no questions that need to be answered. They obviously don't need you to explain any more to them, because they have a firm grasp of all the legal issues you address. They just don't want to waste your time and resources when it's not necessary. This is a good thing, I believe." Katie seemed encouraged by my positive spin, but still disappointed that she didn't get a crack at presenting to the judges.

CHAPTER 14
DOUBLE RAINBOW

Saturday afternoon, the 29th of June 2019, I witnessed a double rainbow up above the hills of Camp Pendleton surrounding our Brig. It was the second double-rainbow display that I had witnessed that year and I immediately sensed it was a good omen from my Higher Power of things to be revealed soon. I was so moved that I recorded it in my diary, "a good omen of things to come?" Also on Saturday afternoon, my niece had brought by her newborn to visitation who had been born on my birthday, seven months prior. She had given her son, my grand-nephew, my same middle name of "Hunter." He was a cute little baby with chubby cheeks and her visit boosted my spirits.

All day on Monday, the 1st of July 2019, I expected to get good news about my case. After all, I had witnessed the double rainbow. However, as the day wore on into the afternoon, I wasn't so sure, and started doubting my premonition. Maybe I had been wrong. Finally, just after 1600, as we were getting ready to march off to evening chow, a staff member came to escort me to see my counselor. He handed me the phone and authorized me to dial my lawyer, Katie. She was beside herself with excitement on the phone, blurting out that the appellate court had unanimously "set aside" my conviction for sexual assault of a child "with prejudice." Literally, a one in a million-type decision that rarely happens in sexual assault cases and almost never when it involves a child. I was overcome with emotion and could barely speak on the phone, but she had plenty to fill me in on, so I just kept my mouth shut and listened. Katie believed I could be released within the week, if not by the end of July. My head was spinning with joy. I was going to be free! I really didn't care how long it took me to get released, because I was going to be free and never be forced to register as a sex offender. It was an amazing feeling. I made sure to express my gratitude to my Higher Power that night for his mercy and grace in allowing me to be exonerated. I thought, after our phone call, "was it odd, or was it God" that I saw the double rainbow and that it symbolized God's covenant with me, Colonel Dan Wilson. I had recently read in the Bible, in the book of Genesis, that God had specifically given the sign of the rainbow to Noah, as his covenant to never again completely flood the earth again, as he had just done. "Thank you, thank you, thank you, Heavenly Father!"

The appellate court's Opinion was written by the senior judge on the three-person panel, a female Navy Commander. It was a lengthy fifty-seven-page document that goes into excruciating detail about their reasons for "setting aside" my sexual assault conviction "with prejudice". Here are some

United States Navy–Marine Corps Court of Criminal Appeals

Before
HUTCHISON, TANG, and LAWRENCE,[1]
Appellate Military Judges

UNITED STATES
Appellee

v.

Daniel H. WILSON
Colonel (O-6), U.S. Marine Corps
Appellant

No. 201800022

Decided: 1 July 2019.

of the highlights from their Opinion:

The appellant asserts six assignments of error (AOEs): (1) that the appellant's conviction under Charge I, Specification 2, for sexual abuse is legally and factually insufficient; We find merit in AOE (1). Our action renders all remaining AOEs moot. Accordingly, in our decretal paragraph, **we dismiss Charge I, Specification 2 with prejudice** and, finding that we are unable to reassess the sentence, remand the case for a rehearing on sentence.

All items were tested for the presence of semen, and all items tested negative...Even advanced low-level DNA analysis at a second forensic laboratory could not yield a profile from which any person could be included or excluded as a match...No witness saw the appellant touch the girl's genitalia. Despite the proximity of others in and around the house, no witness ever heard any cause for concern. The girl did not disclose any abuse to either sister at any point. On cross-examination, the defense counsel impeached the mother who agreed she provided a different version of her conversation to NCIS agents on 14 July 2016...She conceded that she wrote in her NCIS statement that she was the first person to use the word "touch," not her daughter. However, she testified repeatedly, "That's not how I remember it." She also agreed that the rest of her written NCIS statement was accurate, including the fact that her daughter twice stated that the appellant did not touch her genitalia. Having carefully considered the evidence presented at trial and taking into account "the fact that the trial court saw and heard the witnesses," we are not convinced of the appellant's guilt beyond a reasonable doubt. Carefully evaluating all of girl's testimony and statements admitted at trial, we find that her statements were fatally inconsistent and wholly irreconcilable. Faced with multiple descriptions of possible contacts—only some of which are consistent with guilt—we cannot find guilt beyond a reasonable doubt based solely on her statements…We next look to the other evidence admitted at trial for corroboration. We do not find evidence sufficient to overcome the infirmities in her statements. There were no witnesses, physical evidence, or admissions of guilt by the appellant…We next consider the testimony of several preeminent expert witnesses in the field of child psychology, maltreatment, and forensic interviewing. Most were presented by the government…the expert testimony does nothing to resolve our genuine misgivings with the evidence. Rather, the testimony of the government's expert witnesses only further diminishes the reliability of the girl's forensic interview and trial testimony…she testified at trial, and portions of three out-of-court statements were admitted. The four accounts are inconsistent in significant ways and cannot all be true…We must contrast incriminating statements with her first two statements about the appellant, which were both adamant denials. On 13 July 2016, she twice denied that the appellant had ever touched her inappropriately. Those two denials cannot reasonably be reconciled with her later testimony at trial. Based on the four major inconsistencies alone, we cannot be convinced beyond a reasonable doubt of the appellant's guilt. But even if we look at each of her statements separately, we still cannot discern a clear narrative of what abuse she alleges the appellant committed. Expert testimony further erodes confidence in her statements. On 14 July 2016, the girl's father participated in a "controlled call" with the appellant, and NCIS agents recorded the call.

"Last night, my daughter disclosed to my wife that you had touched her in her private parts in between her legs. And, sir—" to which the appellant cut him off and responded, "You know that's crazy. You know that, right?" Through the course of the fifteen-minute phone call, the father insisted he knew his daughter was telling the truth. The appellant consistently and emphatically denied the allegation. The conversation reached an impasse, with the father refusing to accept the appellant's continuous denials. He appealed to the appellant as a "father to [him]" who he had "known . . . for years," asking how the appellant would feel if he were in his shoes and what he should do. The appellant responded: "Brother, you do...what your conscience and your gut tells you to do. That's what I always tell any Marine. And, if that means that I get tarred and feathered with a f[***]ing false label, hey, you know, everything happens for a reason. And I'll work through it. But that's tragic, man, because I would kill for your daughters. I would pull a 'Dexter' on anybody that I had any inclination that had done something like that to your daughters or my daughters." The father said he did not know what he was going to do, to which the appellant replied: "I understand the emotions. And I understand the parental feeling. But I want you to know, man, I would die for those girls just like I would die for my own girls...But I am here to tell you nothing untoward ever happened between me and any of your daughters. And there was no situation where I was alone at any time with any of the daughters. So, you know, you do what your gut and your conscience tells you." On balance, the appellant's statement is a strong protestation of his innocence.

In sum, the government presented no physical evidence and no corroborating eyewitnesses who saw or heard signs of abuse. We have carefully reviewed the government's arguments on the evidence as they view it. We do not find that the proof is "such as to exclude . . . every fair and rational hypothesis except that of guilt."

CONCLUSION...The guilty findings to Charge I, Specification 2 and the sentence are **SET ASIDE** and Charge I, Specification 2 is **DISMISSED WITH PREJUDICE**.

Katie got me a copy within a few days and I read through it every day, sometimes twice or more. Just as I had been reading through her Appellant's Brief for the past ten months. Word spread instantly through the prison, and I was being congratulated constantly by both prisoners and guards. Especially, one young black Marine prisoner who had nicknamed me "Triple OG." When I had first arrived at Camp Pendleton's Brig, some sixteen months earlier, he had said, "damn, sir, you're not just an OG (old gangster), you're a Triple OG, you so old!" The Warden authorized my transfer to a separate squad bay that had no stationary guard watching over us all the time, and I was issued a new prison badge. I also observed one of the guards furtively slip my original Camp Pendleton prisoner's badge into his pocket when I was issued a new

<u>Prisoner – Colonel Wilson # 0012866 Whiskey Delta</u>

prison badge. He wanted a souvenir. The guard was none other than Lance Corporal Benatz who had been transferred up from Miramar's Brig to be a guard at Camp Pendleton's Brig, shortly after I had been transferred up.

By the way, I'm not really 6 feet 4 four inches like it may indicate in the picture. I must have been standing on a two-inch cloud of pure excited energy that had me levitating higher than my normal 6 feet 2 inches. God lifts me higher than I could ever possibly be on my own.

I was on an emotional high 24/7, and no one or nothing was ever going to bring me down. I was going to be like the mythical Phoenix rising from the ashes of prison to an even greater status than before. A man who would have an inspiring story to tell of being falsely accused, imprisoned, convicted, and, yet, in the end exonerated and freed from the "ash pit of despair" to once again experience life, liberty, and the pursuit of happiness.

The government lawyers at the NMCCA quickly put a kibosh to my hopes of getting out of the Brig any time soon. Turns out that they can keep you incarcerated, if they file an appeal to the court's decision. They have thirty days to file an appeal. They waited thirty days before filing their appeal on July 31st 2019. I knew it didn't take them thirty days to draft their three-page appeal. No, they were intentionally sticking it to Colonel Wilson. While waiting, I wrote to the Secretary of the Navy himself, asking that he direct my release from confinement, pending my resentencing hearing on the minor convictions, like sending a prank email. He responded some thirty days later with a two-sentence letter and his signature, saying he would let the process play out and refused to get involved to help out a wrongfully convicted service member. "Stigma", I thought, "if I had just been exonerated of any other serious crime, other than child molestation, he would have released me immediately." I had predicted this to Major _____ in the recorded phone call, more than three years prior, "if that means that I get tarred and feathered with a f[***]ing false label, hey, you know, everything happens for a reason. And I'll work through it. But that's tragic, man, because I would kill for your daughters. I would . . . pull a 'Dexter' on anybody that I had any inclination that had done something like that to your daughters or my daughters."

The NMCCA responded quickly to the government's request for a rehearing of my case by the entire nine members of their court with a resounding "DENIED" stamped right in the middle of the first page of their request on August 13th 2019. I grinned for hours looking at that beautiful red denial stamp and thinking, "in your face, pogue government lawyers!" They then lied to my lawyer, Katie, and her husband, Andy Cherkasky, telling them both that the government would be asking the United States Court of Appeals for the Armed Forces (CAAF) to "certify" my case. They had sixty days to file for certification to CAAF. Forty-four days later on September 26th 2019, the senior lawyer in the Department of the Navy, a three-star Admiral, decided that they would not be submitting my case to CAAF for certification. "Psych, we were just playing around…ha ha…and we got to keep Colonel Wilson behind bars for an additional six weeks…ha ha!" The NMCCA gave control of my case back to the Marine Corps who handed it back to II MEF for final disposition instead of giving it to the more "convenient" convening authority, as in I MEF, which was headquartered right there on Camp Pendleton. I was put in solitary confinement for a day expecting to be flown back out to Camp Lejeune, and still in a prisoner status. Later that day, the deputy-warden paid me a visit and said there was mass confusion at the upper echelons of the Marine Corps on what to do with Colonel Wilson. I was going to remain at Camp Pendleton's Brig until the confusion had subsided since moving me cross-country would have been a logistical nightmare. He therefore authorized my transfer back into general population from solitary confinement.

I then had an entourage of staff from the base general come visit me, assuring me that I was to be released soon, and that he was going to put me back to work on his staff. "Fantastic," I thought. They also had appointed a Lieutenant Colonel I knew to come check up on me as often as required to take care of any needs I may have. The comptroller, a female Chief Warrant Officer, whom I had known for two decades paid me a visit to assure me that she was going to personally ensure that I got all of my back pay restored, and "to make you a full up round again, sir." I was officially moved in status from "post trial" to "pretrial" and I switched from an orange suit back into a blue suit. A Colonel was assigned to be my new IRO (Initial Review Officer) and was going to come determine if I should be released, pending a resentencing hearing. The Colonel was switched out at the last minute by orders from on high by a two-star Major General. Katie and Andy Cherkasky came down to my IRO Hearing on October 2nd 2019. I was in my blue outfit thinking, "exactly thirty-eight years ago this very morning, I was in my full dress blue uniform, getting ready to graduate meritoriously as the Platoon and Series Honor Graduate from Boot Camp and officially become a United States Marine. I just know that I'm going free today. The circle of life. Keep hope alive." It was also the 38th birthday of another friend of mine in prison, and I had already wished him a "Happy Birthday, Warrior…Semper Fi!"

The Major General who was my IRO had to have come down with specific orders from the top echelon of the Marine Corps, "Do NOT let Colonel Wilson go!" Katie and Andy gave great reasons why I should be released and I had a good feeling about it, but after deliberating for two hours, the Major General told me that he was ordering my continued confinement, as he believed that I was a flight risk, if I was to be released. I actually did think about rushing him and strangling his skinny pencil neck with my bare hands, but my God-conscious "voice" kept telling me to "under-react." I thought, "any reaction is not going to change this situation. Suck it up and don't let any emotions show. Right now, think with your head and not with your heart. Be logical, not emotional. You can deal with your feelings later. You can do this. This too shall pass. You are a warrior, Dan!"

I'm convinced that the Major General was told not to release me under any circumstances to put the government lawyers in a stronger bargaining position from which to negotiate my release. Katie and Andy had been negotiating with the government lawyers separately to garner my release prior to a resentencing hearing. The Major General's decision also convinced me that there was no general at all in the Marine Corps who was going to cut me any slack. I was then the most senior Colonel in the entire Marine Corps. A resentencing hearing would be comprised exclusively of general officers, and even with only the minor convictions remaining, they could have conceivably sentenced me to an even longer prison sentence than what I had been previously given. Looking at what that Major General had just decided, I knew that I would be hammered in a resentencing hearing by any group of general officers. Couple that with the concept of stigma syndrome and I wanted to avoid a resentencing at all costs. Therefore, I applauded Katie when she was able to convince the government to scrap the resentencing hearing altogether in their back-and-forth negotiations.

CHAPTER 15
THE DIRTY DEAL

There is signing a flawed contract under duress, and then there is 'virtual duress'. "Sign this, or rot in prison forever!"

Below is a portion of the "Dirty Deal" I was pressured to sign in order to escape the bonds of confinement. After I was released, it became a poison pill, however, because the general whose signature is on the line below, immediately went back, reneged, on our agreement. Here are the important portions of our contract that my lawyers had negotiated with the lawyers of II MEF for my freedom:

> I, Colonel, Daniel H. Wilson, USMC, having been convicted of General Court-Martial offenses now pending rehearing on the sentence, in exchange for good consideration, and after thorough consultation with my defense counsel, do fully understand, and agree to the following terms and conditions:
>
> 1. I agree to submit a voluntary request for retirement.
> 2. In conjunction with my voluntary request for retirement, I agree to submit a request for leave awaiting administrative separation. This request, if approved, will allow me to exhaust all

leave that is previously accrued, and if my administrative processing for separation is not complete when the accrued leave is exhausted, all leave thereafter will be charged as excess leave.

3. I recognize that no Board of Inquiry will be convened to make a recommendation on the characterization of service or my retirement grade to the SECNAV and that the SECNAV may reach a service characterization unfavorable to me and retire me in the last grade in which he determines that I served satisfactorily. I may, however, provide written arguments to the SECNAV, advocating a favorable characterization of service and retirement grade determination.

I understand that if my voluntary retirement request is approved, I will be retired in the rank that the SECNAV determines to be the highest grade in which I served satisfactorily. After entering this agreement, the Convening Authority will release me from pretrial confinement upon completion of all administrative and medical requirements necessary to my retirement request package. I understand that this post trial agreement may become null and void and that the Convening Authority can withdraw from this agreement, if I fail to satisfy any material term of the agreement. The convening authority agrees that on the date of the SECNAV's final approval of my retirement request, in lieu of a sentence rehearing, he will order NO PUNISHMENT in his action on my General Court-Martial. By my signature below, I have acknowledged that I have read this agreement completely, I have discussed it with my

counsel, I understand it in all respects,
and I'm prepared to abide by its terms.

Twist my arm, back me into a corner, whatever…I was ready to take one small step out of the Brig, and one giant leap into my freedom. I signed the agreement with reluctance on October 15th 2019, but it was either sign it, or potentially rot in prison for who knows how long, waiting for a sentencing rehearing that would likely return me back to the Brig for an even lengthier stay. "Let the wheels of justice spin, send that 'guilty' bastard in." Military legal actions are normally slower than molasses. The government had already successfully kept me locked up for 106 additional days, following my exoneration by the Appellate Court. It was time to "pull chalks." I decided to take my "get out of jail free card," collect two hundred bucks, and skip on out of the dungeon. I signed the deal because I was tired of being stuck in prison and I wanted to reunite with my wife and daughters. My wife had been more faithful than any man could ever expect from a beloved spouse. She was the personification of the Marines' motto of "Semper Fidelis," Latin for "always faithful." She was more dependable than the postman, always showing up for weekend visitation, whether in the rain, sleet, hail, or snow. Earthquakes and tornadoes didn't stop her from visiting me. She had supported me loyally from the start, and she deserved to get her husband back. She had suffered enough.

Katie and Andy had brokered the deal with the II MEF lawyers who worked for none other than my nemesis, the pogue lawyer Colonel who had conducted one of the three investigations on me, some three years prior, after NCIS had come up empty handed. Following his hit job on me, he was promoted to the position of Staff Judge Advocate for II MEF. The same guy who had investigated me was then giving advice to the general seeking my prosecution at a court martial. The pogue Colonel had advised my general before, during, and after my court martial. The very same Colonel who was buddies with the Colonel Judge in my trial. He had stuck with a plum assignment and was now advising his third general since this all started. He had his proteges negotiating with Katie and Andy, while he kicked back and micromanaged their interactions. I am sure that he lobbied the legal Beagles at Headquarters, Marine Corps to get my case returned to II MEF so he could exact his revenge for losing the biggest case of his career. I imagine he was seething with dismay on 1 July 2019 when the NMCCA released its Opinion. He was likely going to be awarded a Legion of Merit for assassinating Colonel Wilson with a combat "V" authorized since the pogue had destroyed a warrior on the legal battlefield. My takedown had made him a legend in the annals of Marine Corps lawyerly folklore, but now the appellate court judges had metaphorically slapped him upside the head with a case of wrongful prosecution.

After I signed the dastardly deal on October 15th 2019, there was a mad scramble to out-process me from the Brig and from the Marine Corps. I was escorted by a fellow Colonel all over the base for two days, getting my final medical evaluation and starting to process for retirement. All retiring Marines are required to attend a weeklong session of retirement classes. They telescoped all that into an hour and a half for me in the Brig, bringing in all the various experts to meet with me briefly in a small visitation room, one by one – the "firehose" effect. I never got the benefit of the mandatory weeklong course that sets one up for success in retirement. Rather for me, the retirement process was rush, rush, rush.

My diary entry on October 15th reflected my reluctance to sign the deal…

> **0919**: Spoke for thirty minutes – three separate phone calls – with my daughter about the dirty deal, "not thinking about it," or immediately switching to think of something else. I joked about not thinking about the pink elephant. We discussed predestination and whether or not we really do have choices. She said I could get a job, and I told her I was lazy and didn't want a job…become a hobo! Told her I'm ready to roll the dice (22) if the gov't dithers around with the deal instead of the CG signing it."

The next morning, October 16th, I wrote in my diary:

> **0811**: Linen Exchange this morning…just finished making my rack up with clean sheets. Watched the moon setting this morning over the west end of the Brig. A beautiful sunny day out. What's in store for Dan Wilson today? Good news? More checking out? I have no idea, but plan to embrace anything and everything thrown my way. Please give me wisdom, strength, and discernment today Oh Lord, my God.

Shortly after 1500 on Friday, October 18th, 2019, I was summoned to the office of Receiving & Release (R&R) in Camp Pendleton's Brig. I had just spoken with Katie on the phone and was beyond excited with anticipation of my pending release that she assured me was about to go down. We were waiting in the dining hall, while guards shook down our squad-bay. I was first escorted back to our squad-bay by none other than Lance Corporal Benatz who kept whispering to me not to forget mentioning him in my book. At the squad-bay my possessions were strewn around like the drill instructors did to us in Boot Camp. Guards were still milling around looking for contraband, and eyed me suspiciously when I was escorted in. Prisoners are never allowed around when guards are doing a "shake down." Lance Corporal Benatz announced to them that Colonel Wilson was about to be released and he was there with me to pack my trash. While I quickly threw all my possessions in the military blanket, several guards came over, shook my hand, and congratulated me on my pending release. At R&R, I was given my seabag and told that I could dig out my cammies for wear, departing the Brig. A Colonel I didn't recognize was in the room to escort me from the Brig to his headquarters building. He was the commanding officer of the unit I was to be administratively attached to, while I retired from the Marines. He was thoughtful enough to bring the rank insignia of a full bird Colonel, which I affixed to the collars of my cammies with the precision of one who's done it daily for nearly a decade. After taking off my prison garb and putting on my uniform, I signed a bunch of papers the Brig needed me to sign. I didn't even look to see what any of the paperwork was about. I just signed as fast as I could to get the hell out of the Brig. I walked out of the Brig around 1530, and this time unshackled with no handcuffs. Now I truly know when people talk about "walking on Cloud Nine." It was surreal...kind of like watching yourself from above...detached...like watching a movie clip about it. I was very thankful to my Higher Power as I exited the building, got into a government van, and was driven off that compound. "Thank God...Thank God...Thank God Almighty that I'm FREE at last!" It was 109 days after my exoneration by the Appellate Court, and 1009 days exactly since Friday, the 13th of 2017 when I was put in pretrial confinement – more than 33 months and 5 days, nearly three years. I was also now the most senior Colonel on active duty in the Marine Corps – the Bull Colonel.

Andy met me at the headquarters building and took me over to Ward Lodge on Camp Pendleton where room #36 had already been reserved for my wife and I. Katie couldn't make it down for my release, but her husband Andy had driven down in record time from Irvine. Katie had also called my wife and my daughters to alert them to my release, and my wife arrived while Andy was still catching up with me. Here's what I wrote in my diary that day, and they were to become my final diary entries:

> **0629**: Second morning in a row that I started my diary entry at exactly **0629**, with no forethought or action to sync it purposefully. Last night, I woke up to take a leak at 0321...almost like a good omen of 3, 2, 1, GO! Is today the day, or not? I'd like to portray that I will be equally content, regardless of the decision by the CG, or inaction on his part. However, I'd really like to depart this prison – hence my signature on the dirty deal. The new female Warden this AM said my rack was "mind-boggling." It does look pretty good, but it has every day I've spent in prison! It is a gorgeous day out, clear skies. I just admired the setting moon with the kid from Kenya. He has really taken to me. I wish him the best in his case. Two new kids last night were asking my thoughts on corrections. Once started talking about the topic, it took great effort to stop myself, I can drone on, like the energizer bunny. The millennials are watching Steve Irwin on

TV…finally something decent! Yesterday, I kept looking at the clock in the afternoon when it was 1322, 1422, 1522…201822.

1024: 300 push-ups and five sets of dips x 10 reps each at recreation call…walking laps in between sets. Two kids who came in Wednesday night were cleared by the IRO this morning to depart. Happy for both of them. Another kid eager for a second IRO and release was informed in the breakfast line that there was no IRO today. Charges filed and he has to plead to a Judge now for release. He is very depressed…I feel bad for him! Will I even get any kind of "word" today that will clue me into my likely future? I suppose that no word at all will mean I'm staying. Hang in there, Brother, it will all work out for the best according to His plan.

1425: My counselor asked if I wanted a legal call. I said please. Katie answered and told me she had a signed agreement from the convening authority with one minor change. I can only leave the Brig after the checking out is complete. I assured her that the Battalion Legal Advisor told me yesterday after I got an ID card that I was good-to-go. She was going to try and get me out today. Shortly thereafter Major _____ showed up and had me sign the new agreement. He left in a hurry to try and get the right folk lined up to approve my release today. I have a bad feeling that something will be missing from the checkout that bumps it to next week, or later. I'm hopeful to leave today, but prepared for any eventuality. Major _____ cautioned me about not speaking to the press.

1457: Katie just told me I'm out this afternoon!

1910: At Ward Lodge with Susan and Daisy I'm free! Pinch me! Finally released around

1530. Quite a show at R&R. Went to the battalion with Colonel _____...we chatted admin stuff then Andy showed up and we all came to the lodge setting up in room #36. He gave me lawyerly/fatherly guidance. Susan arrived! Unbelievable! Thank you, my LORD!

Andy & I, shortly after my release   With our beloved Daisy

CHAPTER 16
BREAKING BAD
"BOHICA – the big green weanie!"

I got to spend the next day in the company of my wife and daughters. My daughter had driven seven hours overnight to reunite with me. My daughter and stepdaughter took me to the big PX (post exchange) on base and bought me new civilian clothes and shoes. They lavished me with gifts and love. It was unreal. I kept pinching myself to make sure I wasn't dreaming. My daughter had arranged for my wife and I to spend a week at a posh hotel in Irvine. Before heading up, I had to get a picture of parking in the spot at the Post Exchange, reserved exclusively for Colonels. The prosecutor had mentioned in his closing remarks that I should never be allowed to park in the spot reserved for Colonels, ever – so I had to take pictures to send to him some day.

A day or two after we checked into the hotel, I got a call from the female Major whom I had served with on Okinawa – the one NCIS had tried to get to testify against me. She was overjoyed about my exoneration and release from the Brig. She asked me to be her retiring officer at her retirement ceremony some three years in the future. Of course, I always say "yes" in being of service to others, especially the Marines I've served with. Immediately following our phone call, her husband called to ask me the same question. Would I be his retiring officer? Yes, I would.

Here you go, Pogue Prosecutor and Pogue Lawyer!

I spent hours on the phone catching up with old friends and family members. I really enjoyed my alone time with my wife. The first we had had in three and a half years. My wife and I mostly chatted, were entertained by our dog, and ordered food to be delivered right to our hotel room. Katie and Andy invited us to dinner one evening, but my wife didn't want to leave our dog alone in the hotel room, so I went with my favorite lawyers to chow down. It was the finest meal and best steak I'd enjoyed in many years. In Marine-run Brigs, back in the kitchen, where I had been to several times on a clean-up crew, all canned goods are stamped with "Not Fit for Human Consumption!" They fed us the shit anyway.

I worked with Katie and Andy in the next few weeks to get our rebuttal submitted to the endorsement from my convening authority at II MEF on my retirement package. I appealed to friends on Facebook for letters in support of my rebuttal and was flooded with forty letters in mere days.

Back on the East Coast, plotting his next assassination bid against Colonel Wilson, my nemesis, the pogue lawyer Colonel decided to attack me again, but this time through the administrative retirement process, because trying to take me out with lawfare had failed him. He prepared an endorsement for my new general to sign that would accompany my voluntary retirement package to the Secretary of the Navy's office. The SECNAV's office was in turmoil at the time with POTUS having just fired the SECNAV for trying to stick it to Chief Eddie Gallagher, the Navy SEAL who had been cleared of murder at his court martial, but the Navy was trying to shaft him administratively. POTUS stepped in saying, "I support my warfighters…let my people go…honorably!" Unfortunately, due to the stigma surrounding my original allegation, no one was willing to advocate for me. I was on my own. The pogue lawyer Colonel violated my rights to privacy and contacted my discredited accusers, begging them to write highly inflammatory letters to the SECNAV, pleading that he have me executed me at high noon. Those letters accompanied the general's endorsement that the pogue lawyer Colonel had personally prepared. He also added in a big lie that NCIS had found a thumb drive with secret files on it, and I had therefore violated national security as a Major. He failed to mention that his own government security experts had told my lawyers that there were no classified files or slides on my thumb drive. The thumb drive I had used in Iraq to brief VIPs in 2004-2006. Had there been any classified material on that thumb drive the prosecution would have gleefully added many more charges to the dozens they already had…the more the merrier is their motto. Pogue lawyer also made mention in the endorsement of all the petty convictions that his general had promised no punishment for. A direct breech of our written contract. That was the only stipulation the general had agreed to. His lawyer had my general renege on that agreement that we had both signed. I had lived up to every stipulation on the other hand, going without pay from mid-December through 1 April 2020 when I got my first retirement check. All this is going on, while I'm on the West Coast and unable to go into their offices on base and defend myself. His endorsement to my voluntary retirement request was asking the Secretary of the Navy to put me on the retirement rolls in the pay grade of an O-4, Major, with and "Other-than-Honorable" (OTH) characterization of my service. The most outrageous portion of the endorsement was the pogue lawyer taking a swipe at the appellate court's decision to set aside my Article 120b conviction for child molestation:

> While I recommend approval of Colonel Wilson's voluntary retirement request, partially as an alternative to resentencing for the General Court-Martial convictions of firm by the Appellate Court, I also specifically ask that you consider all the misconduct captured in the enclosures. Colonel Wilson was tried by a seven-member General Court-Martial panel of four generals, and three colonels with over 200 years of collective military experience having been instructed by a military judge regarding their duty "to determine the believability of the witnesses, and how the final determination is to the weight or significance of the evidence and the credibility of the witnesses." In this case, those members were convinced beyond a reasonable doubt that Colonel Wilson sexually abused the child on divers occasions. That the appellate court set aside this conviction, based on its own unique application of the highest, criminal burden of proof does not reduce my belief that this significant misconduct must be considered for purposes of this administrative action. The evidence regarding this offense, and even the results of trial, clearly demonstrate that, more likely than not, Colonel Wilson is guilty of violating article 120b.

Are you kidding me? You're going to take a swipe at the appellate court in the one instance where they get it right? They overturned my conviction for factual and legal insufficiency, not on some vague technicality. It was a lie, and the Appellate Court judges spotted it and fixed it by exonerating me. My general at Camp Lejeune went ahead and rubber-stamped the pogue lawyer's endorsement and sent it on up to Headquarters, Marine Corps. The Manpower Chief of the Marine Corps, another three-star general, disagreed with the whole "mishandling of classified material" bit, and said he felt that I should be put on the retirement rolls as a Lieutenant Colonel with an "Other-than-Honorable" characterization of my service – the last rank in which he believed that I had served honorably:

> Defense counsel further argued that the CG, II MEF endorsement is flawed because the classified Report of Investigation (ROI) in fact, tends to exculpate Colonel Wilson in the mishandling of classified material. Defense explained that the 2nd Marine Division Security Manager reviewed the information on the device and opined to the NCIS Investigator that the information on Colonel Wilson's confiscated thumb drive was not classified…The law permits the Secretary of the Navy to consider the overturned Article 120b offense. However, in the interest of judicial efficiency and administrative clarity, I recommend that Colonel Wilson's retirement request be considered in light only of the offenses for which he was convicted. The charges for which Colonel Wilson stands convicted are sufficient to warrant retirement as a Lieutenant Colonel and characterization of service as Other-than-Honorable.

This general at HQMC, however, recommended that my punishment be based on the remaining convictions for which I was promised "NO PUNISHMENT" by my general in our written contract – the "Dirty Deal." Now military lawyers will make a distinction between legal punishment and administrative punishment, but regular citizen Kane recognizes that punishment is punishment – "a duck is a duck."

This entire package was then forwarded up to the Secretary of the Navy's office that was in turmoil at the time, along with my rebuttal and forty letters from friends asking SECNAV to retire me as a Colonel with an "Honorable" characterization of my service. The Navy's civilian Assistant Secretary of the Navy for Manpower and Reserve Affairs then circled and initialed the Marine Corp Manpower Chief's recommendation. And, there you have it…the "Paul Harvey"…the rest of the story.

BOOK UNDAUNTED GLADIATOR

I was penniless when I first was released from the Brig. I hadn't received a paycheck in over two years. I had survived in prison on thirty bucks a month that the government had allowed us for toiletries, underwear, and socks. My wife sold my Harley for way below the blue-book value to be able to eat. We were forced to foreclose on a condo we owned in Alexandria, Virginia. I had defaulted on all debts. My credit score was at 530, down from 810 when I had checked into Camp Lejeune, back in April of 2016. I wasn't going to be paid until my first retirement check, thanks to the dirty deal I had signed. Although still on active duty, I had agreed to go into an administrative leave status, after the leave I had earned on the books expired. I was also never credited for the sixty days of leave that I had earned while in prison, which, after the judges' decision to set aside my sentence, I should have been immediately credited with. Thank God for my eldest brother who immediately sent us some funds that allowed us to get back on our feet. Unfortunately, it wasn't enough, so I stood in line at the Navy Relief Society (NRS) to see about getting a loan. NRS did give me a loan, but not enough to keep us going several more months. I therefore cashed in most of my IRA from my Thrift Savings Account so I could continue to feed my family for an indeterminate amount of time, taking huge tax penalties in so doing. But we made ends meet, and no one went hungry.

I appealed to the Congressman in my home district, asking him to help me get my backpay from the Marine Corps. I didn't hear back from him. Stigma…crickets. I filed a complaint with the Department of Defense Inspector General's Office, asking them to take my retirement decision out of the hands of my service and the Department of the Navy. Rather, appoint an independent board to review my official evaluation reports in making their determination as to my retirement. I had received only glowing evaluations from my first performance report as a Sergeant in 1983 until the last one I had received as a Colonel, more than three decades later. Nearly all of my performance evaluations were what we used to call "walk on water" reports. Nary one negative comment in any of the several dozen I had received from my various reporting officials. They didn't do a damn thing for me but dither. Again, the stigma thing, leading to inaction.

The waiting game for the SECNAV's office to make a decision

played out through November, then December, then January. At the end of January, I got the word that the decision had been made – I was to be retired as a Lieutenant Colonel with an Other-than-Honorable characterization of my service. In February, my convening authority modified the results of my court martial with this supplemental order.

```
              UNITED STATES MARINE CORPS
                   COMMAND ELEMENT
                II MARINE EXPEDITIONARY FORCE
                      PSC BOX 20080
              CAMP LEJEUNE, NORTH CAROLINA 28542-0080

Supplemental General Court-Martial Order No. M18-02a

In the case of Colonel Daniel H. Wilson, U.S. Marine Corps, in
accordance with instructions from The Navy-Marine Corps Court of
Criminal Appeals and pursuant to Rule for Courts-Martial 1107(f)(2)
(2016 Edition), the action by my predecessor in command on 5 January
2018 is withdrawn and the following substituted therefor:

In the case of Colonel Daniel H. Wilson, U.S. Marine Corps, it appears
the following error was committed: the conviction for Specification 2
of Charge I was legally and factually insufficient. Accordingly,
Specification 2 of Charge I and Charge I are dismissed with prejudice.
The remaining findings have been affirmed. Pursuant to a post-trial
agreement, a sentence of no punishment is approved.
```

They were unable to demote me to Lieutenant Colonel while I remained on active duty. I was unceremoniously retired from the Marines on 1 March 2020. I had been debarred from the base, so I was unable to even turn in my active-duty ID card. Instead, I mailed it directly to my Commander-In-Chief along with a letter explaining my situation and asking for his help. Crickets again – the stigma. Being put on the retirement rolls in the grade of an O-5, rather than as an O-6 is harsh punishment indeed, after being promised no punishment. It's a $2,500.00 fine per month for the rest of my life. Additionally, the Other-than-Honorable designation of my thirty-nine years of honorable service, exempts me from 98 percent of the benefits from the Veterans Administration (VA). Although an OTH is technically a neutral designation for administrative purposes, the VA treats it as "dishonorable time." Were I to get a 100 percent rating from the VA, I'd rate another $3,500.00 per month. So in essence, after being promised in writing by my general "no punishment" for the frivolous convictions, I received harsh punishment. A $6,000.00 per month fine for the rest of my life along with a dark cloud of the OTH characterization hanging over my head. That is the hard one to swallow. I'm banned from all Marine bases for life, and I'm not allowed to show up at functions in my uniform. The sacred cloth I proudly wore in defense of this country for nearly thirty-nine years. I need to find a lawyer some day to file a federal lawsuit on my behalf for breech of contract and wrongful termination from the Marines, as well as wrongful prosecution and defamation of character.

Ironically, just prior to my retirement date, I received two letters and a certificate. All of them mentioning my "honorable" and "dedicated" service to my country. It was a case of the right hand not talking to the left hand at Headquarters, Marine Corps. How could the Commandant of the Marine Corps not be aware of what his subordinate generals were doing to Colonel Wilson? I sent a letter directly to POTUS, my Commander-In-Chief with a final appeal on February 29th, 2020, my last day on active-duty service, which had started back on July 6th, 1981:

Dear Mr. President...my Commander-In-Chief: 29 February 2020

Thank you for your Certificate of Appreciation for my 39 years of service as an active-duty Marine. Much gratitude for your kind words, sir. I also appreciated the nice letter from the Commandant of the Marine Corps, General Berger.

I'm disappointed that General Milley, your Chairman of the Joint Chiefs of Staff didn't send me a retirement letter. A decade ago, he and I served together in the National Military Command Center (the basement of the Pentagon) for two years. I can't tell you how many times he came across the hallway to bum a "dip" off me, and we had many professional conversations.

I am returning my active-duty Identification Card directly to YOU, my Commander-In-Chief. I can't turn it in at Camp Pendleton, because the Base General has debarred me from going aboard any of the Marine Corps bases on the West Coast.

Following my wrongful prosecution for sexual assault, I was exonerated and released from military confinement, after spending nearly three years in prison. I agreed, under duress, to file for voluntary retirement. I say "duress," because it was either sign the agreement, or rot in prison for who knows how long. I also agreed to "waive" my right to a Board of Inquiry, which would recommend to the Secretary of the Navy, my retirement rank and characterization of service.

I retire tonight as the senior colonel in the Marine Corps. I have been a "Mustang" Marine infantry officer with 11 deployments around the globe...5 into combat zones, and 2 involving actual combat...Desert Storm (1991), and Operation Phantom Fury (the Second Battle of Fallujah, Iraq - November 2004). I have been shot at, had rockets, mortars & artillery fired at me, and I've even survived an IED attack on my vehicle in Fallujah, Iraq, during combat operations with the Black Jack Brigade. I also survived being killed during a "friendly fire" incident in Desert Storm, while conducting combat operations to kick Sadaam's troops out of Kuwait. Certainly, God has had a platoon of Angels watching over me!

The bottom line, sir, is that I'm asking you to restore my retirement rank to full bird **Colonel**, with an **Honorable** characterization of my service. Also, please dismiss "with prejudice" the remaining 7 frivolous convictions. They are akin to having felony convictions for "jay walking!"

No one in the civilian world would have felony convictions for the bull sh*t that the government lawyers threw at me in court. I conquered the "swamp government lawyers" and pogue billet holders on the legal battlefield, but they seem to have exacted a "pound of flesh" from me in revenge by weaponizing the administrative retirement process.

Please don't let them get away with this, sir! For the sake of my wife, and two daughters, I ask that you reverse this madness, so that my family doesn't have to live with a dark cloud of "dishonor" hanging over their father's head. After all, they were the ones who truly suffered through my 1009 days of wrongful confinement. They all loyally stuck with me throughout the ordeal, and their belief in my innocence never wavered.

Sir, after you fired the worthless SecNav (aka, Spencer-for-Hire), you declared that you have the backs of your Warriors. I am respectfully now requesting that you have my back too, sir!

Thank you for hearing me out, Mr. President, and I wish you all the very best in your future endeavors! My best also to the First Lady, and may God richly bless your entire family, Sir!

Semper Fidelis,

Colonel Dan Wilson, USMC

Dear Colonel Wilson,

Upon the occasion of your retirement, I extend my sincere appreciation for your dedicated service to the Corps.

During your career, the Marine Corps has been involved in combat, and it has been because of Marines like you that the Corps has acquitted itself so well on the battlefield. High standards of excellence in conduct and performance have long been our hallmark, and with them, a unique spirit that sets us apart. You can be proud to have been a part of that legacy and to have attained your grade in an organization such as ours.

In recognizing your long and dedicated service to the Corps, we cannot fail to acknowledge the contributions of your family over those many years. Long and frequent separations are a way of life for Marines, and it takes a very special kind of family to share the many hardships with us. We owe them our deepest gratitude.

As you leave our active ranks, go with the knowledge that your distinguished service will have a lasting influence and it has earned you a legion of friends and fellow Marines who wish you well in the coming years. The Corps is better because you served, and our Nation can stand proud because it produces Marines like you.

I speak for all Marines in wishing you good health and good fortune.

Semper Fi, Marine!

David H. Berger
General, U.S. Marine Corps
Commandant of the Marine Corps

My Retirement Letter from General Berger

Commandant of the Marine Corps

BOOK UNDAUNTED GLADIATOR

CERTIFICATE OF APPRECIATION

FOR SERVICE IN THE ARMED FORCES OF THE UNITED STATES OF AMERICA

COLONEL DANIEL H. WILSON, USMC

I extend to you my personal thanks and the sincere appreciation of our grateful Nation for your contribution of honorable service to our country. You have helped maintain the security of the Nation during a critical time in its history with a devotion to duty and a spirit of sacrifice in keeping with the proud traditions of the military service.

I trust that in the coming years you will maintain an active interest in the Armed Forces and the purpose for which you served. Those who follow in your footsteps will draw inspiration from your commitment, dedication, and sacrifices made to ensure the protection of our American freedoms.

My best wishes to you for happiness and success in the future.

Commander in Chief

My Certificate of Appreciation from **POTUS**

CERTIFICATE OF RETIREMENT
FROM THE ARMED FORCES OF THE UNITED STATES OF AMERICA

TO ALL WHO SHALL SEE THESE PRESENTS, GREETING:

THIS IS TO CERTIFY THAT

LIEUTENANT COLONEL DANIEL H. WILSON

HAVING SERVED FAITHFULLY AND HONORABLY
WAS RETIRED FROM THE

UNITED STATES MARINE CORPS

ON THE FIRST DAY OF MARCH
TWO THOUSAND AND TWENTY

WASHINGTON, D.C.

GENERAL, UNITED STATES MARINE CORPS
COMMANDANT OF THE MARINE CORPS

My "Honorable" Retirement Certificate from the Commandant of the Marine Corps

BOOK UNDAUNTED GLADIATOR

Although, my retirement certificate from the Commandant is addressed to Lieutenant Colonel Wilson, that's because it is dated on 1 March 2020 when I was put on the retirement rolls to be paid as a Lieutenant Colonel. The day prior, I was on active duty as a full-bird Colonel – an administrative quirk because they can't demote you on active duty, but a tool to stick it to deserving members in retirement. The important thing to note on my retirement certificate is the word "Honorable." The Commandant got that part right in my book! He did get my rank right on his retirement letter to me.

CHAPTER 17
THE LIFE OF RILEY

"I've been rocketed into a fifth dimension of existence –

I am truly living a life beyond my wildest dreams in Paradise!"

The good news is that the Marine Corps finally made amends to me and paid me all that money I was owed for being wrongfully imprisoned for nearly three years. The first person I repaid was my stepdaughter, owing her $50,000.00 that she had unhesitatingly contributed to hiring Katie Cherkasky and paying for the storage of our household goods. I immediately repaid my brother and the Navy Relief Society. I called up my civilian lawyer from the court martial and asked him what I owed him – about 69 grand and some change. I overnighted a Cashiers Check for $70,000.00 to him to make it even-Steven. I then hired two financial experts to track down all my outstanding debts and negotiate settlements. I promptly paid all parties. Inside of two months, my credit score was up 200 points to 730 and I had a feeling of satisfaction in knowing I had done the right thing as a good citizen.

The other good news is that my wife and I decided to move back to South Carolina where we purchased our "forever" home and put down roots in a place we call paradise. My first year in retirement, I rode my Harley nearly every single day. We have so many Marine friends visiting Myrtle Beach who stop by and see us that reunions are a frequent thing that we both enjoy.

Shortly following my retirement, I checked myself in to another alcohol detox facility for a second crack at getting sober. This time, I completed the detox program with flying colors, and was accepted into a treatment facility in Florida, where I graduated with honors and distinction three weeks later. I immediately enrolled myself in a recovery program in Myrtle Beach and have remained sober since 18 January 2021. My medicine for the disease of alcoholism is to attend daily recovery meetings, and seek greater conscious contact with my Higher Power, asking that His will be done in my life for today, and every day I wake up. The maintenance of my spiritual condition is my top priority every day, because I now realize that being in a fit spiritual condition is what keeps this alcoholic from taking a drink. Sobriety and a renewed connection with my Higher Power, allow me to live a life beyond my wildest dreams. My absolute worst day in sobriety is exponentially better than my best day drinking. My only desire now is to be of help to another alcoholic or suffering human being. To keep the gift of sobriety, one must be willing to help your fellow man, or woman. I have legions of new friends, thanks to being a member of sober recovery groups. When I first started, I would walk into a meeting room, and they were all strangers. Now I walk into a room and see not just friends, but family. People who genuinely care about you and want to see good things happen in your life. Every meeting I attend, God speaks to me through one, or more, of my new family members. I always hear exactly what I need to hear in every meeting.

Following my retirement, I adopted a "see food" diet. Eat anything, and as much as I desire. More was better. For all my years on active duty, I had to maintain strict height-weight and body fat standards. Naturally being a large fellow that meant denying myself eating everything on my plate. I always made the cut, because I didn't want to be that guy getting kicked out of the Marines for being a "fat body." Two years after retiring, I stepped on the scale one morning and was shocked to see that I had ballooned up to 309 pounds. I immediately decided to get back to my fighting weight and developed a plan of action with respect to a new diet and exercise routine. Initially, my goal was to lose fifty pounds by my birthday in 2022. I was making such great progress that I decided to go double or nothing – 100 pounds. In the end, a voice in my head of my drill instructor kept yelling at me, "Recruit Wilson, Marines don't just give 100 percent…we put 110 percent effort into everything we do." I decided to go for a 110 pound weight loss. Twenty-two months later, I ended my weight loss journey just prior to Thanksgiving of 2023, weighing in the day prior at 192 pounds for a total weight loss of 116 pounds. I decided then that I would maintain my bodyweight at 199 pounds or below for life, which was 110 pounds lighter than where I began my journey. I will be writing a book in the near future called, "A 110 Percent Mentality"…my 110 pound weight loss journey, wherein I will be simply sharing with the reader how I did it and what worked for me.

The Bible tells an old, retired soldier like me "to beat your sword into a plow-sheer, and your spear into a pruning hook." And "blessed are the peace makers for they shall inherit the earth." Well, I don't have a spear, but I did beat my sword into a Pickleball paddle, as directed by my Higher Power. In retirement, I got into the fantastic sport of Pickleball. I was instantly hooked and became addicted to playing for two hours daily. I now have aspirations of becoming the perennial champion for my age group as I grow older. I played with the national champ for the 88-year-old age group recently and he inspired me. Bill didn't even start playing the sport until he was 77 and has been his age group champion with his partner for the last five years. I want to be like Bill when I grow up, not "like Mike" as in the commercial. The side benefit is that I have made many friends on various Pickleball courts around Myrtle Beach. I also plan to write a book about Pickleball in the future, called "Pickleball Like a Warrior," with a subtitle of "developing killer strategies for conquering any opponent." It will be similar to educating the public about the teachings of Sun Tzu on war. I wanted to call it the "Art of Pickleball," but that title is already taken. "The Art of War" by Sun Tzu was our primer in the Marines. At the Infantry Officers Course, we studied it like the Bible and thereafter in the infantry specialty.

I promised years ago that I would write a book about all the things my dad taught me while growing up in Africa, before I joined the Corps. He truly was an amazing leader of his flock and taught me everything that made me successful as a leader of Marines. Therefore, the next book I intent to write, and I already have a good chunk written, is "Out of Africa, and Into the Corps." It will be a companion book of sorts to Undaunted Gladiator…a prequel if you will. Look for it soon at a bookstore near you. Actually, all joking aside, I will likely self-publish it on Amazon, like this book.

Another book, which I also will consider as a companion book to this one, will be titled "Triple OG." I will tell serious and humorous stories from my nearly three years behind bars. I have many stories to tell that the reader may find interesting, and the book will give you a peek behind the crossbars into my world – what it was like for a full bird Colonel to wear an orange prison uniform, stamped with XXXXL on the back, over Camp Pendleton

Brig. The subtitle will either be, "The Crossbar Motel," or the "Hotel California – Once you check in, you may never leave!"

      I get a chance weekly to spend some time with a 100-year-old World War II veteran of the Army Air Corps. As a C-47 pilot, Bob dropped Army paratroopers, and evacuated casualties, from Operations Market Garden and The Battle of the Bulge. Bob is truly one of the greats of the greatest generation. He has given me priceless advice on how to age gracefully and to continue making a difference in other's lives till you draw your last breath. One thing we agree on is that having a basic daily routine (BDR) is very important in maintaining your spiritual, mental, and physical fitness and growth. With Bob's advice, and from what I learned in the Marines, I've developed a BDR that takes about two hours every morning after awakening. I immediately drop to my knees upon exiting the rack, praying to my Higher Power to keep me sober for today, make me the best version of myself for the day, and that His will be done in my life for the day. I then go do a spiritual reading from "Our Daily Bread," followed immediately by a 1-mile morning run. The run wakes me up and connects me with nature – God's creation. I return to my garage and do a circuit course of seven different exercises for four rounds – except I always do a bonus set of pull-ups, screaming Oohrah! I return to my bedroom where I do a daily reading from the Bible. My Dad created a nifty Bible reading guide some four decades ago that has you reading the entire Bible in one year. The daily readings are typically less than ten minutes. I then do another spiritual reading from "Daily Reflections." I then completely strip my bed and remake it from scratch, because that's how my drill instructors taught me in Boot Camp. I have a "water infusion" of 40 ounces of pure water, also downing a multivitamin and fish oil capsule. This quickly turns into a mood enhancer as the water rejuvenates the cells in my body. I then enter into my walk-in closet, lay on the floor, spread-eagled on my back in total darkness, and meditate, listening for my Higher Power's voice. I haven't heard it yet, but the time helps me organize my thoughts and I often come out of the closet with inspirational ideas that he's imbued in my brain housing group. I shave and weigh myself, then prep myself for a five-minute ice bath. I intentionally introduced a period into my daily schedule where I am doing something that I really don't want to do. I detest the ice bath, but it is good for me in so many ways that I keep it in my BDR. I find that doing something "sucky" builds my self-discipline and strengthens my will power. I listen to something spiritual, while I'm immersed in the ice bath to help distract me from the "suck." In the Marines, we used to say "embrace the suck," and I continue to say it to myself every morning. I get a huge endorphin rush when I leave the ice bath, and I'm thinking "now there is nothing that I can't handle today." It reduces anxiety. It gives me a confidence boost, and also a sense of appreciation for the hot shower that I go into next. That's a dirty dozen list of things I do now every morning that set me up for success in the spiritual, physical, and mental areas of my daily living, with the spiritual given my highest priority. I may write a book about my BDR in case others are interested; sharing what works for me.

I'm busier than ever in retirement and I embrace every aspect of my daily life. I'm excited to get up each morning. A typical day begins for me by 0400. It takes about two to two and a half hours to complete the daily routine I describe above interwoven with feeding my dog and cat, letting the dog out for a bit, watering the plants and cooking my breakfast of oatmeal. Depending on where I will be playing Pickleball for the day, I get a good two hours of book writing done in my office with my trusty dog waiting patiently by my side. I then play Pickleball for two hours, which is pure enjoyment and interacting with friends. On Monday, Wednesday, and Friday, I go to Iron Legacy Gym to pump iron with a local business owner who asked me to train him two years ago. From there I attend a recovery meeting for the day and return home for lunch, then taking my dog out for a walk. If I'm lucky, I get more writing done in the afternoon, before doing some casual reading. My busy schedule keeps me active and constantly on the go. Remember, "idle hands are the Devil's workshop?" I am never idle, because I don't allow myself to be idle. My schedule is packed with exciting, important and interesting activities. And the icing on the cake is that I get to roll around Myrtle Beach on my glossy black Harley Road Glide with a souped-up 131 cubic inch engine with a Screaming Eagle, Stage Four, kit upgrade. I have explosive power at my fingertips for those occasions when "I feel the need for speed." "On my Horse of Steel I do ride." Yes, thanks to the daily blessings from my Higher Power, I am truly living the life of Riley! Thank you, my forever Commander-In-Chief.

CHAPTER 18
POSTSCRIPT

I never did hear back from the President, or any of his officials, regarding my letter and active-duty ID card that I returned to my Commander-In-Chief with my letter of 29 February 2020. Crickets...stigma. I found, however, that God works in mysterious ways, so I am sure that He had a reason for inspiring me to write and send the letter to POTUS, exactly four years to the day...29 February 2020...prior to the "launch" of this book.

In June of 2022, I was honored to retire the Major and her husband in a joint retirement ceremony in Florida, nearly three years after their phone call to me, after being released from the Brig. Unfortunately, I have had to turn down several requests to be the retiring officer for Marines who were retiring on Marine bases. Until it gets rectified, I am barred from all Marine Corps Installations worldwide, including from Marine-funded facilities like the Marine Corps Museum in Quantico. Something for my Higher Power to take care of some day, if it be His will.

I continue to get messages of support and encouragement from many whom I was fortunate to have served with. Here is one I received from a

Camp Lejeune guard, after I retired:

> Well I hope that I will be able to get a copy of your book and I am so happy that you got to retire. Those assholes didn't understand that you were being played as a pawn when you were in fact a knight. As crazy as it seems I actually looked up to you while you were in there. You made me feel like I was more than what I was at the time. I always enjoyed hearing about the Real Marine Corps that you went through with the 36 years of experience and with being a mustang it was truly amazing hearing the stories you would tell me. My first goal when I got in was to stay motivated and be the Marine I was destined to be. You were the first person that I noticed wasn't playing games and was actually what a Marine stood for. If you ever want to have a talk about anything or even a real friend despite the age difference please do not hesitate to reach out. I may be younger but I have the soul of a man that has lived a thousand lifetimes. Thank you for being a role model to me and Semper Fi sir!!!!

Messages like these inspire me to always strive to be a better version of myself each day. You just never know who is looking up to you as a role model.

A GAO-directed inspection of my retirement out-processing revealed that they had overpaid me for leave and Marine officials turned over collection of the alleged $10,000.00 debt to the Defense Finance & Accounting Office (DFAS). DFAS contacted me in April of 2023, fully three years after retiring and threatened to take it out of my paycheck in one lump sum unless I immediately set up a repayment plan. I'm guessing the inspection failed to reveal that the Marine Corps actually still owes me $45,000.00, which includes at least sixty days of leave for which I was never compensated, and for my stepdaughter's out-of-pocket expenses to store our household goods. I contacted the Marine Corps IG Office for help but was given a cold shoulder. No one on the inside risks advocating or lending a hand to a Marine Colonel who was accused of being a child molester – the stigma.

NCIS was quick to enter me into the National Crime Information Center (NCIC) data base, following my conviction in 2017, but they never bothered to scrub me from the NCIC database upon my exoneration in 2019. Imagine my surprise when I was detained for three hours at Peterson Air Force base in Colorado, while I was stopping by to visit a general friend of mine, returning to California from the Sturgis motorcycle rally in 2020. I popped in their data base as a convicted felon, and the gate guards had my motorcycle hemmed in with steel barriers. I felt a case of PTSD overwhelming me and thought, "wow," I just may be back in a Brig tonight until this clears up. I was finally cleared and linked up with the general who had not yet seen any of my frantic text messages, asking him to come get me at the front gate immediately.

Following my retirement, I appealed the retributive retirement decisions to the Board for the Correction of Naval Records. Fourteen months later they got back to me with essentially, "you're lucky that's all you got – next case." Had I been exonerated of anything else, I'm sure they would have rectified matters, correcting the record, and retiring me as a full bird Colonel with an "Honorable" characterization of my service. I am convinced that in His good time, and according to His plan, my Higher Power will some day restore honor to my career. Or, in the words of one of the Marines I led, "Sir, those of us who served with you know that your service was 'honorable' in spite what anyone else says." Thank you for the kind words, Marine…Semper Fi!

M U S T A N G…………over and out!

Retirement Pics

ABOUT THE AUTHOR

Colonel Dan Wilson enlisted in the Marine Corps on 24 June 1981, serving as an Electronic Warfare Operator, following his graduation from Boot Camp and his military occupational specialty (MOS) school. He was the Platoon and Series Honor Graduate from Boot Camp – Platoon 2051, Golf Company, 2nd Recruit Training Battalion, graduating in Dress Blues as a U.S. Marine on 2 October 1981. He was the top student at his MOS school and meritoriously promoted to Corporal. Wilson was the Honor Graduate from Non-Commissioned Officer (NCO) School with the highest grade ever achieved at the course of 99.6%. Subsequently, he was recognized as the NCO of the month for October 1982, by 2nd Marine Aircraft Wing, Cherry Point, NC. Wilson earned meritorious promotions to PFC, Lance Corporal, Corporal, and Sergeant – being promoted to Sergeant on 2 February 1983, just sixteen months following his graduation from Boot Camp. He applied and was accepted into the Marine Corps Enlisted Commissioning and Educational Program, attending the University of Arizona in Tucson, and graduating Magna Cum Laude with a Bachelor of Science Degree in Business Administration. Staff Sergeant Wilson was commissioned an officer on 22 December 1988, graduating third in his class of 221 Marine officers from The Basic School in July of 1989, and as the "top shot" with the pistol. He subsequently graduated from the Infantry Officers Course on 22 November 1989, as the recipient of The Wheeler Award for infantry excellence. Wilson led legions of Marines in training and combat, having commanded four platoons, three companies, and four battalions, including the vaunted Spartacus Battalion in Iraq – callsign "Spartacus 6." Lieutenant "Dan" Wilson led infantry machine gunners into combat during the first Gulf War in 1991 as the Heavy Machine Gun Platoon Commander, 1st Battalion, 5th Marines, Task Force Ripper – Desert Shield & Desert Storm. Additionally, he served three years aboard the USS Kitty Hawk as the XO and CO of the Marine Security Detachment, as the CO of Recruiting Station San Diego, as the XO of 3rd Recruit Training Battalion, San Diego, as the Current Operations Officer and VIP Briefer for I MEF Forward in Iraq, as the Afghanistan Division Chief on the Joint Staff, as the Chief-of-Staff for 3rd Marine Division, Okinawa, as the Officer-in-Charge of Special Operations Training Group for III MEF, Okinawa, and as the Operations Officer (G-3) for II MEF, Camp Lejeune, North Carolina. Major Wilson attended the Marine Corps Command and Staff College, graduating as a Distinguished Graduate with a Master's Degree in Military Strategy. Lieutenant Colonel Wilson attended the National War College, graduating as the top student in 4 of 9 courses, and with a second Master's Degree in National Security Strategy. Wilson was promoted to Colonel on 1 May 2010, serving his final ten years as the senior Colonel in the Marine Corps, and retiring on 1 March 2020, after nearly 39 years of active-duty service. Wilson deployed eleven times into combat zones, or in support of our national security objectives around the globe. One of the most highly decorated officers of his era, with 52 individual medals and ribbons, Colonel Wilson's awards include the Defense Superior Service Medal, the Legion of Merit, the Bronze Star, three Meritorious Service Medals, two Combat Action Ribbons, two National Defense Service Medals, two Navy & Marine Corps Commendation Medals, the Navy & Marine Corps Achievement Medal with combat "V", two Marine Corps Good Conduct Medals, eleven Sea Service Deployment Ribbons, a Marine Drill Instructor Ribbon, a Marine Recruiter Ribbon, the Arctic Service Ribbon, ten individual Certificates of Commendation, ten Letters of Appreciation, and the "Order of the Combat Spur" from the Army's Black Jack Brigade, following the Second Battle of Fallujah, Iraq. Wilson was certified as a "Conning Alongside Officer" aboard the USS Kitty Hawk (CV-63). Colonel Wilson was certified as a Marine Combat Instructor of Water Survival, and as a Lifeguard, graduating from the training course with the "leadership award." He was a certified "Master" of Helicopter, Rope, and Suspension Training. He additionally earned his "Black Belt" in the Marine Corps Martial Arts Program at Parris Island, SC. Wilson and his wife currently reside in Myrtle Beach, South Carolina.

Made in the USA
Columbia, SC
24 May 2024

5bb99e55-ed68-46cd-84ad-ed861445ebbcR01